Reflections on Big Spring

A History of Pittsford, NY and the Genesee River Valley

DAVID MCNELLIS

authorHOUSE®

AuthorHouse™
1663 Liberty Drive
Bloomington, IN 47403
www.authorhouse.com
Phone: 1-800-839-8640

First published by AuthorHouse 10/13/2010

ISBN: 978-1-4520-4358-6 (e)
ISBN: 978-1-4520-4356-2 (sc)
ISBN: 978-1-4520-4357-9 (hc)

Library of Congress Control Number: 2010911740

Printed in the United States of America

This book is printed on acid-free paper.

Cover art by: John C. Menihan, AWS, ANA, 1908-1992.

For Seneca Chiefs Segoyewatha (Red Jacket), Kaintwakon (Cornplanter) and Okanyatarariyau (Handsome Lake).

Contents

Prologue

"For what is a man's lifetime, unless the memory of past events is woven with earlier times?"

Cicero

This story begins around 40,000 BC and concludes in the mid 20th century AD. It is an historical account of the Genesee River Valley of Upstate New York with a particular focus on the Village of Pittsford. This material has been distilled from a broad array of hard copy references, online sources and anecdotes of oral history captured from members of the community. The result is a fresh, unique narrative of the settlement of the area. This chronicle will appeal to past and current residents as well as those simply interested in the fascinating history of the Genesee River Valley and Pittsford, New York.

While the facts presented here are based on information deemed reliable, the reader is cautioned that portions are based on accounts as told by those with clearly biased views regarding controversial issues including: slavery, religion, indigenous people, capitalism, civil rights, suffrage, the Civil War and wars with Great Britain, France et al. Additionally, because the primary written historical account of the area between 600 BC and the fifth century AD depends on a single, narrow religious orthodoxy, the reader must reconcile how those views mesh with their own beliefs. Therefore, some may decide to characterize this work as fiction. Not withstanding the above caveats, great effort was made to use reliable, factual information in retelling the history of Pleasant Valley and Big Spring.

The naming rights to an area legitimately belong to those who reside in the region over the most extended period of time. "Genesee" translates from the Seneca language to "Pleasant Valley" and was the name ascribed by the Seneca Tribe of the Iroquois Confederacy to the Genesee River Valley during the five hundred years they called it their home. By this standard, the village of Pittsford, New York should be forever known as "Big Spring"; the name used by the Seneca in recognition of its plentiful supply of clean, fresh water ascending from its substantial natural spring.

The defining topographical features of the area are the parallel riparian corridors formed by the Genesee River and Irondequoit

Creek. Both are contrarian; flowing south to north before entering Lake Ontario. The hearty, independent minded pioneers that settled Pleasant Valley also refused to be bound by tradition. They departed the relative safety of New England to take on substantial risk and uncertainty to make a new life on America's western frontier. They were greeted with predictable trepidation by the equally proud and independent Seneca Indians; the primary fighting force of the mighty Iroquois Nation.

There are hundreds of handsome river valleys in North America; many are far grander than the Genesee. There are thousands of small communities whose settlement were prompted by the pool created by a gentle bend in a stream, by the confluence of rivers, the intersecting of paths, highways or railroads or the natural occurrence of a fresh water spring or deep water port. Each area has a story to tell; many are significant and some fascinating.

The topography, riparian features, soil and climate is the stage on which this story unfolds. The cast consists of an amazing cadre of imperfect but inspirational warriors, chiefs, pioneers, farmers, politicians, clergy, civil rights leaders, inventors, volunteer firefighters, culinary artists and entrepreneurs. Their story is remarkable.

1

Pleasant Valley – It's the Water

"It's the Water" so proclaimed the ads for Genesee Beer in the 1960's. Madison Avenue contended that the pristine waters of Genesee Lake distinguished the local beer from the competing "imports" from the Midwest or New York City. It was, in fact, "the water", in its various states, that largely shaped the Genesee Valley.

In 40,000 BC, a west and, more substantive, east tributary of the mighty Genesee River flowed north 158 miles from its source near present day Genesee, Pennsylvania before emptying into the Ontario River; now Lake Ontario. The larger eastern branch followed a course that now forms the valleys of Conesus and Hemlock Lakes and the path of present day Irondequoit Creek before entering Irondequoit Bay and Lake Ontario.

Around 38,000 BC, the last of four glaciations crept across what is now North America. The surging headwaters of the eastern branch of the Genesee was no match for the crushing lobe of this last Wisconsonian glacier as it marched southward to a point just north of the current Pennsylvania state line. The river's flow was redirected southward into the present day Susquehanna River just south of present day Danville.

As the glacier continued moving south, the remaining branch of the Genesee was pushed westward and forced to cut a new path through limestone escarpments. Variations in density of the earth's crust created a series of three waterfalls as the Genesee River approached Lake Ontario. Present day Rochester, New York exists because of these waterfalls. Pioneer entrepreneurs harnessed the river's power at these points and built mills to process grains harvested from the surrounding fertile valley. Rochester became The Flour City!

Geologically, the area now containing the towns of Pittsford, Perinton, Penfield and Brighton is known as the Valley of the Irondequoit. The valley was not formed by Irondequoit Creek but rather by the glacier that pushed sand and gravel to the border of the valley. Irondequoit Creek is entirely within the boundaries of the former District of Northfield (Eastern Monroe County). Its headwaters are the spring fed ponds in Mendon Ponds Park. It flows thirty four miles, dropping 416 feet, before entering Irondequoit Bay.

Water's seminal impact on the area began with the glacier that sculpted the local topography. Its influence continued with the underground springs that fed Big Spring in what would become the Village of Pittsford. The spring's clear water became a natural meeting place for the local Seneca. A village, foot paths and transportation routes subsequently emerged.

Minor variations in pre-glacial weather patterns would have left the Genesee River's eastern tributary intact. With a bountiful water supply, there would have been no need for the local Seneca tribe to seek out Big Spring and establish a settlement there. A village, perhaps called Pittsford, would have been located on the river's bank somewhere along where Irondequoit Creek now meanders. Or... perhaps Pittsford would have become the Flour City?

At the opposite end of North America, the Wiscon-sonian glacier was concurrently reshaping the earth's surface; an activity that would facilitate the migration of a broad range of Asian animal species including bison, camel, horse, mammoth, mastodon, opossum, sloth, weasel, wild dog and...homo sapiens. Sea levels in the world's oceans receded in the range of 150-200 feet exposing heretofore submerged land masses. Where Alaska's Seward Peninsula had been separated from Siberia by fifty miles of Bering Sea, a land bridge emerged connecting the two continents. Hunters and hunted ventured across this isthmus in search of new territories to hunt, explore and reside. Sometime between 6500 and 8500 BC, the mammoth, mastodon, sloth and camels perished in the new environment.

Driven by their insatiable quest for adventure and discovery, the first North American bipedal primates migrated south from Alaska and Canada into what would become the Western United States. From there, they gradually moved eastward to the plains and Great Lakes areas and subsequently to the eastern part of the continent. Simultaneously, these first North American human explorers settled what would become the Southern U.S., Mexico, Central and South America.

The earliest white settlers were attracted to Pleasant Valley when they heard it described as an "agricultural el dorado". The prolific farmland resulted from combining the fecund soil with a dependable source of water supplied by river, creek, lake and precipitation.

Water in the form of Pleasant Valley's ubiquitous winter snow tested the will, character and ultimately the survival of the area's earliest inhabitants. The "winter of the deep snow" which struck western New York State in 1779-1780 was one significant element in the series of fateful events leading to the tragic downfall of the Iroquois Confederacy whose shelter and food stocks had been destroyed at the direction of General George Washington.

In the eighteenth century, the deep, fast moving water allowed for the harnessing of energy to fuel industrial development along the mighty Genesee and beside the smaller, but more manageable, Irondequoit Creek. In the early nineteenth century, the first waters flowed through the Erie Canal and significantly enhanced the area's economic prosperity by allowing the expansion of the market for locally produced commodities. Humid water-laden summer air contributed to the combustible atmosphere of the Rochester street dance that erupted into the first of a series of urban civil rights riots to rock America in the nineteen sixties.

Over the centuries, Pleasant Valley's characteristic heavy winter snows and excessively sultry summers played a role in altering the area's demographics. The harsh climate provided the impetus for some of the increasingly mobile residents to permanently flee for milder and drier climates.

It was the water.

2

The Iroquois Confederacy

Between 3500 BC and 2000 BC, New York's indigenous people were of the Lamoka culture. These hunters and gatherers were drawn to the area from the upper Great Lakes area by the bountiful supply of fish and game. This ready supply of indigenous nourishment provided little incentive to clear the land, cultivate and grow food. The Lamoka culture was eventually absorbed by a succession of other hunter/gatherers: the Frontenac, Laurentian l and Laurentian ll.

The first native people of New York to cultivate and grow substantial portions of their food were the Owascos. While they continued the centuries-long tradition of hunting and fishing, they were the first culture in the area to discover that the climate and soil were ideal for growing beans, squash and corn as well as their discretionary crops of tobacco and herbs. Anthropologists generally agree that their culture immediately preceded the Iroquois and date their presence in the area over three centuries beginning about 1000 AD.

Tribal pride deterred the Iroquois from subscribing to the anthropologic theory that they were descended from a succession of earlier native people who had emigrated from Asia. According to Iroquois legend, the Great Spirit released six families of indigenous people from below a mountain adjoining Oswego Falls. After traveling east to the "great ocean", the six families faced the afternoon sun and walked west. Immediately upon entering what would become Eastern New York State, the first of the families settled the area and became the Mohawk Nation. Next the Oneida, then the Onondaga, Cayuga and Tuscarora families likewise established home lands as they marched westward. Finally the Seneca made their home in the Valley of the Genesee and assumed their responsibilities as "Guardians of the Western Door".

The Seneca tribe has a proud legend of origin separate from the Iroquois Confederacy. According to their oral tradition, Seneca forefathers began their worldly existence in an ancient cave hidden

4

in present day Clark's Gully adjoining Canandaigua Lake. The first Seneca emerged from the cave and appeared on the steep slope of South Hill that had been formed when the Great Spirit opened the earth to form the lake. This sacred site is on the lower southeast side of the lake just south of Bare Hill; twenty two miles from where the Seneca would eventually build their capital at Ganondagan (near Victor) and an additional ten miles from Big Spring. The Iroquois Confederacy, also known as the Haudenosaunee Confederacy, was formed about 1575. It represented the successful consolidation of five native Indian nations residing in New York State into a single social, cultural and governmental entity. The original catalyst for joining forces was to quell intertribal skirmishes and end cannibalism. Within two hundred years, concerns regarding the encroaching white settlers provided added impetus to retain the strength created by the union

These five powerful independent nations dominated the area now containing the State of New York at least since 1300 AD and their ancestors for several thousand years prior. The Seneca, Cayuga, Onondaga, Oneida and Mohawk people were ultimately convinced that a joining of nations would be to their mutual advantage by The Great Peacemaker; known by his native people as Deganawida. A sixth tribe, the Tuscarora, joined the confederacy in 1715.

Collectively the Iroquois Confederacy had no peer north of Mexico. They were the best organized and most militarily astute. When attacked or threatened with violence, the Seneca Tribe was the first charged to take up the defense of the confederacy. While the Seneca was the largest single tribe at the time the confederacy was formed, they garnered particular respect and honor because of their unparalleled skills on the battlefield and their role as the primary fighting contingent of the Confederacy. In times of threatened hostility, it was the Seneca war chiefs (sachems) that were responsible for organizing and leading warriors from all nations into the conflict.

At any given time, they were expected to marshal fully one half of the confederacy's fighting force; as many as 10,000 warriors from the ranks of Seneca.

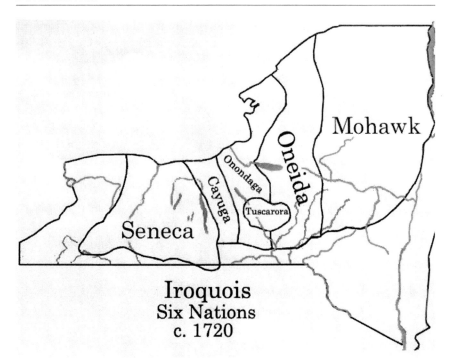

Iroquois Six Nation Map by R. A. Nonenmacher.
This image is released to the public domain.

Deganawida (The Great Peacemaker) is credited with consolidating the tribes of Upstate New York to form the Iroquois Confederacy. He was often described as being originally from the Huron Nation. Others proclaim that he was Onondaga by birth but adopted and raised by the Mohawks. Many of his contemporaries believed he was born of a virgin.

The native people consider him a prophet. His prophecies included... the "white serpent" (the white man) would befriend his Iroquois brothers and sisters and, after gaining their confidence, betray that trust. According to The Great Peacemaker, the "red serpent" would then rise up against the white man. Ultimately he predicted that a "black serpent" would intercede and destroy both the reds and whites. He preached that salvation was reserved for those who obeyed the one "Great Maker" and fostered peace among all. As his name suggested, The Great Peacemaker was a staunch advocate of harmony among all nations. He was highly influential in ending the practice of cannibalism among the Iroquois.

Deganawida's first disciple was the gifted Onondaga orator Hiawatha. After securing an agreement to join the fledgling confederacy from the Onondaga, he convinced Hiawatha to join him in preaching the benefits of peace and consolidation among the remaining, often hostile, nations of New York Indians.

Together they ventured to the Mohawk Nation. Deganawida was immediately rebuffed by the tribal elders. In order to garner attention and respect, he decided to perform a modest miracle. After climbing a tall tree at the edge of what is now known as Cohoes Falls on the Mohawk River, The Great Peacemaker ordered that the tree be chopped down, casting him over the raging falls. The bemused onlookers were certain that he had been pummeled to death on the rocks at the base of the falls or drowned. The next day, they found him warming at a riverside campfire. Word of his great power spread rapidly and the Mohawk Nation immediately declared their intent to align with the emerging Iroquois Confederacy. With the help of Hiawatha, the remaining nations joined to form the dominant organized Native American Indian entity in the Northeast.

This Iroquois Confederacy, known as "People of the Longhouse", was an early representative democracy with a single chief representing his tribe. Each tribe could cast a single vote and decisions required a consensus. The women, who were the leaders of each clan within the nations of the Iroquois, selected male representatives to attend tribal council meetings and vote on behalf of the tribe. Each tribe could have as many representatives as they wished in attendance at tribal councils but when it came time to vote, it was strictly one vote per tribe. The confederacy created a constitution called the Gayanashagowa. Five hundred years hence, this constitution remains operational for the surviving Iroquois people. Many believe that the Iroquois constitution provided the model for the earliest drafts of the United States Constitution.

Because the histories of indigenous peoples were largely passed down in the oral tradition, there are considerable voids in our knowledge base. Such is the case in the naming of certain tribes of people based on their prevailing characteristics or practices. Prior to the formation of the Iroquois Confederacy, the Seneca were known as the "People of the Great Hill". While earlier tribes preferred to build their villages near streams and springs, the Seneca's reputation as fierce warriors resulted in a propensity to build their villages in strong defensive positions; hence on the crest of "great hills". Many of these villages were protected with wooden palisades; some included watch towers. After joining the Iroquois Confederacy, they were alternately known as "People of the Longhouse".

The "People of the Longhouse" moniker had two derivations. First was the Iroquois proclivity to reside in such houses. Long was an understatement. In order to accommodate the twenty to thirty families of a clan they were designed to house, a typical longhouse measured eighty feet in length, 18 feet in width and had a roof that peaked at 18 feet. Straight trees were felled and erected vertically to form the walls. The tops of these trees were bent toward the center of the longhouse to form a sloped roof to shed water and snow. The roof was covered with overlapping bark layered like shingles. Smoke holes were incorporated at the roof peaks every fifteen feet along the longhouse's length. Openings in both ends accommodated egress and were covered with animal skins in cold months. With only the smoke holes emitting light, the longhouses were typically dimly lit.

Iroquois Longhouse
Courtesy of New York State Museum, Albany, New York
Copyright of the New York State Museum, Albany, NY

Iroquois Longhouse
Courtesy of New York State Museum, Albany, New York
Copyright of the New York State Museum, Albany, NY

Normally a single clan occupied a longhouse; its symbol engraved and painted red above each entry. Seneca clans included the bear, wolf, turtle, snipe and hawk. Within the longhouse, individual clan families were assigned small private spaces measuring approximately six feet by nine feet that were defined by curtains made from animal skins. Personal tools, weapons and clothes were stored under seats built into the exterior wall. Mats of corn husk covered with furs buffered the sleeping families from the frigid floor.

The second derivation of the "People of the Longhouse" was a symbolic reference to the fact that the original five nations of the confederacy lined up geographically in an east to west alignment. The eastern most Mohawk nation was called the Keeper of the Eastern Door while the western most Seneca were called the Keeper of the Western Door. The centrally located Onondaga nation was the Keeper of the Fire and hosted the Tribal Council in what was considered the capital of the federation. Collectively these three tribes were known as the Three Brothers.

Seneca Chiefs Cornplanter and Red Jacket were among the most accomplished and respected members of the Seneca Nation. Both were born in 1750, fought for the British in the Revolutionary War and served with the Americans in the War of 1812. Cornplanter's reputation was established as a brutal but effective warrior chief fighting the Colonists. Ironically, he was awarded his own tract of land (The Cornplanter Tract) for exemplary service in ultimately helping bring peace between the Colonists and his people.

Cornplanter greatly admired the Mohawk Chief Joseph Brant and despised the whiskey (known as "firewater") supplied by the British. Red Jacket despised Joseph Brant and loved firewater. Red Jacket was awarded his heavily decorated "red jacket" by a thankful British officer for his services as a speedy and reliable messenger during the Revolutionary War. Red Jacket avoided dangerous battles on more than one occasion and, accordingly, was called a coward by many fellow Iroquois Chiefs. This had little effect on Red Jacket as he proudly professed his staunch advocacy of peace between the British and Americans. Likewise, he promoted peace between the Iroquois Confederacy and the American Colonists.

While contrary to a thousand years of tradition, Red Jacket did not share the life goal of the majority of young Seneca males; to be recognized as a brave warrior. What surely must have seemed odd at the time, Red Jacket aspired only to become the most respected orator in the land.

Gaiant'wake (c.1750-1836) or Kaintwakon, generally known as Cornplanter,
Portrait by F. Bertoli, 1796.
This image is in the public domain.

Chief Cornplanter (Kaintwakon) was born of a Seneca mother and Dutch Fur Trader father in 1750 in Canawagus on the Genesee River. Canawagus would later become Caledonia. Kaintwakon (Seneca for "by what one plants") would later become the influential Seneca Chief known as Cornplanter. When it seemed to serve his purposes, he would also answer to John O'Bail; his fathers name. Cornplanter's mother continued to live as a Seneca and raise her son while his father reverted to his fur trading vocation and resided mainly with fellow Dutch trappers.

RED JACKET,
SENECA WAR CHIEF.

Red Jacket, Seneca War Chief, 1835. Library of Congress Prints.
This image is in the public domain.

"Keeps them awake" is the English translation of Segoyewatha; Red Jacket's Seneca name. He was born in Geneva, New York in 1750. His father was a Cayuga and his mother a member of the Wolf Clan of the local Seneca Village. By matrilineal tradition, Red Jacket was therefore a member of the Wolf Clan of the Seneca.

He lived his entire 80 years in the lands of the Seneca. He was proud of his service to Great Britain and wore his namesake "Red Jacket" for many years after the war. His fame as a loyal comrade of the British was dwarfed by his eventual notoriety as the greatest Native American orator of the time; perhaps of all time. His eloquence is captured in several speeches contained in Bartleby's List of the World's Famous Orations.

Cornplanter's half brother was Handsome Lake (Okanyatarariyau). While he is thought to have squandered the first two thirds of his life, in his later years, Handsome Lake became the most highly respected religious leader of the Iroquois Confederacy. He led a renaissance of the confederacy; a renaissance that was nearly successful in saving the proud heritage of his people. Known as the "Peace Prophet", his gospel, called the Gawwioo, advocated reasonably balanced tenets which included: 1) the retention of much of the Iroquois tradition 2) retaining all remaining tribal land for Iroquois use 3) learning English so as to peacefully coexist with the white man 4) using the white man's building and farming technologies to enhance the tribes standards of living and 5) abstinence from alcohol. His legacy lives on in the many "Handsome Lakers" that continue to follow the Gawwiio.

Seneca food, their land and traditions

Among the six nations of the Iroquois Confederacy, the Seneca became known as the "Keepers of the Western Door"; due to the fact that they occupied the western most section of New York State. While official stewards of a large swath of what would become western New York State, most Seneca lived in the area loosely defined as north of Canandaigua Lake to Lake Ontario and west to the Genesee River. The area contained generous natural resources that prompted the Seneca to make the area their home. Irondequoit Creek attracted abundant game, the area's fertile soil yielded plentiful bounty of the Seneca's favorite crops and Big Spring provided an infinite supply of clean, clear water. As a result, the area within a twenty mile radius of what would become Pittsford was the epicenter of the Seneca Nation.

The Seneca lived in villages whose locations were initially scouted and secured by male members of the tribe. Evidence has been found that suggests that these villages were often protected from potentially warring neighbors by sixteen foot wooden palisades. Men cleared the land around the village so that the women could cultivate, plant and harvest the "three sisters" of their diet; squash, beans and corn.

Soups were a common entrée. Corn combined with the other "sisters" of squash and beans were standard fare. Available meat, seasonal fruits, herbs and grasshoppers were added to provide zest. Salt was not part of the chef's condiment tray. In leaner times, dried corn was pounded into meal which could be stored until it was boiled into hot mush. Variations included baked corn dumplings which was considered a delicacy when spread with bear oil or maple syrup.

While they strove for variety in their diet, the Iroquois were mainly corn-fed. This food staple had a long history with the indigenous people of North America. Archaeologists and ethnobotanists agree that the first signs of domestication of corn occurred 9000 years ago in central Mexico (Mesoamerica) in the highlands of Oaxaca and Jalisco.

Around 1500 BC, corn cultivation began to spread and become a dietary staple through much of Mexico, South America and the Caribbean islands. By 1000 AD, corn (or maize) cultivation had spread to the North American Southwest and, shortly thereafter, to the Northeast and lower Canada. The emergence of corn in the Iroquois diet changed the landscape of New York State as forests were cleared to accommodate the planting of fields of corn. Corn found its way to Europe and the remainder of the world in the late fifteenth and early sixteenth centuries as Europeans returned from visits to North America.

Time permitting; tobacco was grown as the sole indigenous recreational drug. Firewater would come later; its impact so devastating that it threatened the Seneca Nation's survival.

By today's standards, the Iroquois had a progressive sense of women's rights. Sole guardianship of the land was placed in the hands of the villages' women. This made sense as it was the women who were accountable for producing two thirds of the food. If there had been a concept of holding "title" to the land, clearly such title would have been held by the female clan leaders.

While not eligible to become "chiefs", the Iroquois women were the official leaders of each clan within a tribe. If you were born of a Wolf Clan mother, you were forever a Wolf Clan member as would be all the children of Wolf Clan mothers.

There were forty nine Iroquois Chiefs. When one died, the women of the confederacy nominated his successor. Accordingly, those males aspiring to hold office within the tribe were well advised to curry favor among their female constituents.

In addition to child rearing, women of the tribe were responsible for the less glamorous chores of gathering berries, medicinal plants, nuts and wild fruit. They were charged with breeding and raising domestic animals. These included deer, various fowl and dogs. The latter were not deployed as playful companions for entertaining Seneca youth but rather, were coveted for adding variety to the diet.

Iroquois men spent their time supplementing the "three sisters" with a broad variety of local game and the fishing bounty of nearby lakes and streams. As they traveled afar in search of fresh meat and fish, they evaluated sites for future villages. Every ten to twenty years, they orchestrated the relocation of their home village to a new site. This became necessary as hunting and fishing grounds were depleted and soil became less fertile without crop rotation and fertilization; practices that would be learned subsequently from white settlers.

New village sites were determined based on the availability of a dependable source of water, game resources and fertile soil. Surely Irondequoit Creek, Canandaigua Lake and Big Spring provided steady water and attracted game animals. The soils of the deciduous forests of the southern section of Seneca lands offered superior crop yields compared to the coniferous forests to the north near Lake Ontario. Accordingly most Seneca villages were located in the southern portion of the Valley of the Genesee.

Proud Iroquois parents inculcated their children with traditions that remained unchanged for centuries. This yielded a seemingly harmonious culture where all were expected to contribute to the maximum of their capabilities for the good of the tribe and, in return, each individual would share equally in the bounties of the collective efforts. This essentially socialist society dictated a clear division of labor, particularly between the sexes, but a collective effort where it seemed to make sense from an efficiency perspective. The result was often analogous to an old fashioned Midwestern barn-raising. The system worked. Hunger was rare. Early white settlers marveled at the efficiency of the Iroquois in feeding their people.

Like their communal "ownership" of the land, the Iroquois worked together to maximize the productivity of farming, hunting and fishing. The women typically worked in large teams, moving from one clan's assigned tillable land to another, performing the more arduous chores in mass under the direction of a female clan elder.

As warriors, Iroquois men were accustomed to working collectively. They tapped those cooperative skills in the area of food gathering as well. They learned that hunting yields could be substantially enhanced by aligning fences of woven brush in large "V" shapes. They spread a phalanx of hunters across the widest breadth of the "V" to herd wild game into the narrowing apex where others awaited the kill. Reports of hundreds of harvested deer in a day were not uncommon when using this cooperative method.

Fishing was often done in teams as well. Dozens of Iroquois men, paddling canoes, spread nets across the breadth of a stream that trapped migrating fish. The daily bounty of such operations often numbered in the thousands as compared to far more modest amounts that would result from a like number of tribesmen with spears or bone hooks and line working independently.

Although community celebratory feasts were common after particularly successful days of hunting or fishing, consistent with cooperative fundamentals, the bounty of such activities was viewed as community property to be spread evenly amongst tribe members. Despite the lack of individual incentives of a materialistic nature, there was strong familial pressure for all members to contribute fully to the sustenance and well being of the tribe. Regardless of an individual's contribution, he or she shared equally in the output of the tribe. Parents held sons and daughters to high standards with regard to their contributions to society. Men were expected to be capable hunters and fishermen. Women of the tribe were judged on their farm yields and housekeeping acumen. A person's esteem within the tribe was commensurate with their perceived contribution to the community.

While socialist societies have traditionally been characterized as stifling individual ambition, the Iroquois imbued a strong sense of individualism, self-discipline, stoicism and pride among its members. Independence and responsibility were stressed as desirable traits from an early age.

The concept of "parental pressure" has worked effectively for thousands of years. Iroquois elders made it clear that bringing honor to the clan via each member's contribution to the community was the centerpiece for determining an individual's worthiness.

Consistency in parenting style prompted significant pressure to conform to the tribe's expectations of behavior. In a commune-like environment, it was hard for youth to escape watchful adult eyes. The fear of potentially bringing shame upon one's family or clan was sufficient deterrent to most youthful indiscretions. Petty crime, common in today's contemporary society, was almost nonexistent.

Despite the high expectations placed upon their young, Iroquois parents were also characterized as indulgent and permissive. Infants were carried on cradleboards, securely swaddled, until they were too heavy to carry to the fields. The cradleboards were hung from trees with the infant's line of sight positioned to observe their mother working in the fields. Diapers of moss were changed regularly and babies were not weaned until their third or fourth year.

Permissiveness characterized the parenting style during the adolescent and teen years as well. The traditional awkwardness existed between the sexes but premarital sex was common and allowed among the young. Such activities were solely the providence of youth, however. Once adulthood was reached, chastity for single people and marital fidelity for committed couples was the expectation. Divorce was easily facilitated and remarriage was common.

Fidelity was a challenge because couples were typically separated for extended periods during the hunting season. Able bodied males adopted a nomadic lifestyle during this period of the year. They often traveled as far as the Ohio Territory in search of game and fur bearing animals and, accordingly, were absent for several successive months. This tended to test the fidelity of both partners. It was not uncommon for hunters to take up with women from the community located in close proximity to that year's chosen hunting grounds. Predictable trauma occurred when the husband returned from the hunt to discover his wife had decided to cohabit with another man. Consistent with the influence afforded women in the confederacy, the man was expected to abide by her decision regarding mate selection; amicably granting a divorce if one was requested.

"Ondinnonk" was the word that described the "secret desire of the soul" contained in dreams. Iroquois felt compelled to publicly discuss the implications of their dreams and often to take action to either assure that those dreams became reality or preclude them from becoming so. On occasion, sexually explicit dreams were acted out in public orgies that were thought to be therapeutic. This was inconsistent with the characteristically modest behavior and dress of both genders.

Moccasins were the only drab element in the Seneca wardrobe. Clothing of bright colors, often red or blue, were the choice of both genders. Breechcloth and a calico shirt covered tight leggings. Men wore their short leggings above the knee while a woman's extended below the knee. Females usually wore blue skirts tied at the waist. Winter weather prompted the classic and popular blanket-over-the-shoulder look or jackets and waist coats made from blanket cloth. Silver was the jewelry of choice for finger, ear and nose rings. Various bangles were typically attached to the clothing to add a touch of individual panache.

By contemporary standards of the white man, the personal grooming habits of the Iroquois were substandard. Making soap was not a high priority; they seldom bathed or washed their clothes. Women wore their hair in long ponytails lathered with bear grease. Men painstakingly plucked every hair from their scalps excepting the crowning scalp lock.

Iroquois neighbors had little to covet as few items were individually owned. Perhaps a few farm tools or cooking implements were the sole property of the person who crafted these items but these were typically in plentiful supply. Accordingly, the risk of theft of personal property was not something the Iroquois spent time contemplating.

When the Europeans arrived in the Americas, the concept of individual ownership of land was unknown in the Iroquois Confederacy. Five hundred years hence, in 1981, The Council of Chiefs described similar beliefs: "the earth is sacred...was created for all to use forever—not to be exploited merely for this present generation. Land is not just a commodity and in no event is land for sale." Twenty-first century Iroquois retain a similar perception of private property ownership. They publicly state that their people "have no absolute right to claim territory for purely monetary purposes. Our Creator gave us our aboriginal lands in trust with very specific rules regarding its uses. We are caretakers of our Mother Earth, not lords of the land. Our claims are valid only so far as we dwell in peace and harmony upon her."

"Guardianship" was the closest adjective to describe the Clan Mothers responsibility towards the land. The Iroquois did not consider the white man's concept of land "ownership" legitimate…the Great Spirit had simply entrusted the land to the Iroquois Confederacy for their collective use during their lifetime.

The Seneca property system was in fact a hybrid. When the Iroquois Confederacy was formed, it was agreed that all of the lands of the five tribes would become common land for the use of all member tribes. In practice however, it was understood that each of the tribes would retain a "special interest in its historic territory". Furthermore, individual clans and family groups were assigned specified sections of tribal lands to inhabit and farm.

Distribution of the land within the tribe was determined within the Clan Mothers' Council. Some of the land was reserved for the common good of the entire tribe. This land was planted, tended and harvested on a communal basis with all females participating. The food harvested from the communal tract was called *kĕndiŭ"gwă'ge' hodi'yĕn'tho* and was served at council meetings and other tribal celebrations.

The tribe retained the right to all of the land within the confines of the tribal area and, once it was agreed which tracts would be reserved for communal purposes, the Clan Mothers' Council allotted specific areas for each clan to farm. The clan, in turn, divided their assigned area between their member families.

An element of competition did exist within the clans because the individual clan tracts were redistributed every few years. Clan mothers could allot additional acreage or more desirable lands to those clans who they deemed had been superior guardians of the earth and reallocate lands from clans that had shown comparable neglect.

It is no surprise that when Oliver Phelps and Nathaniel Gorham introduced the concept of "buying" Seneca land, in the area that would become Pittsford, tribal leaders were puzzled by the concept. From their prospective, this was an unprecedented practice. Clearly the indigenous people were at a significant disadvantage in determining a fair price. After all, they had never "sold" land before and were simply "caretakers" of this property which was on loan from the Great Spirit.

3

Iroquois Entrepreneurs - Dining on the Enemy

While living independently in terms of life's staples, the Iroquois did engage in their own form of commerce in order to obtain items in more limited supply. It was a form of trading without the formality of establishing a pre-agreed rate of exchange. They considered the process analogous to an exchange of gifts between tribes with whom they occasionally interacted. For instance, the tribes to the north typically had a surplus of furs but corn and tobacco was less plentiful. The Seneca clan leader would arrange for a gift of corn to the northern tribe with the expectation that some commodity of value to their tribe would be forthcoming. There was no specified quid pro quo however. The recipient tribal leader would appraise the gift and assess the desirability of a long-term "trading" arrangement in deciding the quantity and quality of furs sent south. As each side chose to or not to continue this relationship, the strength of the trading partnership was established.

The Iroquois were not void of free enterprise spirit. There was a significant hint of entrepreneurship in the establishing of trading routes. An individual who developed a new trading route was considered to henceforth have proprietary rights to that route. From a practical standpoint and consistent with the communal tradition, such exclusive rights were more often relinquished to the tribe to retain.

Dehuntshigwa'es roughly translates to "men hit a rounded object" in Onondaga. In the fifteenth century, the "rounded object" would likely have been the head of a recently dispatched enemy warrior. The loosely defined field of play could range from 500 yards to several miles in length. Individual games could last days and involve 100 to 1000 players. The French initially observed this Iroquois "game" in 1640 and described it with the French term for a bat or stick "crosse". They ultimately called it lacrosse as an abbreviated version of "le jeu de la crosse" or "the game of the stick".

Lacrosse served as an important release for the competitive spirit of young warriors. Excelling on the lacrosse pitch was a method to bring honor to your clan or tribe and had the added benefit of usually not proving fatal for the losing contestant. If contemporary lacrosse looks simply like a game of no rules, the earliest version of Dehuntshigwa'es was abjectly brutal. The object of the game was to (in today's jargon) "beat the crap" out of your opponent possessing the "round object" until he relinquished such object; then to facilitate the movement of the captured object toward the goal. Significant injuries were not uncommon and fatalities occurred occasionally. Human heads proved to be quite heavy (and perhaps distracting) so later versions of lacrosse used balls of various combinations of indigenous materials; normally clay, stone, deerskin and wood.

The game had deep meaning within the Confederacy. It was viewed as a non-lethal substitute for war and as training and conditioning activity for young warriors. Sometimes a lacrosse match was used as a means of settling tribal disputes sparing the downside of lethal combat. Not unlike the game-day exuberance of Notre Dame football fans, the game had a near spiritual significance as it was "played for the pleasure of the Creator".

Impact of the fur trade

Europeans developed a seemingly unquenchable thirst for the furs of North America. The Dutch India Company agreed to purchase their furs from the Iroquois Confederacy and, within a few years, the fur trade became an integral part of Iroquois life. While initially enamored by the availability of heretofore unknown European-made goods that appeared to enhance their lives, the growing dependence on such products served to jeopardize the Iroquois Nation's independence. Prior to this time, their sole focus had been on hunting, growing adequate food stocks and building secure and reasonably comfortable longhouses. Now their lifeblood became the beaver pelt that could be redeemed for guns, ammunition, manufactured tools and alcohol.

Pelts were described as the "gold of the woods". In retrospect, they were simply "fool's gold". Did this growing dependence on the "white serpent" ultimately strip the Iroquois of their dignity and lead to the downfall of their proud culture. In hindsight, it is far easier to discern this pivotal point leading to the precipitous decline of a once proud, independent, peaceful hunter/gatherer society

Rather than hunting game animals for food and clothing, the Iroquois warriors began to focus their attention on securing pelts; pelts that could be traded with the English or Dutch for goods that a decade ago were unknown to them. If previously unknown, perhaps these new commodities were not truly essential to their continued happiness and prosperity? Then, as now, the temptation of a perceived "better life" was compelling.

Initially the Iroquois seemed to have access to a near infinite supply of pelts; the common currency of the trading process. In exchange, short lists of products were produced expressly for bartering with the native people. The calico shirts, linen breechcloths, blankets of wool, pipes, armbands, ear/nose rings, steel hatchets/knives and guns were starkly similar. They were produced to specifications deemed desirable to the Iroquois Nation and bartered exclusively in exchange for pelts.

Prompted by the predictable depletion of their own beaver population concurrent with rising demand for pelts from the Dutch West India Company, the Iroquois determined that their continued new found "prosperity" depended on expanding their trapping territories. To this end, they looked at the thriving beaver populations in the homelands of their neighbors to the north and west. Within a six year period beginning in 1649, they easily neutralized the Huron, Tobacco, Neutral Nation and Erie tribes and assumed full control of their combined lucrative trapping areas.

The defeat of the Huron provided the Iroquois a generous supply of beaver pelts to perpetuate trading with the Dutch and, ultimately, the English. It also facilitated the continued loss of independence of the native people. As the Iroquois grew accustomed and began to prefer the European manufactured goods, they gave up their traditional tools and weapons. When rifles became the minimum standard to wage war, they were hopelessly dependent on trading for gunpowder and bullets. Warriors that formerly spent their peaceful times hunting and fishing, now focused on trapping and trading.

The Beaver Wars continued as the Iroquois proved their military prowess over the Conestoga in 1675 and the Illinois in 1700. By the turn of the century, the Iroquois controlled the fur trade and were the prevailing force within an area bordered by the Ottawa, Kennebec, Illinois and Tennessee Rivers. They were clearly the dominant tribe on the field of battle.

Tradition dictated that Iroquois women who lost sons in battle were entitled to either retribution or restitution. She alone decided the fate of a warrior captured from the opposing tribe. Should she choose restitution, not only would the captive's life be spared but they would be adopted by the bereaved mother. Adoptees were totally assimilated into the clan and tribe, treated as equals, awarded a clan name and afforded all the rights and privileges of a naturally born offspring.

While a clan mother could choose to exact revenge on a rival tribe responsible for the death of one of her clan's warriors, more often she chose to take pity and attempt to replace a lost son or clan member. So prevalent was this practice, that the Iroquois adopted entire tribes and, in one case, an entire small French colony. The Seneca image as brutal warriors was partially mitigated by this reputation for compassion for the defeated, the homeless and the downtrodden.

A captured warrior faced drastically different fates depending on the disposition of the effected clan mother. If she chose not to adopt, the range of options were abjectly bleak for the captive. The most desirable outcome for the captured warrior was summary execution. The alternatives were a range of tortures, all ultimately lethal. A captive, whose fate was so decided, might pray for just a single day of torture ending with swift execution. The alternate schedule might begin with a day of slow roasting on a fire. Towards nightfall, as the amused observers grew hungry and tired, the victim might be fed and hydrated in hopes that he might survive the night. If he was so "lucky", he would be exposed to a second day of a variety of brutal fire tortures. In most cases, the victim was dispatched after the second day; his head and preferred organs awarded to a tribe member selected by the bereaved mother who was then responsible for the preparation of a feast. By comparison, this treatment makes a day of water boarding at Guantanamo Bay seem bearable.

The French priest LaSalle visited the Seneca Capital of Ganonagan near present day Victor in 1667 hoping to recruit a guide to accompany his party to the Ohio River Valley. This was two decades before French belligerence towards the Seneca began so LaSalle was welcomed as a special guest. To his horror, this "special" treatment included the torture, sacrifice and ingesting of a prisoner captured in a recent skirmish.

Because adoption was the prevalent choice, the Iroquois Nation's population grew to 16,000 by the beginning of the 18th century. Surviving Seneca have a complex web of adoptions to untangle to clearly follow their genealogy. Their nation was a melting pot of eleven or more tribes that were defeated, overpowered or voluntarily assimilated into the Seneca Nation during the warring years of the seventeenth century.

Trading was the primary gambit of the British in attempting to convince the Iroquois to join their side in the Revolutionary War. Perhaps the greatest long-term evil wrought at the bargaining table was alcohol; a substance unknown to the native people prior to trading with the Europeans. Iroquois Chief Scarrooyady was prophetic when he petitioned the Governor of Pennsylvania in 1753 to stop the barter of firewater.

"Your Traders now bring scarce anything but Rum and Flour; they bring little powder and lead, or other valuable goods . . . and get all the skins that should go to pay the debts we have contracted for goods bought of the Fair Traders; by this means we not only ruin ourselves but them

too. These wicked Whiskey Sellers, when they have once got the Indians in liquor, make them sell their very clothes from their backs. In short, if this practice be continued, we must be inevitably ruined."

Where was the Great Spirit during this period of crisis? Did he/she not send dream-borne revelations to his mortal disciples warning them not to stray from five hundred years of tradition; tradition that had rewarded the Iroquois with plentiful game, fertile soils, warm clothes, dry shelter, clear heads unadulterated by the poison of "firewater" and relative peace? The coveting of the fur of a helpless rodent by the European gentry coupled with the Iroquois obsession to satisfy that demand would ultimately force strategic alliances that would prove fateful.

4

Choosing Sides in the White Man's Wars

Because the Seneca had at least five hundred years to move to sunnier climates on their own volition, it is reasonable to assume that they quite liked living in region. The area's bountiful natural resources allowed them to live independently in relative comfort. The forests were abundant with game and held an endless supply of logs to construct longhouses. The lands were fertile and the drinking water clean and plentiful. They called it Pleasant Valley. Life was good!

The Seneca apparently did not tire of the constantly menacing mosquitoes of the dank summers; nor were they driven out by the heavy snows that encumbered the winter hunt. They did not seek the ease provided by more moderate climates. Rather, they were beaten down and slowly driven out over a period of one hundred years.

On July 10, 1687, Marquis DeNonville swooped across Lake Ontario from Montreal accompanied by three thousand French and Indian warriors. He had been commissioned by King Lois XIV of France to eliminate the Seneca as competitors in the fur trade. DeNonville landed at the current location of Ellison Park and marched along a route approximating the course of Irondequoit Creek. This took him on a route that would later include the villages of Webster, Penfield, Pittsford and Perinton in present day Monroe County and onto Victor in present day Ontario County. His destination was the heavily fortified (with palisades) Seneca Village of Ganonagan; the largest village and "capital" of the mighty Seneca. His army crossed what is now Oak Hill Country Club and camped at Mendon Ponds (later to become Mendon Ponds Park) on July 23, 1687. DeNonville razed all Seneca villages he encountered en route.

At one point, DeNonville reportedly feared a surprise attack at the Big Embankment on Marsh Road in Pittsford. While this skirmish did not occur, the decisive battle ultimately took place at Ganonagan near present day Victor. As the French and Indian army approached the village, they were ambushed by Seneca warriors. Casualties were high on both sides with the French reporting one hundred dead and the Seneca eighty. During their retreat, DeNonville's troops burned three other Seneca villages and their stores of foodstuffs.

Ganonagan was considered the contemporary "capital" of the Seneca Nation. Twenty years earlier, French priest La Salle had described the hilltop village as consisting of 150 longhouses and estimated the population at 4500 persons; a number exceeding the size of the emerging settlement at the mouth of the Hudson River which would become New York City. DeNonville referenced four additional local Seneca settlements in recollections of his humbling campaign. Two were major villages containing upwards of one hundred longhouses each. The smaller settlements each consisted of twenty to thirty longhouses. The presence of an estimated 400 longhouses in the area; containing an estimated twenty to thirty families per longhouse is clear indication that the area in and around Big Spring was the heartland of the Seneca Nation.

While the Seneca victory over DeNonville was decisive, Ganonagan was damaged beyond repair. New villages were built along Canandaigua Lake, Seneca Lake, the Genesee River and probably at Big Spring. Some migrated along the Allegheny River as far as Ohio. Had the Senecas not defeated DeNonville at Ganonagan, today Thirsty's tavern might well have been called François's and the patrons be arguing in French.

DeNonville returned to his fort at Lake Ontario via Pittsford and bivouacked at Big Spring. This popular site was located just behind what is now Pittsford's 38 State Street. The benevolence of the victorious Seneca in allowing an apparently leisurely retreat is difficult to reconcile. Having been attacked without provocation, their capital decimated and suffering significant casualties at the hands of the French, henceforth the Senecas allied themselves with the invaders traditional nemesis; the British. This would prove to be a logical but portentous decision.

The first opportunity to do so did not occur for sixty seven years. Despite the passage of many decades and the absence of a written, recorded history, the oral history of the French belligerence towards the Seneca was passed to succeeding generations. In 1754, the entire Iroquois Nation, including the local Seneca, allied with the British and British American forces in the French and Indian War. The Algonquin and Huron tribes aligned themselves with the French and the French colonists in Canada, the Great Lakes area and in the territory of Louisiana.

At the time, what was called the Ohio Territory, was in dispute. This area included the giant swath of land between the Appalachian Mountains and the Mississippi River running from the Great Lakes to the Gulf of Mexico. Both Britain and France desired exclusive rights to this vast territory so as to continue their lucrative beaver trapping. The French Empire in North America was centered in its four major cities that linked the area in dispute; Montreal, Quebec, Detroit and New Orleans. Neither side recognized claims by Native Americans who had considered the land their home for thousands of years.

While there may have been skirmishes in the Valley of the Genesee, no major battles are known to have occurred there. The area played a significant role however as a link in the Seaway Trail connecting France to her inland colonies. Control of this communication and supply route would prove critical to the outcome of the war. Prior to the conflict, there were both French and English trading posts on Irondequoit Bay. The French General Prideaux camped with his army first at Sodus Bay and then Irondequoit Bay on his way to taking siege of Fort Niagara in 1759. Important battles occurred at Youngstown, Lewiston and Niagara Falls.

At this time, the area that would become Pittsford was squarely in the heart of Seneca lands. There were no white settlers in the area. Many Americans from the eastern colonies received their initial military training and experience in the French and Indian War and traversed Seneca lands en route to battles on the Niagara Frontier. Twenty years later, George Washington and others would use training received in the Genesee Valley in their leadership of the Revolutionary War.

These excursions through Seneca lands provided perhaps the first glimpse of the pleasing terrain, bountiful forests, fertile soils and clean waters that made Pleasant Valley so appealing to the indigenous people. These favorable impressions would be recalled a few years later when many of these soldiers sought a new life in the "American West".

In 1759, nineteen-year old Mohawk brave Theyendanegea was sent to Moor's Indian Charity School in Connecticut by his English benefactor William Johnson. Moor's would eventually be moved to New Hampshire and become Dartmouth College. Theyendanegea would be known mainly by his English name Joseph Brant; most respected chief of the Mohawk Nation and ...the Iroquois Nation's first Dartmouth graduate!

Brant's older sister married the successful trader, land speculator and local Superintendent of Indian Affairs William Johnson. Brant was close to his sister, her husband and their family. In 1754, when the last battles of the French and Indian War were imminent, Johnson requested help from the Mohawks. Among the warriors sent to Lake George to join the British in fighting the French was 13 year old Joseph Brant. He followed Johnson into combat again at Fort Niagara. As a result of his extraordinary leadership of victorious British and Indian forces, William Johnson was knighted by the King of England.

Johnson had observed remarkable emerging battlefield leadership talent in the young Joseph Brant. He was not surprised when young Brant excelled in his English skills at the Moor's School. Upon graduation, he asked Joseph to be his interpreter with the Iroquois. When Johnson died in 1774, his successor convinced Brant to stay on as his interpreter and personal secretary. He traveled with the new Superintendent of Indian Affairs, Guy Johnson, to England where he met King George lll. He deeply impressed the king with his diplomatic acumen and English speaking skills. Upon returning to North America, Brant vigorously lobbied the Iroquois Confederacy to ally themselves with his longtime friends, the British. His leadership and oratory skills were generally considered to have been influential in swaying four of the six tribes to ultimately align with the British; a fateful decision.

As it became clear that the colonies would seek their independence from Great Britain and that armed conflict would result, both the Colonial Continental Congress and the British attempted to sway the Iroquois Confederacy to their side. Either would have settled for neutrality on the part of the indigenous people, but were intent on not allowing the Iroquois to ally with their enemy. The Iroquois were literally "caught in the middle" as the majority of their villages, farms and hunting grounds were located between the American Colonies and British Canada.

Based on years of fur trading with the Iroquois, the British were acutely aware of which material goods were most coveted by the Iroquois; particularly the women clan leaders. This knowledge allowed them to make appealing offers of material goods in exchange for their allegiance.

The Iroquois League met in July 1777 to make an alliance decision. Joseph Brant was vehement in his advocacy for supporting the British. Cornplanter continued to promote neutrality but ultimately aligned with the four tribes that voted to join the side of the British. While only one of six votes, as official War Chiefs of the Haudenosaunee, the Seneca vote swayed some indecisive tribes to side with the Great Britain. Ultimately, disagreement among the Six Nations resulted in what amounted to a civil war amongst the native people. The Mohawks, Cayugas, Onondagas and Senecas agreed to fight with the British while the Oneidas and Tuscaroras sided with the Americans.

The conflicts began shortly after the British surrender at Saratoga in 1777. British Loyalists joined with their four newly allied Iroquois tribes in raiding the villages of the Americans as well as those of the Oneidas and Tuscaroras who had aligned with the colonists.

Seneca Chief Cornplanter and Mohawk Captain Joseph Brant joined Tory Commander Colonel John Butler at Fort Niagara. From this secure position, they conducted Tory-Indian raids throughout western New York State.

Cornplanter and British Colonel Butler were joined by a band of Cayugas in July of 1778 as they massacred 360 armed patriots defending Forty Fort in Pennsylvania's Wyoming Valley near present day Wilkes-Barre. The ancillary slaughter of many women and children was a wake-up call for the colonists. The blended army of British and Iroquois was not inclined to follow the more gentlemanly war protocols of a strictly British fighting force.

Joseph Brant and 30 Mohawks joined forces with Cornplanter and 320 Seneca warriors on November 11, 1778. Among the warriors were Cornplanter's half brother Handsome Lake and Red Jacket. Before entering into battle, Red Jacket complained that too little remained of the summer fighting season to make this campaign worthwhile. He returned to the safety of his village before a shot was fired. This continued Red Jacket's pattern of last minute avoidance of danger; a disturbing trait for someone anointed as a chief of the mighty Seneca. Red Jacket's reputation as a warrior was placed in further jeopardy when he turned tail at the sound of the first gunshot in one of the earliest battles of the war.

Red Jacket was an early pacifist at a time when manhood was defined by the adolescent warrior eager to fight and die for the honor of his clan. His first contribution as a warrior was at the age of 29; only when his own village was attacked.

Cornplanter, Joseph Brant, Handsome Lake and their Seneca/Mohawk force attacked the fort at Cherry Valley led by Loyalist Captain Walter Butler, the son of John Butler. With the fort under siege, the Iroquois and Mohawks proceeded to kill and scalp 33 civilians in the adjoining village. Brant attempted to stop further carnage in, what became known as, the Cherry Valley Massacre. He is credited with showing mercy to noncombatants; women, children and men who had failed to take up arms.

By amazing coincidence, one of the homes burned was the residence of Dutch fur trader John O'Bail. Even though Cornplanter had seen his father only one time in his youth, he miraculously recognized him. After rescuing him from the fate of many of his fellow villagers in Canajoharie, Cornplanter offered him a choice of safe passages; either to live once again with the Senecas or to return to his fellow Dutch. When he chose to continue to live with the non-native community, Cornplanter graciously provided his father a Seneca warrior escort.

The fact that women and children were again among the brutally slain, exacerbated the reaction from General Washington. He felt compelled to redirect troops and resources to the New York frontier.

Even as the British were attempting to concentrate troop strength in the southern colonies, he decided to take decisive action to eliminate the "Iroquois threat". Washington turned to Major General Sullivan. His eighteenth century version of "shock and awe" orders to Major General Sullivan was clear.

Sullivan Expedition

"Orders of **George Washington** to General **John Sullivan**, at Head-Quarters May 31, 1779"

"The Expedition you are appointed to command is to be directed against the hostile tribes of the Six Nations of Indians, with their associates and adherents. The immediate objects are the total destruction and devastation of their settlements, and the capture of as many prisoners of every age and sex as possible. It will be essential to ruin their crops now in the ground and prevent their planting more.

I would recommend, that some post in the center of the Indian Country, should be occupied with all expedition, with a sufficient quantity of provisions whence parties should be detached to lay waste all the settlements around, with instructions to do it in the most effectual manner, that the country may not be merely overrun, but destroyed.

But you will not by any means listen to any overture of peace before the total ruinment of their settlements is effected. Our future security will be in their inability to injure us and in the terror with which the severity of the chastisement they receive will inspire them".

Because General Washington's orders were directed to Major General Sullivan, this operation is most often referred to as the Sullivan Expedition. General Sullivan actually led only one of the three prongs of the attack while General James Clinton and Colonel Daniel Brodhead headed up the remaining two allied forces. In total, 5000 soldiers were deployed.

General Sullivan was ordered to lead his men north up the Sesquehanna River to Tioga Point which is present day Athens, Pennsylvania. General Clinton was to meet Sullivan's forces at that location after traveling west from Albany via the Mohawk River to Canajoharie and via land to Otsego Lake and south down the Sesquehanna. The plan was to have Colonel Brodhead lead his troops up the Allegheny River and join Generals Sullivan and Clinton at the Seneca Village located at Geneseo. After joining forces, they intended to attack Fort Niagara.

During the summer of 1779, Sullivan and Clinton laid waste to over forty Iroquois villages. Nothing was spared. Adhering to General Washington's directive, crops, orchards and livestock were destroyed. Meanwhile, Colonel Brodhead's forces leveled ten additional Iroquois villages en route to the planned rendezvous at Geneseo. Brodhead met with little resistance as the main force of Iroquois warriors were preparing to fight Sullivan and Clinton. Joseph Brant, Cornplanter, Old Smoke and Loyalist Colonel John Butler attempted to delay the Sullivan-Clinton armies so as to allow many of the Iroquois to escape with their lives if not their homes, lands and winter provisions. Brodhead never met up with the Sullivan-Clinton forces; instead returning to Fort Pitt in Pennsylvania.

The devastation wreaked by this campaign prompted the Iroquois to assign the Iroquois nick-name of Caunotaucarius, or "Town Destroyer" to General Washington. Much to the General's disappointment however, only a single significant battle was fought during the Sullivan-Clinton Campaign. On August 29, 1779, the Battle of Newton occurred just south of Buffalo on the Chemung River. It was a decisive victory for the Continental Army. Washington was particularly irritated that Fort Niagara was not taken. When General Sullivan learned of Washington's displeasure, he promptly resigned his commission.

Their villages and food stores destroyed, the surviving Iroquois were totally dependent on their British Allies for sustenance and housing during the long, cold winter of 1779-1780; the season forever known as "the winter of the deep snow". Many Iroquois refugees joined the British Loyalist in marching to over-crowded Fort Niagara in search of safety, food and shelter. At the conclusion of the war, an estimated 2000 Seneca had sought sanctuary at Fort Niagara and the adjoining area along Buffalo Creek; the land that would become Buffalo, New York.

The total devastation of most of their villages and the loss of all traditional means to support themselves broke the spirit of the surviving Iroquois. Despite many more deaths from exposure and starvation over the winter, Cornplanter, Handsome Lake, Red Jacket and other surviving Iroquois warriors stubbornly continued their retaliatory attacks well into 1780.

Humbled by the devastating losses to the soldiers from the newly formed "Thirteen Fires" (the Iroquois name for the thirteen colonies), Chief Cornplanter decided that the survival of his Iroquois people depended on achieving peace with the colonist enemy.

He worked diligently in earning the respect of the American government by becoming a highly effective negotiator between the U.S. and Indian tribes (both Iroquois and others) spread over a broad stretch of the American frontier. The respect gained over the years with the Iroquois Confederacy allowed him to keep his people out of the Indian Wars in Ohio and Indiana. He also is credited with skillfully representing the US in negotiations with the Shawnee Nation.

Cornplanter's most famous oration was directed to President George Washington ... "When your army entered the country of the Six Nations, we called you Caunotaucarius, the Town Destroyer; and to this day when that name is heard, our women look behind them and turn pale, and our children cling to the knees of their mothers... when you gave us peace, we called you father, because you promised to secure us in possession of our lands."

In order to better understand his antagonists, Cornplanter studied the Americans in great detail. He seldom missed an opportunity to visit their villages and engage in dialogue to promote mutual understanding. The Quakers provoked a special interest in Cornplanter. He greatly admired their peaceful beliefs, respect for all mankind and rigorous system of education. He was so impressed with the latter, that he asked for their help in educating his son and assistance in establishing Indian schools for the Seneca.

The conclusion of the Revolutionary War brought relative peace to Pleasant Valley. As the New England soldiers returned to their homes from the Sullivan Campaign, they told friends and family of the rich soils of the Genesee Valley and the bountiful harvests they were sure to yield. Early promoters spoke of an "agricultural el dorado". As decades past, New Englanders felt at greater ease in braving the earlier uncertainties and dangers of the western frontier. The lure of the untamed, yet affordable fertile land to the west held considerable appeal to second and third generations much as the voyage to the new world had to their British parents and grandparents.

Despite aligning with the losing side, the Mohawk Nation reaped some benefit from their alliance with the British. The British, feeling indebted, awarded them a substantial land grant on the Grand River in Southern Ontario, Canada. The Haldimand Proclamation of 1784 granted 950,000 acres contained in a very long twelve mile wide swath of Canadian soil to Brant and his Iroquois followers. It stated:

> "I have at the earnest desire of many of these His Majesty's faithful allies purchased a tract of land from the Indians situated between the Lakes Ontario, Erie and Huron, and I do hereby in His Majesty's name authorize and permit the said Mohawk Nation and such others of the Six Nation Indians as wish to settle in that quarter to take possession of and settle upon the Banks of the River commonly called Ouse or Grand River, running into Lake Erie, allotting to them for that purpose six miles deep

*from each side of the river beginning at Lake Erie and extending in that
proportion to the head of the said river which them and their posterity
are to enjoy for ever."*

Captain Brant led his wounded warriors from the Mohawk Nation
to their new home along the Grand River. They landed their canoes
at a shallow within the grant which became known as "Brant's Ford".
As European settlers immigrated to the adjoining area in the early to
mid-nineteenth century, they named their village after the original
Indian landing site, Brantford, Ontario[1]. Brant died in 1807 on the Six
Nations Reserve. Despite the British crown's commitment that this land
would belong forever to the Iroquois, within a hundred years, all but
about 47,000 of the original 950,000 acres of this tract reverted to British
control or had been lost to squatters.

At the beginning of the Revolutionary War, it is estimated that
there were between eight and ten thousand members of the Iroquois
Confederacy in New York State. Twenty years later, the number
had dwindled to 3500 in New York State and 500 at the Six Nations
Reservation in Ontario.

A combination of events caused this rapid decline. The war itself
was costly to the warriors fighting on the side of the British. The
culminating Sullivan Campaign destroyed their villages, crops and
food stores and left them ill prepared to survive the particularly harsh
winter of 1779 – 1780. The British did not have facilities to house and
feed most of the surviving members of the tribe. With very limited food
and only make-shift shelters, a large portion of the confederacy failed
to survive the winter. Subsequent epidemics of measles and small pox
sapped the weakened population still further. A single outbreak of
dysentery accounted for 300 deaths during this period.

[1] Among Brantford's most notable native sons are Wayne Gretzky ("The Great
One") born in 1961 and Philip McNellis born in 1904. The Great One had his number
99 jersey retired by the National Hockey League in 1999 and is considered the "greatest hockey player of all time". Mr. McNellis (father of the author) was regarded as the
"greatest steel buyer" at General Motors. He retired in 1963 and relocated to nearby
Paris, Ontario. His jersey was never retired. He and his wife Dorothy Greville McNellis are buried in Brantford.

5

Seneca Capital in Pittsford?

Was there a major Seneca village located in Pittsford? Could that village have been the capital of the Seneca Nation? If so, were Red Jacket, Cornplanter and Handsome Lake regular visitors? Yes, very likely and certainly!

An abundant supply of clean water was perhaps the most critical element in determining specific settlement locations for the first indigenous people and subsequent white settlers. The Village of Pittsford sits on a limestone dome. Beneath this surface runs an underground stream that feeds a spring. The Seneca's called it "Big Spring" and located a primary village here; on the north side of State Street a short distance from what is now the Four Corners of the Village of Pittsford.

Other villages in Pleasant Valley were likewise founded based on naturally occurring clean water. Nearby Brighton was settled where the soggy marsh on a hill top in Ellison Park marks the source of an earlier spring. Deep Rattlesnake Spring, which is now part of Brighton, was on the road from Canandaigua to Indian Landing and provided a convenient rest and refreshment stop. Penfield was settled based on the availability of dependable spring water. John Hipp purchased one of the first pieces of land in the town which had a spring popular with Seneca traveling to their villages at Big Spring, Ganonagan and the Finger Lakes.

Big Spring clearly played the pivotal role in the establishment of the community that would become Pittsford. In addition to providing a source of drinking water, it fed a pond at the site that attracted game animals. Indian trails radiated from Big Spring to local hunting grounds. One trail followed present day Washington Road toward Penfield. Another passed through Powder Mill Park which contained a reliable source of spring water. That spring now feeds the fish hatchery in the park. Ganonagan, the Seneca capital, was located near present day Victor; a distance from Big Spring that could be traveled in a few hours.

But where exactly were the major Seneca village sites in the Genesee Valley? Identifying these specific sites is challenging for several reasons. With no knowledge of fertilization or crop rotation techniques, Seneca farm yields diminished over time. This prompted the relocation of entire villages about every ten years.

Incredibly fertile soil was in abundance as dense, old growth deciduous forests had been composting for centuries throughout the lower Genesee Valley. Once the clan mothers selected a new site, the forests would be cleared and the deep, rich soil planted with the Seneca staples of corn, beans and squash. New villages would typically be relocated within a day's hike of the original sites

Armed conflict was a second factor causing the displacement of Seneca villages. The fortification of their villages combined with a well-deserved reputation as the most formidable fighting force in the Iroquois Confederacy was normally adequate deterrent to keeping territorial disputes from escalating into lethal battles. While they lost an occasional skirmish fighting adjoining tribes over fur trapping territories or perceived slights, entire villages were rarely, if ever, destroyed.

The Seneca were not so fortunate when attacked by the French and Colonists forces that were equipped with superior arms. DeNonville's campaign of 1687 destroyed the Capital of Ganonagan and three substantial "nearby villages". DeNonville ostensibly bivouacked at Big Spring during his retreat so it is unlikely that a significant village existed there at that time. In 1779, the Continental Army commanded by General John Sullivan laid waste to forty Iroquois Villages. Because the primary fighting force of the Iroquois Confederacy was the Seneca Nation, the Sullivan Campaign focused their slash and burn tactics on the Seneca homeland in the lower Genesee River Valley.

One of the few objective records that identify the locations of local Seneca Villages was prepared by the French military officer Captain M. Pouchot (1712-1769). After successful assignments to engineer and build the fortifications at several French Forts in Canada, Captain Pouchot was awarded the commandment of Fort Niagara. There he developed a favorable reputation based on his ability to earn the respect and loyalty of the local Indian populations. He was so admired that he successfully enlisted a significant contingent of the native Algonquin and Huron to ally with the French in the French and Indian War.

Captain Pouchot was fascinated by the North American Indians. In 1758 he drew a series of maps of what would become western New York State. One focused on the lands of the Seneca Nation in the Genesee

Valley. Though drawn by hand and not to a consistent scale, it provides insight into the location of several major mid-eighteenth century Seneca Villages.

Pouchot's map identified five thriving villages within Pleasant Valley. (See map on page 49 which is based on content on Pouchot's map) Two of these villages were on the eastern shores of Finger Lakes; the Village of Kendae was located on Seneca Lake and the Village of Goyogoin on Cayuga Lake. Two were on the Genesee River; the Village of Kanavagan was located just north of present day Avon and the Village of Kanonskegon was situated at the sight where Geneseo is located today.

The fifth settlement was shown on his map between Irondequoit Bay and Honeoye Falls. It was called the Village of Anjagen. Given the casual hand-drawn nature of Pouchot's maps and the scale inaccuracies, the Village of Anjagen could have been located anywhere between Big Spring and Honeoye Falls. Pouchot depicted its location as due east of the former location of Ganonagan; the Seneca Capital near Victor. (Ganonagan has been added to the revised Pouchot map as a reference point.) If accurate, this would place Anjagen just south of Big Spring. Because the Seneca located their villages at a source of fresh water, it is safe to postulate that Anjagen was either located at Mendon Ponds or at...Big Spring. If Anjagen was, in fact, located at Big Spring, is it not reasonable to posit that it replaced the former capital of Ganonagan that had been destroyed by DeNonville? Presumably the original capital site was chosen for its central location and easy access to the prevailing trail systems that connected the major trading and trapping routes; all attributes shared by Big Spring. The long-composted timbers of the last Seneca longhouses of Anjagen perhaps lie in the sterile darkness beneath the Phoenix Hotel.

With only five villages located in the heart of the Seneca lands and the Big Three Chief's propensity to travel, it is certain that they spent considerable time in Anjagen. And...if Anjagen was the capital of the Seneca Nation, it is safe to postulate that Red Jacket, Cornplanter and Handsome Lake were, at one time or another, residents of Big Spring/ Pittsford.

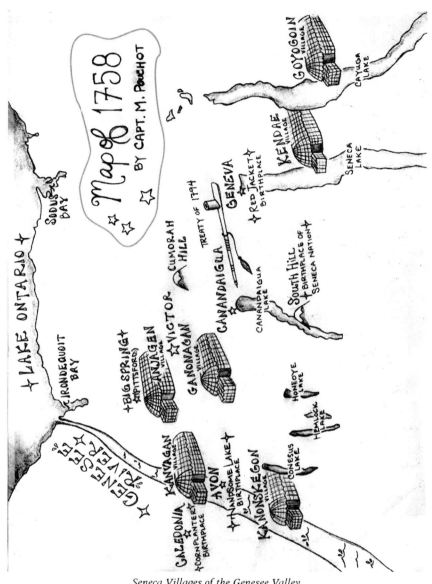

Seneca Villages of the Genesee Valley
Map by Alicia Ivelich

6

The White Man's Upstate New York

At the time the colonies were formed, both New York and Massachusetts asserted that the boundaries of their states extended from the Atlantic to Pacific oceans. Both claimed title to the lands in present day New York State; specifically including the six million acres west of Seneca Lake extending to the Niagara River and Lake Erie. The Hartford Treaty of 1786 attempted to resolve this issue through the compromise of both parties. In exchange for agreement that the lands in question would be forever governed by New York State, Massachusetts obtained "pre-emptive rights" to the entire area. "Pre-emptive rights" meant that only Massachusetts could purchase and obtain full title to the subject lands from the Iroquois Confederacy. Or...they could sell these "rights" to a third party and allow the buyer of these rights to negotiate with the Iroquois.

The Commonwealth of Massachusetts was staggering under its Revolutionary War debt and preferred cash to the uncertainty of the value of land on the frontier. Two years after the Treaty, in 1788, Massachusetts chose to sell their pre-emptive rights to Oliver Phelps and Nathaniel Gorham for one million dollars; a little less than 17 cents per acre. This was to be payable in three annual payments.

On July 8 of that year, Phelps and Gorham successfully negotiated an agreement with the Iroquois Confederacy to obtain full title for all 2,250,000 acres east of the Genesee River plus the 185,000 acre Mill Yard Tract located west of the river. The Mill Yard Tract consisted of a swath of land adjoining the Genesee River extending 24 miles south from Lake Ontario and 12 miles west from the river. It was Phelps and Gorham's intentions to tap the power of the mighty falls and build a gristmill and sawmill on the western shore.

This purchase agreement included one third of the lands contained in their pre-emptive rights purchased from the Commonwealth of Massachusetts. In exchange for forever giving up title on the subject acreage, the five nations of Iroquois, received a payment of $5000 and an annuity of $500. Phelps and Gorham had paid seventeen cents per acre for the "rights" to negotiate with the Iroquois and paid them just one penny per acre to purchase their land; a bargain even in inflated contemporary dollars. Thus began the pattern of unjust compensation in the acquisition of Seneca lands.

One hundred and sixty years earlier, in 1626, Manhattan Island was sold by the resident indigenous people for twenty four dollars or about ½ cent per acre. Since then the value of Manhattan has appreciated approximately seventeen billion percent. The Louisiana Purchase of 1803 resulted in a transfer of land at the rate of three cents per acre. Alaska was acquired for two cents per acre in 1867. Accounting for eighty years of inflation, the price per acre, was lower than what Phelps and Gorham paid the Seneca for the lands surrounding and including, what is now, Pittsford. Phelps and Gorham sold Township Number Thirteen to a group of speculators from Berkshire County, Massachusetts in January 1789. Within weeks they resold the lands that would become Pittsford and Perinton to two former officers of the Revolutionary War.

The shrewd buyers were cousins, Simon and Israel Stone of Salem, New York (Washington County) and Seth Dodge. They purchased 13,296 acres for 18 cents per acre. As the fertile land attracted more settlers, land prices rose significantly and Phelps and Gorham tried to repurchase the land they had previously owned. A deal was ultimately struck whereby the Stones and Dodge returned one half of the acreage in exchange for complete relief of their indebtedness on the original purchase. The net result was that the threesome became the unencumbered owners of roughly 6000 acres for a sum of about thirty dollars. This amounted to an ultimate purchase price of about one-half cent per acre.

By the summer of 1789, the Stones and Dodge had resold at a handsome profit a key creek-side location to John Lusk. The site, on Irondequoit Creek in present day Ellison Park, was known then (and now) as Indian Landing and served as an important Indian transportation hub. Because the surrounding land was so heavily forested, canoe travel was the prevalent mode of long distance travel for the Seneca community. The falls on the Genesee were a significant hardship to a water travel network that ran from the Atlantic Ocean to the Gulf of Mexico. Canoes traveled from the Atlantic, through the St. Lawrence River, Lake Ontario, into Irondequoit Bay and into Irondequoit Creek. By disembarking at Indian Landing and portaging to the Genesee River, the three falls on the upper Genesee could be avoided. Travelers and fur traders continued on their southerly water route to the Mississippi and, ultimately, to the Gulf of Mexico. This was a prized route that the French and English fought to control as it had been the main commercial passage of the fur trade for one hundred and fifty years prior to the settlement of the area by whites.

This portage route, known as the Iroquois Trail, led from the point where Red Creek emptied into the Genesee River in present day Genesee Valley Park and followed a path which later became Highland Avenue. The biography of Solomon Aldrich contained a description of travel on the Iroquois Trail:

> *"The Indians knew that from the bay they could, by water, find their way to the eastern ocean or the waters we know as the tropical Gulf of Mexico. To the Gulf from here by way of the trail was a three league portage 'round hill and dale then beyond the rapids at Red Creek's mouth to the Genesee and upstream to the south. Far upstream was a spot they could seek where canoes could be set in a very small creek. Then, with the current, they were swept on south by the Allegheny and Ohio to the Mississippi's mouth"*

John Lusk planned to develop the commercial potential of this route and purchased several parcels necessary to complete his plan. He acquired land above the falls on the Genesee River, at the bay end and several locations along the route.

Orsamus Turner told of the trip west by the Lusk family in his "History of the Phelps & Gorham Purchase".

> *"Mr. Lusk was a pioneer in improvement and settlement, and in fact bore that relationship to all of what is now Monroe County...With his son Stephen, then fifteen years of age and Seely Peet, a hired man, he came to the new region early in the summer of 1789. Arriving at Schenectady, he embarked with a small stock of provisions, in a bateau, the son and hired man coming by land, and driving some cattle. The son, Stephen Lusk of Pittsford, says he remembers very well, that upon the present site of Utica, there was only an opening of about half an acre in the forest – and that the pioneer there, John Post, was just finishing his log cabin. They came upon the Indian Trail, via Skaneateles, Onondaga Hollow and from there to Cayuga Lake had little more than spotted trees (blazed) as a guide. They crossed Cayuga Lake on a raft, swimming their cattle. The father, son and hired man reunited at Canandaigua and constructing an oxen sled, made their own road to their location in Brighton...While they were clearing their land and sowing their wheat, they saw none of their own race but the surveyors of the township. Indians often came from Canada in canoes to the Bay, on their way to Canandaigua....They returned to Massachusetts in the fall. In the spring of 1790, Mr. Lusk brought out his family, coming all the way from Schenectady to the head of Irondequoit Bay by water, the sons Stephen*

and Erastus coming by land with stock …the family of John Lusk may be said to be the first (white) family located upon the territory now embraced by Monroe County…"

The Lusk's were the first white settlers in Monroe County. Like many of the first local pioneers who settled the area, John Lusk was from Berkshire County, Massachusetts. The present county seat of Berkshire County is Pittsfield which is located forty miles east of Albany; just over the New York and Massachusetts border. When Lusk arrived with his son Stephen and hired man Seely Peet, they discovered a "mulatto squatter" by the name of Asa Dunbar and his family living on the property.

Asa Dunbar was born in Plainfield, Massachusetts in 1754 a few miles east of John Lusk's home in the Berkshires. He too migrated to the western frontier of Pleasant Valley probably just months prior to Lusk's arrival to claim his land. Most historical accounts dismiss Asa and his family as "mulatto squatters" on land owned by the Lusk family but there is no specific account of exactly what transpired when the Lusks first encountered the Dunbar family at Indian Landing. The inference was that they were not allowed to remain.

While John Lusk's family legitimately laid claim to being the first land-owning, white settlers, Asa Dunbar and his family received little notoriety for being the first non-native settlers of Pleasant Valley. It is clear that Asa Dunbar and his family did not simply relocate further west on the frontier upon being discovered living at Indian Landing. In fact it appears that he was accepted and perhaps even embraced by his fellow pioneers. In "Rochester: A Story Historical" published in 1884, the author described the struggling Town of Tryon (on the old Indian Landing site) where four families were attempting to make it commercially viable in 1799: "Asa Dayton, was mine host of the popular tavern, while Stephen Lusk was at the head of the leather concern, leaving John Boyd, and Asa Dunbar, a mulatto, to look more particularly after the general commercial interests of the town".

Several historical anecdotes confirm that Asa Dunbar was quite industrious in his pursuit of these "commercial interests". Dunbar Hollow contained a brine spring whose water could be boiled down to salt for preserving meat and fish. Apparently Asa was seen so frequently producing salt from the spring's water that the hollow was named after him. Others described the fruit from Asa Dunbar's "farm" at Indian Landing being shipped down Irondequoit Bay and across Lake Ontario to be sold in Kingston, Ontario, Canada.

While repeatedly described as "mulatto", there was some question as to whether Asa was, in fact, of mixed-race. In William Peck's "Semi-centennial History of the City of Rochester" (Published in 1884) there is a discussion regarding the disclosure of the secret location of a spring "to three or four white friends, Asa Dunbar being one of the number". Adding to the confusion was the fact that census records sometimes described Asa and his family as "free white", other times as "all other free people" and occasionally Asa as white and his family as "free colored".

The 1790 U.S. Census for Plainfield, MA reflects the following population mix:
- 109 free white males of 16 years and upward
- 120 free white males under 16 years
- 224 free white females and
- 5 all other free persons

Asa is listed as the head of family of the five "all other free people". The same year's census lists Asa's father Sampson as the "head of family" consisting of four "all other free people" residing in the Town of Stoughton, MA. Sampson's family represented four of the eight "all other free people" in a town of 158 people.

Stephan Lusk and his family are shown in the 1800 Census as residents of the Township of Northfield. Asa and his family are listed as "free white" residents on the next line. Given that the population of Northfield at the time was 414, there is little doubt that this Asa was the "squatter" encountered at Indian Landing by Stephan Lusk. The fact that Asa and his family were residents of Pittsford (then Northfield) is further collaborated by the Northfield Town Records. Asa is listed as a participant on March 2, 1802 "at meeting of freeholders and other inhabitants of the Town of Northfield assembled at the schoolhouse in said town for the purpose of electing town officers ..." A "freeholder" is defined as "a registered voter who owns local property and has been a local resident for a specified period of time".

Further confusing the issue of racial identity is the fact that the Census of 1810 for the Township of Boyle (Pittsford area's name at the time) lists Asa Dunbar and his family in the "all other free persons" category. His family represents four of only five persons contained in that column.

According to court records, Asa fell behind on his mortgage payments on 200 acres of land he had purchased in 1807 and lost the property through default. Within a few years, the family moved to Canada where Asa died in 1815.

It is reasonable to conclude that Asa and his family were mixed race because of the continued references to the "enormous mulatto" who had "gigantic strength" and his own choice to declare he and his family as "other free people" on multiple census reports. It is safe to assume that his wife Elizabeth Odle was black or mixed-race because

41

their 1784 marriage is duly recorded in the State of Massachusetts; at a time when interracial marriages were not permitted by law. And...it is reasonable to assume that both were descended from southern slaves.

We are left to speculate how Asa and Elizabeth managed to bush-whack and/or navigate via canoes or log rafts the 283 miles from Plainfield, MA to Indian Landing with three small children in tow; only to arrive without assurance of a place to camp or means of support. All pioneers were brave to pursue the challenges and uncertainties of carving out a new life on the frontier but, to do so as perhaps the only mixed-race family within many miles, took an extra measure of fortitude and spirit of adventure.

The impetus to move from the civilized Berkshires of Massachusetts to the western frontier was largely prompted by a taxpayer revolt among the small farmers of the area. After the Revolutionary War, these farmers were facing foreclosure and possible prison time for failure to pay their debts. These delinquencies were mainly a result of the war debt, leading to high taxes and devaluation of the local currency. Led by Daniel Shays, they "revolted" in a major protest movement in 1786. A number of skirmishes ensued with the state militia. Rather than face likely criminal charges, several hundred residents decided to start their lives anew in the fertile valley of the Genesee. Many of these protesters ultimately settled in the area that would become the Village of Pittsford. Not unlike the sordid past of the original immigrants to Australia, Pittsford's original founders were escaping criminal charges in their "homelands". Perhaps present day civic pride is a remnant of these renegade roots.

John Lusk pined for western Massachusetts and returned there before fully developing his planned commercial enterprises to serve the travelers along the Iroquois Trail. He died in Massachusetts in 1814. His son Stephen remained in the Genesee Valley and built a tannery and distillery at the Indian Landing site. Eventually he sold the land in present day Brighton to the Tryon Company, moved to Pittsford where he opened another tannery and began the first of the Lusk farms.

In 1789, Israel Stone built his log cabin at the Big Spring at the current location of the home at 38 State Street. His brother Simon erected his first home a little to the south at what is now the corner of South and Locust Streets. Family and friends from the Salem area soon joined these pioneers on the new frontier. The Stone-Plumb-Newcomb House on State Street was believed to be built sometime between 1800 and 1825. The house stands today on the north side of State Street, one block east of Main Street just past South Street In 1845, Thomas Plumb purchased the home and farmed land that now includes the east end of Schoen Place and the Powers Farm. The house was severed from the farm when the Erie Canal was built and further eroded when the canal was widened and deepened between 1910 and 1912.

The Stone cousins soon aspired to upgrade their residences from the common, primitive log cabins they originally erected. While the log structures could be easily constructed from abundant indigenous supplies of trees, their inherent design flaws made them very difficult to heat in the long, harsh winters common to the area. Three years after their arrival, Simon built both a gristmill and sawmill on Irondequoit Creek at the eastern edge of Pittsford. The latter could accommodate the production of framing lumber to satisfy his personal needs and serve the growing demand for conventional housing. At the time, the closest sawmill was near Canandaigua Lake.

Phelps and Gorham failed to make the 1790 installment of their debt on the pre-emptive rights to the Commonwealth of Massachusetts. Due to this breach of contract, the commonwealth reclaimed the remaining rights on lands west of the Genesee River in 1791. Within two days, they had resold those rights to Robert Morris, who, at the time, was believed to be the richest man in America.

Robert Morris (1734-1806) paid $333,333.34 (one third of a million dollars) for these pre-emptive rights. For most of his life, Mr. Morris was the Sam Walton of the eighteenth century. He was born in Great Britain but moved with his family to the colonies as a teenager. He became a successful merchant and trader; including two modest attempts at the slave trade. Seeking to utilize Morris' international connections, the Continental Congress contracted with him to purchase and secure arms and ammunition in anticipation of war with Britain.

His business acumen was so well recognized, that he was appointed to be Superintendent of Finance of the colonies. As a result of his accomplishments in this role, he is credited with being one of the pioneers of the financial systems of the United States. He was the catalyst in forming a national banking system and the chartering of the first such bank; Bank of North America. The bank was made possible only as a result of a substantial loan that Morris negotiated from France. The bank's primary role initially was to finance the Revolutionary War.

During the war, he occasionally met the army's payroll out of his personal account. Accordingly, it is no surprise that he became known as the "financier of the American Revolution". His significant wealth was augmented during this period from his ownership of a fleet of privateers that seized and sold the bounty of English ships caught in the waters claimed by the colonies.

Morris was so well respected, that he was asked to be a signer of the Declaration of Independence, The Articles of Confederation and the U.S. Constitution. Washington asked him to be Secretary of The

Treasury but he declined preferring to serve as a U.S Senator for six years. Morris's contributions were recognized when his likeness was selected to adorn the US $1,000 notes and the $10 silver certificates in the nineteenth century. He is also credited with participating in the creation of the U.S. dollar sign ($).

Robert Morris was not a long-term investor. In December of 1792 and July of 1793, he successfully negotiated a two-part agreement with the Holland Land Company to sell a large portion of his holdings. But... these sales were contingent on him successfully gaining full title from the Seneca Nation.

This land sale included 3,250,000 acres west of the Genesee River. It included all lands west of the river except: a) the 185,000 acre Mill Yard Tract that Phelps and Gorham had successfully purchased from the Seneca along with their large tract east of the river and b) a 500,000 acre tract that Morris intended to retain for his personal use. The latter which would become known as the Morris Tract, consisted of a swath of land 12 miles wide extending from Lake Ontario to the Pennsylvania border and following the border of the Phelps – Gorham lands on the east.

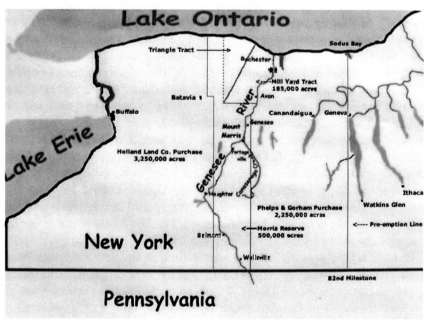

Map of Western New York (c. 1791) showing Phelps and Gorham Purchase (including old Mill Tract), Holland land Co. Purchase and Morris Reserve (including Triangle Tract).
Author: User:Bill 745. Permission to use under terms of GNU Free Documentation License.

Of the lands that Robert Morris retained for his exclusive development, most was subdivided and promptly sold. While most were in relatively small increments, two large tracts were carved out of the northern most area adjoining the Phelps and Gorham Mill Yard Tract. One large 87,000 acre tract known as The Triangle Tract was sold to Messrs. Leroy, Bayard and McEvers. A second adjoining 100,000 acre site was sold to the State of Connecticut. Morris managed to obtain some remaining lands east of the Genesee River from Phelps-Gorham and he sold this land to The Pulteney Association.

The Holland Land Company consisted of thirteen land speculators from Amsterdam, Holland who had never seen the property. At the time, foreigners were not allowed to own land in the United States so American trustees operated on behalf of the Dutch investors.

It is important to remember that Robert Morris only acquired the "pre-emptive rights" to the land secured from the Commonwealth of Massachusetts when Phelps and Gorham failed to make a required progress payment. The Holland Land Company required, as a condition of the sale, that Morris acquire clean title from the Seneca Nation; exactly as Phelps and Gorham had succeeded in doing.

7

Canandaigua Treaty of 1794

Seneca Chief Cornplanter grew disillusioned by the inequities he perceived in the treaties and contracts signed between his people and the white man. In retrospect, he questioned the merit in allowing the descendants of the first European explorers, who had arrived only over the previous three hundred years, such power at the negotiation table. Had not the Great Spirit appointed his people the exclusive and rightful guardians of these North American lands thousands of years ago? Why should the Iroquois Confederacy now be restricted to only a portion of the lands on which they formerly had unlimited rights and access?

By 1790, Cornplanter clearly recognized the pattern... as the white man's unquenchable thirst for more and more of the Seneca's best farming and hunting lands continued unabated, the colonists would initiate a series of cordial meetings. Firewater for the native people and trinkets for the Seneca women would be followed by the proposal of a new treaty wherein more Seneca land would be bartered for the short term gratification of receiving colorful clothing, trinkets and tools. Concluding offers of cash stipends directed to the most influential tribal decision makers combined with a promise of a new "permanent" home for their people would usually consummate the deal.

Cornplanter's distinguishing leadership strength was his rabid opposition to the use of alcohol by his Seneca brothers. He recognized its devastating impact on the collective judgment of the tribe at the time treaties were negotiated and how the white man exploited these vulnerabilities. His opinion was reinforced by his half brother and the tribe's religious leader, Handsome Lake, who recognized first hand, the devastation wrought by alcohol abuse.

In 1790, in the company of his brother, Half-Town, Cornplanter met with President George Washington and the Governor of Pennsylvania Thomas Mifflin in Philadelphia. Perhaps with the telltale recollection that four of the six Iroquois Nations had allied with the British, Washington and Mifflin agreed in principal with Cornplanter and

Half-Town that the lands of the Iroquois needed to be protected for their sole use in perpetuity.

In that same year, accompanied by Handsome Lake, Red Jacket and Joseph Brant, Cornplanter addressed Congress and sought similar assurances. He had additional talks with Washington and they agreed informally that remaining Iroquois lands should forever remain in the hands of the native people.

It is interesting to ponder the interpersonal dynamics, anxiety levels and questions of trust in the minds of President Washington, the members of Congress and the invited Iroquois guests. Just fourteen years prior to these meetings, Cornplanter had helped lead the raids on the Cherry and Wyoming Valleys that resulted in the massacre of unarmed men, women and children. Likewise the Iroquois leaders could clearly recall the devastation imposed on their people by the Sullivan Campaign ordered in retaliation by then General Washington.

There is no doubt that President Washington and the Members of Congress had a clear recollection of these events. Perhaps the term "terrorist" was not coined until the twentieth century, but descriptions such as "ruthless, child murdering savages" may have been uttered by some in preparatory sessions preceding the congressional meetings. There must have been considerable uneasiness in both camps when in the presence of their former enemy.

President Washington, perhaps sensing Red Jacket's pacifist tendencies, presented him with a silver medal engraved with the likeness of Red Jacket and The President smoking a peace pipe. Exclusive of his red jacket, the medal was Red Jacket's most prized possessions. It is now on display at the Buffalo Historical Society Museum.

While George W. Bush may have categorically rejected the option of "negotiating with terrorists", George Washington and the U.S. Congress apparently saw it quite differently. Perhaps they felt it was more prudent to know your enemy than not.

Cornplanter believed the assurances proffered by Washington and his government leaders. He returned to the lands of the Seneca with sanguine expectations and committed to a path of peace and reconciliation. His full intention was to spend his remaining time on earth consistent with the spirit of his Anglicized name; farming the land and growing corn.

President Washington remained uneasy regarding the safety of a growing number of settlers wishing to begin a new and prosperous life in Upstate New York. In an attempt to mitigate these fears, he prompted a summit conference with the Iroquois Confederacy in 1792. Red Jacket was one of the chiefs representing the Seneca Nation. It culminated in the Canandaigua Treaty of 1794. This treaty attempted to establish a "firm and permanent friendship" and "perpetual peace" between the Iroquois and the United States. Further, it clearly defined the boundaries of the Iroquois Reservations and assured the Confederacy that such lands would be their home until such time they chose to sell those lands to "the people of the United States". It did allow however, for the free passage of non-Iroquois through their reservations on wagon roads and waterways.

The greatest amount of detail in the treaty involved the clear definition of the boundaries of the Seneca Reservation. This was essentially all the lands of present day western New York State from west of the Genesee River, north to Lake Ontario and west to the Niagara River and Lake Erie. The southern boundary was the Pennsylvania border. The north-south boundary on the east was, in fact, described as the lands the Seneca had previously sold to Oliver Phelps which contained present day Pittsford.

The Treaty precluded the Iroquois from ever claiming any other lands within the United States beyond the boundaries of the specified reservation. In consideration for their signatures, the United States also committed to a single payment of "goods" with a value of $10,000 and a perpetual annuity in the amount of $4500 for the purchase of various items at the Confederacy's discretion.

Key portions of the treaty are reprinted below.

The Canandaigua Treaty of 1794

Preamble of...

"The President of the United States having determined to hold a conference with the Six Nations of Indians, for the purpose of removing from their minds all causes of complaint, and establishing a firm and permanent friendship with them; and Timothy Pickering being appointed sole agent for that purpose; and the agent having met and conferred with the Sachems, Chiefs and Warriors of the Six Nations, in general council...the parties have agreed on the following articles...shall be binding on them and the Six Nations"

Article 1. Peace and friendship are hereby firmly established, and shall be perpetual, between the United States and the Six Nations.

Article ll. The United States acknowledge the lands reserved to the Oneida, Onondaga and Cayuga Nations, in their respective treaties with the State of New York, and called their reservations, to be their property; and the United States will never claim the same, nor disturb them or either of the Six Nations, nor their Indian friends residing thereon and united with them, in the free use and enjoyment thereof: but the said reservation shall remain theirs, until they choose to sell same to the people of the United States who have right to purchase.

Article lll. The land of the Seneca nation is bounded as follows: Beginning on Lake Ontario, at the north-west corner of the land they sold to Oliver Phelps, the line run westerly along the lake, as far as O-yong-wong-yeh Creek at Johnson's Landing-place, about four miles eastward from the fort of Niagara; then southerly up that creek to its main fork, then straight to the main fork of Stedman's Creek, which empties into the river Niagara, above Fort Schlosser, and then onward , from that fork, continuing the same straight course, to that ; (this line, from the mouth of O-yong-wong-yeh Creek to the river Niagara, above Fort Schlosser, being the eastern boundary of a strip of land , extending from the same line to Niagara River, which the Seneca Nation ceded to the King of Great Britain, at a treaty held about thirty years ago, with Sir William Johnson) then the line runs along the river Niagara to Lake Erie; then along Lake Erie to the north-east corner of a triangular piece of land which the United States conveyed to the state of Pennsylvania, as by the President's patent, dated the third day of March, 1792; then due south to the northern boundary of that state; then due east to the south-west corner of the land sold by the Seneca nation to Oliver Phelps; then north and northerly, along Phelp's line to the place beginning on Lake Ontario, Now, the United States acknowledge all the land within the aforementioned boundaries, to be the property of the Seneca nation; and the United States will never claim the same, nor disturb the Seneca nation, nor any of the Six Nations, or their Indian friends residing thereon and united with them, in the free use and enjoyment thereof: but it shall remain theirs, until they choose to sell the same to the people of the United States, who have the right to purchase.

Article lV. ...Now the Six Nations, and each of them, hereby engage that they will never claim any lands within the boundaries of the United States; nor ever disturb the people of the United States; nor ever disturb the people of the United States in the free use and enjoyment thereof."

Article V allowed for the US to build wagon roads through specified sections of the territory as well as permitting free passage through these lands as well as the latitude to ply the rivers and harbors therein.

Article Vl provided "in consideration of the peace and friendship hereby established" for the delivery of unspecified "goods" having the value of $10,000. Additionally it committed the US to make an annual payment to the Six Nations of $4500 "forever" for their purchase of "clothing, domestic animals and implements of husbandry".

The "permanent friendship" and "perpetual peace" committed to by both parties in The Canandaigua Treaty of 1794 relegated members of the Iroquois Confederacy to the confines of their prescribed reservation while allowing white Americans to build roads and travel freely through these lands. The treaty relieved some, but not all, of the considerable anxiety experienced by adventurous New Englanders with thoughts of exploring and settling in the new western frontier of the fertile Genesee Valley. Only 14 years had passed since Cornplanter's Iroquois war party had scalped and murders civilians at Cherry and Wyoming Valleys. So it was not without trepidation that the flow of immigrants to the area resumed.

In 1796 Cornplanter was awarded a 1500 acre tract of land in recognition of his efforts at peaceful coexistence and contributions to the state of Pennsylvania. The tract was located on the Allegheny River in Northern Pennsylvania, three miles south of the New York State border. It became known as the Cornplanter Tract.

By 1798, he was joined by 400 Seneca followers. Among those who descended on the Cornplanter Tract was his half brother Handsome Lake. He and his family shared a house with Cornplanter.

Despite the fact that the land had been "granted" to him and his heirs "forever", the State attempted to impose taxes on the land in 1821. The dispute was ultimately decided in Cornplanter's favor. This settlement would ultimately create an important precedent for the future ability of the U.S. Government to tax Native Americans.

Despite the favorable resolution, Cornplanter tired of the white man's ways. He decided to follow Handsome Lake's advice and return to the traditions of his Seneca people. He closed the Quaker- inspired schools he had created, burned his military uniform and discarded his war medals.

Even though he had been a well respected chief over many decades, Cornplanter lost substantial support among his followers when the Phelps-Gorham purchase agreement was later recognized by his fellow Iroquois for what it was; a tipping point that began the gradual sale of the vast majority of Iroquois homeland. Because Cornplanter was signatory to that agreement, some described his actions as a betrayal of his people. The resultant death threats deeply disheartened the once proud Iroquois Chief.

Cornplanter died on The Tract in 1836. Consistent with his request, he was buried in an unmarked grave on the Tract. The graves of both Handsome Lake and Cornplanter were moved to higher ground in 1965 to accommodate building the Kinzua Dam. The complete Cornplanter Tract is now covered by the waters of Kinzua Lake; the deepest lake in Pennsylvania.

8

The Fall of the Iroquois Confederacy

The ink was barely dry on the Treaty of Canandaigua when discussions between the Seneca Nation and representatives of Robert Morris and The Holland Land Company began in the summer of 1797. The parties met at a location on the Genesee River known as Big Tree; later to become Geneseo, NY. Cornplanter, Red Jacket and Handsome Lake were among the Chiefs and Sachems representing the Seneca Nation. While originally they were all opposed to the sale, eventually they succumbed to the promise of 200,000 acres that was to be preserved as Indian reservation lands in perpetuity and the lure of $100,000 in cash.

The initial discussions lasted two weeks and yielded no significant progress. Whether he was simply tired or attempting a clever negotiating gambit, Red Jacket decided at that time to "cover up the council fire" and thereby terminate discussions. Cornplanter and Handsome Lake agreed publicly with Red Jacket's actions but Cornplanter had already committed his support of a sale in earlier personal discussions with Morris.

Morris reportedly brought many gallons of spirits to soften the Iroquois will. One day was dominated by drunkenness and fighting. A report at the time described Red Jacket and a group of drunken Seneca "pulling hair...biting like dogs".

Without gaining Iroquois agreement to relinquish all title to the land, Robert Morris' investment had little value; perhaps none at all. Robert's son Thomas Morris, cleverly chose to exploit newly acquired knowledge regarding the balance of power within the Seneca Nation. He learned that, while chiefs and sachems were authorized to negotiate treaties, it was the Seneca clan mothers who held the power relating to all uses of and dispositions of land. Consistent with the long-held tradition within the Iroquois Confederacy, the women held control and authority over land, raising crops and animals. Men were charged with hunting, fishing and fighting. As a result, the clan mothers, along with warriors, could overrule decisions made by chiefs pertaining to native lands.

Morris utilized this knowledge to curry favor with the women of the tribe. Silver brooches, beads and colorful clothes were promised should a successful treaty be signed. He also appealed directly to them and suggested that the generous cash offer could be used to hire white men to tend the fields of the reservations and allow more leisure pursuits by the clan women. He described his approach with the clan mothers as follows:

"… informed them of the offers that had been made to their Sachems; I told them that the money that would proceed from the sale of their lands, would relieve the women of all hardships that they then endured, that, now they had to till the earth, and provide, by their labour, food for themselves and their children; that, when those children were without clothing, and shivering, that their sachems would always supply their own wants, that they fed on the game they killed, and provided clothing for themselves, by exchanging the skins of the animals they killed, for such clothing, that therefore the Sachems were indifferent about exchanging for their lands money enough every year, to lessen the labour of the women, and enable them to procure for themselves and their children, the food and clothing so necessary for their comfort."

Cornplanter replaced the discouraged Red Jacket as the primary negotiator and the Treaty at Big Tree was signed on September 15, 1797. It effectively passed title of the vast majority of remaining Seneca land (3.75 million acres) to The Holland Land Company. In exchange for forever relinquishing title to its heartland, the Seneca Nation was given $100,000 that was to be invested in "bank stock" yielding approximately $4 per Seneca man, woman and child per year. Additional immediate cash grants were awarded to key signers of the treaty; Cornplanter received $300 and Red Jacket $600. Annuities were also awarded to Cornplanter and Red Jacket of $250 and $100 respectively. Handsome Lake was listed third on those signatory to the treaty but the record does not reflect a cash payment to him.

The Seneca Nation was dispersed and relegated to eleven comparatively small reservations ranging in size from two to forty two square miles totally 311 square miles or 200,000 acres. Six of these reserves were on the Genesee River: Canawaugus, Big Tree, Little Beard's Town, Squawky Hill, Gardeau and Caneadea. One reservation was adjoining Cornplanter's Tract in Northern Pennsylvania and the remaining ones were located near Buffalo, along the shores of Lake Erie (Buffalo Creek, Cattaraugus and Tonawanda) and in very Southwestern New York State (Oil Spring).

Even if you consider two hundred plus years of price inflation, it is exceedingly difficult to comprehend the short sightedness of the Seneca and the unmitigated greed of Robert Morris reflected in the final terms of this treaty. Perhaps it was a vivid manifestation of the Seneca's complete lack of understanding of the material world, their naivety of the European concept of land "ownership" and the value of money as a medium of exchange. Maybe it was simply a lack of experience. Recall this was only their second treaty dealing with the disposition of land; the first being the Phelps - Gorham purchase in 1788. Or...was it acquiescence to the growing fear that the cancer of the encroaching white man was simply unstoppable and any material benefit was more than would be realized if they were ever forced to defend in battle their sovereign right to native lands

It is difficult to find any expressions of compassion in the conduct of Robert Morris' agents in their dealing with the Seneca Tribe in The Treaty of Big Tree. Comparisons with NYC landlord Lorena Helmsley may ring appropriate.

While he may have begun his entrepreneurial life as a young merchant like Wal-Mart's Sam Walton, Morris's later years were quite a contrast. Walton bequeathed individual fortunes to his wife and children upon his death. Robert Morris' life did not follow such a storybook ending.

Perhaps overly confident as a result of his very profitable prior business accomplishments, Morris became highly leveraged in speculative land development projects in Washington DC and the Southern U.S. He was dependent on substantial loans committed by Dutch investors to underwrite these projects. When Napoleon invaded Holland, the investors quickly altered their priorities and reneged on their loan commitments. Morris' company became insolvent; he was arrested and placed in debtor's prison from 1798 to 1801. His congressional friends passed the first bankruptcy legislation, at least partially, to allow for his release. Perhaps there is some truth to the adage "what goes around comes around". Morris died a man of modest means.

The ensuing years took their toll on the disenfranchised Iroquois confederacy. In 1817, Erastus Granger, the Indian Agent assigned to the Buffalo area reported:

"The situation of the Indians is truly deplorable. They have exerted themselves for the year past in trying to raise crops but have failed in their expectations. Their prospects have failed. Their hunting grounds are gone. They have availed themselves of their money arising from their public funds but they fall short. They are in fact in a state of starvation".

The impact of "firewater" on the Iroquois was devastating. Drunkenness was pervasive among many of their most respected leaders. In fact, those few who drank in moderation earned a reputation for that singular noble trait. Joseph Brant and Cornplanter's stellar reputations were, in part, a result of their moderation and self-control in the use of alcohol.

Red Jacket, on the other hand, had a life-long battle with the white man's firewater. He publicly acknowledged this weakness and believed that the Great Spirit exacted punishment upon him for his weakness. In response to being asked if he had any offspring, he once replied:

> *"Red Jacket was once a great man, and in favor with the Great Spirit. He was a lofty pine among the smaller trees of the forest. But, after years of glory, he degraded himself by drinking the firewater of the white man. The Great Spirit has looked upon him in anger, and his lightning has stripped the pine of its branches".*

Even Handsome Lake, through most of his life, was known for his tendency to drink in excess. Fortunately, his outstanding reputation as a sober prophet in later life largely overshadowed his youthful indiscretions.

The Treaty at Big Tree was the seminal act of resignation by the once proud Seneca Nation. It pushed them over the edge onto a slippery slope of continued degradation of their independence and self-sufficiency. They no longer had free access to their historic hunting grounds nor the latitude to move to fresh fertile soil every few years to assure the productive growth of food crops. The lands of the Seneca had provided far more than sustenance; they had defined their culture for five hundred or more years. No wonder many turned to alcohol; a short term elixir to dull the pain.

Holland's employees spent three years surveying their purchase and building roads. In 1801 they opened a sales office in the County Seat of Batavia which was centrally located within their property.

Ten years later, there was much discussion regarding the possibility of building a huge canal through the Holland owned land. If approved and successfully built, this engineering marvel would effectively connect the Atlantic Ocean to all of the shipping lanes of the Great Lakes and the western frontier. Holland's local representative, Joseph Ellicott recognized the impact on the desirability of Holland's land holdings and began strong lobbying efforts directed at then Governor DeWitt Clinton. Those efforts were well rewarded when ground was broken to begin the Erie Canal in Rome, New York in 1817; thereby assuring the long-term commercial vitality of Pleasant Valley. Having sold all their land to investors, the Holland Land Company liquidated its remaining U.S. assets by the 1840's. None of the thirteen investors ever set foot on the property.

9

Jesus Pays a Visit to Pleasant Valley

The history of the indigenous people of North America relies mainly on the oral tradition. There is sparse written record of Pleasant Valley prior to incursion by the white man. This historical void extends from the glacial period to the fifteenth century AD.

The exception is an account proffered by the Church of Jesus Christ of Latter Day Saints (LDS). That rendition is offered here because it is the sole historical account of Pleasant Valley during this period and posits a remarkable series of local events culminating in a personal visit to the area by Jesus Christ.

Followers of the LDS Church reject the traditional history text's versions of Christopher Columbus's "discoveries" of 1492. They believe that North America was originally settled in 600 BC by a band of Hebrews who came from Jerusalem.

At some point discord split these early North American inhabitants, into two groups. The Lamanites rejected their Jewish faith and evolved to become the American Indians. Those remaining faithful to Judaism were called the Nephites and built a prosperous civilization. Sometime in the first three hundred years AD, Jesus Christ visited North America and inspired the Nephites with his teachings. During this period, Mormon, the prophet, captured Christ's teachings on a series of gold plates.

In 421 AD the gold plates created by Mormon were buried by Mormon's son, an angel named Moroni, at the northern point of a hill called Cumorah located two miles north of the Village of Manchester near Palmyra, New York. This site adjoins present day Highway 21, two miles north of Interstate 90; fifteen miles down Palmyra Road from the Village of Pittsford.

In the early fifth century AD, the Lamanites (American Indians) destroyed the faithful Nephites and every remnant of their society. Theologians may wonder why there are no indications of disdain or hostility for the American Indians in the teachings of the LDS

Church. Perhaps they have read the DNA studies that clearly prove that American Indians are descended from Asian; not Middle Eastern bloodlines?

Archeologists do not spend much time seeking evidence of the steel swords, chariots, elephants and domesticated cattle, horses, sheep and pigs referenced in the Book of Mormon. The Smithsonian Institute grew tired of fielding such questions and, in 1996, issued a statement stating in part that there was "no direct connection between the archeology of the New World and the subject matter of the Book of Mormon".

Fourteen hundred year later, on September 21, 1823, Moroni reappeared in a series of dreams delivered to Joseph Smith. There is no record that Smith was aware of the revelations which had been delivered via dreams to Handsome Lake in 1799 and Cornplanter around 1820; all three occurrences within a few miles of each other in the heartland of the Seneca Nation.

In each dream, Smith was told that he was chosen to restore the one true God's church on earth. Smith himself remained skeptical until the incarnate Moroni appeared as a mortal and delivered the gold plates to him on September 22, 1827.

Written in a combination of Arabic, Chaldaic, Syriac and Egyptian, Smith was instructed to translate the teachings contained on the gold plates by using divinely inspired stones (peers) set in silver bowls. This resulted in the publication of The Book of Mormon in Palmyra, New York in 1830. The plates were returned to Moroni in May of 1838. They have not been seen again.

To the followers of the LDS Church, the area in and around Palmyra, New York not only has a rich history, but is considered perhaps one of the single most important places on planet earth. Indeed the figurative foundation of their church; Joseph Smith's first visions, the discovery of the golden plates and the writing of the Book of Mormon all occurred within a day's hike of the Village of Pittsford. Accordingly, faithful Mormons consider the Palmyra area as significant as Bethlehem and Jerusalem are to contemporary denominations of Christians and Jews.

With the limited transportation options of 200 - 300 AD and Jesus' pension for prophesizing, is it reasonable to assume he spent his time in the area traveling the prevalent local system of footpaths? Perhaps during this second incarnation he stopped to bathe at a wide spot in Irondequoit Creek (later to become Jaeschke's) or refreshed at Big Spring just a few hundred feet from where Thirsty's Tavern resides today?

To non-believers, this may seem unconvincing and Palmyra just another agrarian based village contributing to the county's twentieth century reputation of growing more potatoes per acre than any place east of Idaho. Regardless, during the second week of July each year, the population of Palmyra expands exponentially as the faithful, and the merely interested, converge on Cumorah Hill to fill nine thousand seats and celebrate the annual Mormon Pageant.

If we are intent on establishing a date when the first "white man" settled Big Spring, we are left with a very broad range of nearly 2400 years. The Church of Jesus Christ of Latter Day Saints contends that there existed a robust white population in the area beginning in 600 B.C. Alternately, main stream historical accounts describe the "white man" as settling the area around 1788; a few years after the Revolutionary War. According to the latter, more popular account, this settlement process initiated the gradual displacement of the lone inhabitants at the time; the Seneca Nation.

Nineteenth century Pleasant Valley had very few African Americans among its population. It is ironic that, during this period, it would be both the founding home of a religion that cast the Black man as an inferior descendent of Cain whose eternal glory would be to serve the white man in heaven[2] and... the home of the world's greatest abolitionist leader who orchestrated the clandestine movement of hundreds of escaping slaves to freedom via the area's extensive Underground Railroad network. Palmyra, in fact, emerged as an important home to multiple "stations" on the North-South Underground Railroad route connecting Bath in the South to Naples, then Canandaigua, Palmyra and Pultneyville on Lake Ontario.

---

[2] See Exhibit #1 for a brief summary of Mormon theology with regard to the "African Race".

10

Early Pittsford

The United States did not invent slavery; "credit" the Greeks, Egyptians or Romans. The practice gained a substantial foothold in the seventeenth century when Portuguese sea captains embarked on the African continent to discover a non-Christian society with weak central government that actively practiced slavery. They rationalized their actions in the name of Jesus Christ; heathens were not worthy of their freedom.

The South, like Pittsford, was mainly an economy dependent on agriculture. Pittsford had grain crops; grown on family farms and access to a steady supply of immigrant laborers eager to start a new life on the American frontier. In order to understand the emergence of slavery in the South, one only has to "follow the money".

Immigrant white men and women were equally available to the southern plantation owner as they were to the northern farmer. These "indentured servants" generally agreed to work a specified number of years (up to a decade) in exchange for passage to America. Once the terms of their indenture were completed, they were free to seek paid employment elsewhere and almost always did so. This system required the perpetual recruiting, hiring and retraining of new farm laborers. The southern plantation owner sought a cheaper, more dependable source of farm labor.

Once the first large plantation owner converted his labor force to slaves, the die was cast. In order to have equally low labor costs, adjoining plantations were compelled to follow suit. The practice spread quickly throughout the South. As the supply of slaves increased to meet the growing demand, their prices declined and the cost of producing and harvesting a bale of cotton became more "efficient". The economics of slavery was turned upside down in 1807 when it became illegal to import slaves from Africa or the Caribbean Islands. Runaway slaves could not be immediately replaced at the local slave sale where heretofore they were in abundant supply for less than one hundred dollars each.

There were about four million slaves and seven million free whites in the Southern States in the first fifty years of the nineteenth century. Of the white population, somewhere between three and four hundred thousand were the landowning gentry; most of whom depended on the labor of slaves. While the majority of Southern Whites did not own slaves, their livelihood was tethered to the economy of the South and its dependence on the cheap labor afforded by the shackles of slavery. Accordingly, this broader constituents of whites remained in favor of retaining the status quo.

The owners of the Southern plantations had grown rich using unpaid slaves to harvest their labor intensive crops; mainly cotton, sugar cane and tobacco. Slaves who chose to escape to freedom threatened not just the pride of the South but the heart of its economy and the primary source of its affluence.

New York State law mandated that any slave children born in the state after July 4, 1799 be allowed their freedom; men at age 28 years and women at age 25 years. Smallwood (soon to be re-named Pittsford) resident Caleb Hopkins bought a young "negro boy" by the name of Titus Lord in Canandaigua for $150 in 1813. Thirteen year old Titus integrated Pittsford's School No. 1. In 1815 Caleb purchased another ten year old boy for $140. Public records are sparse relating to further slave ownership but local Quaker Gideon Ramsdell reported that a "negro" resided at his home in the 1810 census. The Asa Dunbar family, discussed earlier, resided in the village early in the century. There is clear evidence that they were landowners at one time. They had emigrated as "other free persons" from Massachusetts but were listed as white in the 1810 census. The Hargous-Briggs House had "slave quarters" behind the home at the time.

Anecdotal evidence includes Alice Ray moving to Brighton and "taking her slave woman with her" and Lawrence Whitbeck buying Little Jack, Big Jack and Big Jack's family when he lived in New Jersey and bringing them with him when he moved to Pittsford. Big Jack's children attended school in Pittsford.

Consistent with state law, Big Jack was offered his freedom upon reaching his 28th year. "Big Jack declined his freedom at first, saying that he had as much to eat and drink as Mr. Whitbeck, and didn't work any harder than he did; but he left soon after, and Little Jack left as soon as his age qualified him to leave."

In 1796, the District of Northfield was formed by combining the seven townships northeast of the Genesee River and northwest of Canandaigua into a subunit of Ontario County and, on April 5, 1796, the Town of Northfield was established. The first town meeting was held in, what would later become, the Village of Pittsford.

By contemporary standards, the Genesee Valley's first white settlers were well educated. They did not intend to allow their adventure to the western frontier to preclude their offspring from benefiting from first-rate cultural and educational opportunities. Accordingly, the area's first libraries and schools were built in Northfield. Deeds signed in the early years of the area's settlement confirm that most of the early inhabitants were educated or could at least sign their name. Original records of town meetings indicate that "school commissioners" were among the first elected officials.

John Barrows was Northfield's first teacher. Simon Stone donated three acres of land at the corner of Mendon and Mendon Center roads for the express purpose of building the area's first school house. An historical marker designates the location in Pittsford today. The original log building was built in 1794 and funded by taxing local families in proportion to the number of school age children each intended to have benefit. About 1806, it was replaced by a frame structure, presumably built with lumber supplied by Stone's local mill. This structure was replaced by the brick building (Number One Mile Post School) that survives today one mile south of the village. It shares the original site with the Pioneer Cemetery.

John Lusk's sons Norman, John, Aaron and Stephen and their families remained in the area and continued to prosper. In the earliest decades of the nineteenth century, Stephen developed a successful tanning business at Indian Landing and vertically integrated into making shoes and boots. He sold some portion of his land at Indian Landing, moved to Pittsford where he lived until his death at age 85 in 1860. His brother Norman also moved to Pittsford. The Lusk farm was located just south of the village and, until 1992, was farmed by Lusk descendents.

The Tryon Company was convinced that the Indian Landing site and the portage trail to the Genesee was an ideal location for the areas first planned unit development. They built an ashery, a distillery and four cabins in preparation for the traveling crowds they presumed would be embarking at the site. John Tryon's grand plan anticipated that his site at Indian Landing would ultimately become the commercial center of the Genesee River Valley. In his view, it had the important transportation elements necessary for the influx of settlers; namely both land trails and water routes to connect to the remainder of the country and, ultimately, the world.

The masses did not come. Tryon City remained a city only on paper. Due to its superior lake-side location, Rochester logically declared

Charlotte its official port city in 1805. John Tryon died three years later.

In 1807, as the second war with Great Britain seemed imminent, President Thomas Jefferson placed an embargo on foreign trade. This was followed by the Non-Intercourse Act of 1809 and, a year later by the Napoleonic Embargo. Traffic along the Iroquois Trail declined precipitously. Finally, the opening of the Erie Canal a few miles south in Pittsford, provided more efficient transportation options that effectively sealed the fate of "The Lost City of Tryon." Current historical markers designate the City of Tryon site as the "first white settlement west of Canandaigua, founded – 1797, abandoned – 1818".

Settlers to the area came mainly from New England. Migration often occurred in the late winter while ice covered streams were easy to ford and before the spring thaws made the primitive roads less hospitable. While colorful wagon trains made memorable movies, horse drawn wagons were rarely used by the first local settlers. Rather, a substantial sleigh pulled by a team of oxen proved far more practical for negotiating the trip from Massachusetts or Vermont over primitive trails. The designation as "trails" is important as these passageways could not be characterized as true roads. Upon arrival, the strong, versatile oxen were well-suited for clearing the land in preparation for farming. Eventually, as roads were improved and taverns and inns built to accommodate the tired, hungry and thirsty, wide wheeled wagons replaced the ox drawn sleighs.

The first record of a true public tavern in the District of Northfield occurred around 1789. It was owned and managed by Orringh Stone. The date is an estimate deduced from the fact that Stone's tavern was roofed with the second batch of wood shingles to be produced at the shingle mill established at Indian Allen's mill that same year. The tavern was located on what would become East Avenue as it approached the falls on the Genesee. Probable second place goes to Asa Dayton who quenched the thirst of local travelers from his tavern that was one of four buildings at Tryon near Indian Landing. His tavern is now a residence at 319 Landing Road North. Simon Stone was granted a whiskey license in 1793 and purportedly ran an establishment within the confines of Northfield but the precise location of his establishment remains unclear.

The second local school house was built in 1802 in Tryon on Landing Road. That site has contained a succession of school houses; each named Indian Landing School. Present day Indian Landing School is located at 702 Landing Road North in Rochester.

Penfield grew around the falls of Irondequoit Creek which were called "Sgoh-sa-is-thah" by the Seneca. Daniel Penfield built a saw mill in 1800 where the creek drops ninety feet in one mile. This initial development prompted the building of distilleries, asheries, soap mills, clothing mills and flour mills. Prior to the building of the Erie Canal, flour was shipped to Canada across Lake Ontario.

Daniel Penfield was intent on encouraging settlers to purchase property in his development. In order to compete with adjoining areas, he built a school at the corner of Five Mile Line and Penfield Roads in 1804. When Pittsford was known as Boyle, a second school was added on Mendon Road in 1804 or 1805. These four schools preceded the first to be built in the section of Brighton that would become Rochester (Midtown Plaza) in 1813.

Pittsford was the home of the county's first library. In 1803, forty four villagers agreed to contribute one dollar each to fund the establishment of a lending library to be operated from Erza Patterson's home. Logically, Mrs. Patterson was elected as the first librarian in the year of its founding. Within two years, the library contained seventy seven books. While there seemed to be a heavy emphasis on the French Revolution, the library also contained copies of Robinson Crusoe, the History of America, American Geography, Hume's History of England, Goldsmith's Rome, Pope's Essay on Man and Cook's Voyage.

Stiff fines prompted library patrons to treat the library treasures with great care and respect... "any person that shall blot or creese (sic) or soil any book in any shape or turn down any leaf shall forfeit six cents, and taring (sic) of every leaf shall be left to the discretion of the directors and every leaf that shall be tourn (sic) out shall forfeit double the price of the book." The village founders may have been literate but the same can not necessarily be assumed of the author of the library fine schedule.

Early settlers cleared the dense hardwood forests and planted grain crops. The soil was so fertile, that they soon realized that their harvests would yield more grain than could be consumed or sold locally. Not a problem...the excess wheat and rye grain was promptly distilled into whiskey for the thirsty populace. The benefit of distilling was recognized early on; a far greater dollar value of distilled spirits could be stored indefinitely in a substantially smaller space than what was necessary for rye or wheat of equal value. With distilled spirits, there was no fear of spoilage or vermin infestation. Because this was prior to the building of local rail or barge infrastructure, the whiskey could be stored, consumed at a later time or sold and transported more easily than bulky grain shipments. A single packhorse could transport whiskey of greater dollar value than multiple wagon loads of grain crops. It made sense that distilled spirits were one of the area's earliest cash crops.

Why were Northfield and, specifically the area that would become Pittsford, settled before Rochester? The latter had a seemingly more attractive lakefront site and direct access to the shipping lanes of the Great Lakes. Complimenting the advantages of the lakefront location was the powerful and picturesque falls of the mighty Genesee River. The deciding factors were mainly: 1) the relative efficiency (i.e. lower cost) of harnessing local water power combined with 2) the significant disparity in soil fertility of the two areas.

While the Genesee was surely far mightier than the gentle Irondequoit, early settlers to the area preferred the latter to the former. Irondequoit Creek was more accessible and its adequate power more easily tapped. An undershot wheel could be easily built and placed safely in the stream to power rudimentary flour or saw mill in a short amount of time.

It was easy to erect a modest dam across the creek and produce a mill pond. Creation of a flume allowed for the use of the more efficient overshot wheel which yielded 2.5 times the power of the undershot wheel. Even small tributaries, like nearby Allen's Creek, contained adequate latent power to operate small mills.

Secondly, the sandy soil adjoining Lake Ontario supported a broad range of coniferous softwood species. This was quite different than the southern part of Northfield that was covered with hardwood forests. Over the centuries, the decaying deciduous hardwoods yielded rich alluvial soil that was far superior for the desired grain crops of the first white inhabitants. Two men could clear just ten acres a year of the dense hardwood forests. Oxen, that originally brought the pioneers to the area, were called upon to hall the fallen trunks to selected hedgerows where, those trees not needed for constructing log homes and barns, were burned.

While the oilfield wildcatters of the twentieth century may have popularized the "black gold" moniker for petroleum, the first such valuable black chemical was a byproduct of the clearing of North American hardwood forests a century earlier. That period's black gold was...potash.

The availability of potash has been critical to the continuing industrial development of the civilized world for thousands of years. It has been an essential ingredient in making soap and glass, the baking process and the dyeing of fabrics. It is a key component in saltpeter, which in turn, is required in the manufacture of gunpowder.

In the early eighteenth century, the woolen mills of Great Britain were running at full speed. Freshly shorn wool fleece contained about 50% yolk; the gummy secretions of the sheep. Potash based soap was the highly preferred cleansing agent to prepare the wool. Because the English had long ago cleared their land of desirable hardwood species, they depended on imported potash from the U.S., Canada and Russia. Due to their strong preference for American- made product, Great Britain took action to encourage its production in the former colonies. They reduced or eliminated tariffs and provided funding for the building of potash asheries.

"Potash" was America's first industrial chemical. The name was derived from the process. Ash from the trees felled to clear the land for grain crops was mixed with water and boiled down in large "pots" yielding crude black potash. This was a critical cash crop that provided local settlers a stream of income; cash that was needed to pay taxes and purchase staples in the years immediately following the American Revolution.

One large Elm yielded forty pounds of premium potash and garnered $4.00 to the settler. At the time, $4.00 could buy an acre of land. Accordingly, the production and sale of potash was an important element in financing local family farms. The flip side of this prosperity was that, the dense hardwood forests were decimated at a rate greater than what was needed for additional farmland. Millions of acres of dense hardwood forests were cut, burned and converted to "black gold" in just twenty-five years.

While it is comforting to envision idyllic scenes from a Currier and Ives print when imagining Pittsford's first family farms, Norway Tidings' description paints a less pleasant picture.

> "Potash products found a ready cash sale. The cremation of the forest into ashes not only kept the wolf from the door of the pioneer cabin, but enabled many to pay the purchase price of lands. By night the fires, and by day the smoke could be seen from a hundred choppings."

Norway Tidings April, 1887

A comparison to the twentieth century burning of the South American Rain Forests may be valid. Both were products of desperate frontier people trying to eke out an existence in inhospitable surroundings. Had John Muir been born a few decades earlier, perhaps this wholesale raping of old growth hardwood forests would have ceased or the land clearing managed in a more sustainable manner.

Most farmers eventually concluded that twenty percent of each farm should be left wooded so as to provide a continuous supply of building materials and firewood. As the finite forests were depleted, the potash industry was thrown into crisis mode. Farm families began experimenting with ways to extract more potash from a given quantity of ash. They dreamed of ways to milk the waste ash at the bottom of pot for additional pounds of salable product.

Samuel Hopkins found a solution. He was a pioneer in inventing innovative techniques to extend the yield of each pound of raw ash delivered to his potash factory. On July 31, 1790, he applied for and was granted the first U.S. Patent for "making Pot ash and Pearl ash by anew Apparatus and Process". This was the first patent; Patent Number One and was signed by President George Washington and Secretary of State Thomas Jefferson. Just two additional patents were granted in 1790; one for a candle-making process and the other for machinery to mill flour.

Hopkins' new and improved process substantially increased the yields of domestic potash operations. The efficiency gain was so great that, eventually, the United States became the world's dominant supplier of the chemical.

There were two components to Hopkins' innovative process. First, he discovered that he could increase the ultimate carbonate formation by burning the raw ashes in a furnace prior to them being dissolved in water. His second discovery came while he was trying to create a use for the insoluble residue remaining after a batch of potash was cooked. He found that he could mix this residue into the next batch of raw, unprocessed ash and thereby further increase the yield.

From a 21st century perspective, the rewards for Patent # 1 should have been significant. Because he was the true pioneer of patent holders, Hopkins did not fully appreciate the value of protecting his creation or how to benefit from this protection. Later industrialists fully understood the value of patents. Ninety years hence, George Eastman secured patents on his revolutionary photographic plates, films and cameras that became critical elements in Kodak's long-term prosperity. In the 1940's Chester Carlson likewise patented his proprietary processes of xerography and forever change the nature of information exchange.

Beyond his technical breakthroughs in potash processing, Hopkins made equally significant contributions to the world of business by creating and popularizing unique new sales and marketing concepts. Because there had never been protected ideas and technologies, Hopkins was largely on his own in deciding how to capitalize on the intrinsic value contained in the patent he had been awarded.

Rather than attempting to run his competitors out of business by building more cost efficient plants throughout the country, Hopkins created the concept of selling licenses to those wishing to use his process. He licensed the use of his patented process for five year periods. Licensees paid Hopkins either $200 or two tons of potash over the five year period. Recall that an acre of land could be purchased at the time for $4. Each license to process potash by the Hopkins method therefore could have created for him the equivalent of fifty acres of wealth. His innovative licensing arrangement established the precedence for marketing patented processes over the next two centuries.

As the lands were cleared, it made little sense for each individual farmer in the Genesee Valley to process potash. They were consumed by their real mission of becoming America's granary. Accordingly, ash was taken and sold to local asheries. They in turn, could justify the investment in Hopkins's licensed furnaces that produced the greater yields necessary to meet the growing demand of woolen mills being built in The United Kingdom and New England.

While the original patent was lost in a devastating fire that that swept through the U.S. Patent Office in 1836, biographical details emerged as early as 1847 referring to the holder of the first patent as being a Samuel Hopkins; resident of Pittsford, Vermont and, ultimately, Pittsford, New York. This information was affirmed in 1932 in a well respected research published by the Stanford University Press that chronicled the achievements of a long line of descendents of one John Hopkins of the Massachusetts Bay Colony. As recently as 1988, the U.S. Patent and Trademark Office recognized the groundbreaking contributions of Pittsford's pioneer patent holder.

Pittsford's Samuel Hopkins was the son of Lt. Noah Hopkins and Sarah Paine Hopkins. He was born in Amenia, New York in 1765. In 1781, he moved to Pittsford, Vermont where he resided for thirty years. Consistent historical accounts describe that when an inventor named Samuel Hopkins sought patent protection for his proprietary potash process in 1790, he chose to do so in Philadelphia. This was ostensibly due to the fact that Vermont was not yet a state and he was unsure of the protection afforded a patent holder who was not a resident of a recognized state. Around 1810, Hopkins moved from Pittsford, Vermont to Pittsford, New York. His first wife Betsey died there in 1813. Some time later he married Pittsford resident Sarah Dunn. Hopkins died in Pittsford, New York in 1840 and was buried in the Pittsford Pioneer Burying Ground.

The proud citizens of Pittsford, Vermont and Pittsford, New York quite reasonably claimed Samuel Hopkins as their own. In 1956, Pittsford, Vermont history buffs erected a historical marker on their village green funded by the Vermont Historical Sites Commission that lauded the accomplishment of their Samuel Hopkins. The Governor, joined by two hundred proud residents, attended the ceremony. They basked in the repeated praise of their native son and first patent-holder in a wide array of highly respected main stream magazines and esoteric journals.

Not to be outdone, at a bicentennial ceremony in Pittsford, New York in 1989, a historical marker paid for by the Rochester Patent Law Association was unveiled near the Pittsford Pioneer Burying Ground where Mr. Hopkins lies, no doubt amused, by the posthumous praise. This ceremony took place during "Samuel Hopkins Week" as proclaimed by the Monroe County Legislature to honor one of their native sons.

Not so fast. In 1998, Patent historian David W. Maxey discovered a host of inconsistencies in the records pertaining to the holder of the first U.S. patent. Among the discrepancies was the statement that the original patent holder was born in Maryland, not New York. His birth year was shown as 1743; not 1765. His death was recorded as having occurred in the year 1818 in Philadelphia; not 1840 in New York State. Finally, there was no indication that this alternate Samuel Hopkins ever resided in Vermont or Upstate New York.

The holder of the first U.S Patent named Samuel Hopkins was, in fact, born in Maryland of Quaker parents in 1743. He moved to Philadelphia as a child and at age 16, became an apprentice potash maker. During his early adult years in Philadelphia, the local census described his occupation as "shopkeeper" or "merchant". After turning forty, he declared his profession as "inventor". He lived most of his adult life in Philadelphia and enjoyed the initial spoils of his successful licensing venture.

Despite his conservative Quaker roots, Hopkins speculated extensively in the booming market for land. So much so that he squandered the considerable wealth accumulated from his lucrative licensing fees. Near the turn of the century, the homeless Hopkins moved in with his daughter and her family in Rahway, New Jersey. He and his wife Hannah returned to Philadelphia in 1814. Hopkins died there in 1818. Prior to his death, he was awarded two additional patents; both for "a preparation of flour of mustard". The record does not reference any link to Pittsford's French's Mustard but it is an interesting coincidence.

The definitive research on the controversy to discover the "real" Samuel Hopkins was surely a disappointment to residents of both Vermont and Upstate New York. Mr. Maxey's findings were summarized in a 1998 article titled "Inventing History: The Holder of the First U.S. Patent". He is emphatic in stating that there has never been any indication that the Samuel Hopkins that did reside in both Pittsfords ever attempted to personally claim to be the first patent-holder. Likewise, he describes the path taken by the well intentioned local historians as "quite simply, the compounding effect of uncontested error". But what to do with those sturdy historic markers designed to last a century or more? Patent Historian Maxey said it best: "There is no reliable precedent or prescribed ritual for decommissioning two roadside markers put up in good faith to honor the wrong man."

The seed of this error was probably sown by the overzealous genealogist, Timothy Hopkins, who had been contracted to trace the progeny of John Hopkins; a resident of the Massachusetts Bay Colony. Pittsford's Samuel Hopkins was, in fact, descended from this John Hopkins. In 1932, young Timothy discovered a mistaken reference to THE first patent holder being a resident of Vermont - no city specified. That sufficed however for Timothy to anoint his Samuel as the holder of Patent #1. This error was propagated and remained "uncontested" until 1998.

Hopkins did not live to see the demise of the American potash industry that occurred twenty years after his death. At that time, rich natural deposits of potash were discovered in the dry lake beds of Europe; mainly in Germany. Germany then became the dominant supplier to the U.S. market until World War I when an embargo ceased all German imports. The U.S. had to scramble to meet domestic demand and did so by eking out potash from various wastes of the mining, kelp and food processing industries. After the First World War, Germany again became an important supplier but discoveries in Russia, France and Poland supplemented those supplies. Before World War II, America became self-sufficient in potash as naturally occurring deposits were discovered in New Mexico, California and Utah.

In the twenty-first century, the market for potash has rebounded with vigor. In recent years the high energy costs associated with producing potash had caused the market to languish. As the demand for food crops has accelerated concurrent with growing demand for corn based ethanol, the demand for fertilizers to increase the output per acre has jumped. Potash sales and prices have increased as a result.

It was clear to the first white settlers that the Seneca could dependably rely on an abundance of wild fish and game for sustenance. The deer population remained robust; pioneer William Hencher, the first white man to build a "hut" at the mouth of the Genesee and hunting partner of Asa Dunbar, reported bagging six deer in one day. He regularly hiked to Braddock Bay on Lake Ontario where otter and mink were plentiful. Hencher harvested all the eggs his family could eat from the shores of Irondequoit Bay; a favorite breeding ground for massive flocks of geese and ducks. He also spoke of the hazards of traversing the shore of the Genesee River where he reportedly dispatched forty rattlesnakes in a single day. An article in the "Rochester and Post Express" described Allan's Creek as "so full of trout that one could catch a hundred of them without changing position".

While grain crops were the early focus, many of the areas first inhabitants of Anglo Saxon descent, herded domestic farm animals with them on their trek from New England. The quality of life was clearly enhanced with the prospect of fresh beef, pork or chicken on the homestead's menu. Providing these luxuries did not come easily. Not only did the early pioneers have to herd the breeding stock hundreds of miles from New England but once settled, the animals had to be fed, protected from the elements and from the indigenous bear and wolf populations. The latter surely found domesticated animals easy targets compared to the deer, ducks, turkeys and squirrels that were hardwired to elude such predators.

Both the Stones and Lusk's lost pigs to the "call of the wild". After escaping, they transitioned from domestic to wild boar. Once their tusks grew to their natural state and provided potentially lethal protection, they were not intimated by the local black bears. Eventually, however, they caused such damage to crops, that they became a favorite target for local hunters.

The grain crops provided ample food for local squirrel and pigeon populations and caused a quantum leap in their numbers. Farmers had to remain diligent to scare off the masses of passenger pigeons seeking seeds in newly planted fields. These were no doubt the ancestors of Bunny Bonhurst's passenger pigeons that roamed the Pittsford skies in the third quartile of the twentieth century. As the grain matured, the local squirrels feasted and hoarded for the bitter Upstate winter. Young men were enlisted to thin the squirrel population, hone their hunting skills and provide meat for the table. This tradition continued into the twentieth century as local youth were encouraged to hunt squirrels.

While the economic vitality of twentieth century Pleasant Valley was measured by product development announcements and sales forecasts at Kodak and Xerox, in the prior century, water was the lifeblood of the family farm and a key determinant of the area's prosperity. For good reason, there was much talk about the weather; specifically rain. It either seemed to be inadequate in volume, arrive too early or too late.

The Ontario Repository of October 10, 1809 reported a disappointing year for crops:

> *"We have taken some pains to collect information relative to the crops this season, from which it appears that wheat – our prime commodity, comes in much short of a middling crop, smut has injured many fields, and many 'tares (weeds) among the good seed' in general. Rye hurt much by cold spring weather, weighs very light. Flax in some parts good, in others will scarcely pay securing; seed very sour. Oats not gathered, but from an observation will come very light. Planted late, ears*

not well filled and some low fields greatly damaged by September frosts. Hay good yield in general, but the extensive rains in July destroyed the produce of whole meadows; hundreds of tons floated and spoiled in the Genesee flats, much hay damaged in curing. Apples scarce."

Despite the unpredictable weather and challenging growing years of the first decade of the nineteenth century, the bountiful wheat crops of the Genesee Valley caused the area to become known as the "nation's granary".

Local Seneca had propagated seeds from indigenous apple trees into small local orchards. Recognizing the value of adding fruit to the pioneer diet, Jesse Perrin is credited with establishing the first local orchard in Perinton around 1790. Shortly thereafter, Josial Farr gathered seeds from a Seneca orchard at Seneca Point on Canandaigua Lake and started the first apple orchard in Pittsford.

11

The Iroquois Renaissance

"Our religion is not one of paint and feathers; it is a thing of the heart"
Handsome Lake

Cornplanter's half brother Handsome Lake was the Iroquois Confederacy's great nineteenth-century prophet. He ministered to brethren at the Coldspring, Tonawanda and Cornplanter Reservations. Like Red Jacket, he strongly encouraged his Seneca brothers and sisters to continue in their native tradition and remain faithful to the one Great Spirit of the Iroquois.

He parted with Red Jacket in advocating that the Iroquois learn the English language so as to facilitate peaceful coexistence with the white man. He promoted the selective adoption of specific aspects of the white mans' technology that could improve the living standards of his people; particularly as it related to farming. He advocated silent prayer, the performance of good deeds, abstinence from alcohol and continued formal education as the foundation of his "Longhouse Religion". His doctrine, known by the Iroquois as Gawwiio, encouraged a return to the communal nature of their roots and against the individual accumulation of wealth. While, Handsome Lake died in 1815, many present day Iroquois continue to practice the Gawwiio as they gather in longhouses of worship.

Handsome Lake was a minor chieftain for most of his life. He was born in 1735 in the Seneca village of Conawagas on the Genesee River opposite the current site of Avon. At the time of his birth, the Seneca Nation was at the pinnacle of its prestige, power and prosperity. By his fortieth year (1775), morale was abysmally low, alcoholism was rampant and the Iroquois people had been stripped of their last remnants of dignity. Relegated to reservations, their culture was spiraling to extinction.

Through much of his life he was guilty, along with many others, of excessive use of distilled spirits. His leadership blossomed just as the morale and cultural values of his people were deteriorating to its lowest point in history. In his final fifteen years, he became supreme leader of the Six Nations (1801), emerged as its spiritual leader (the "Peace Prophet") and was the driving force in a veritable cultural renaissance of the Iroquois Confederacy.

When Handsome Lake was sixty four years old and living with Cornplanter, he fell into an alcohol induced coma. While in this unconscious state, he was inspired by a series of dream-based revelations. His resulting "religion" was a thoughtful blend of elements from the traditional pagan theocracy and the beliefs of Quaker Christians. His visions began in 1799 when he was visited by a series of angels; one of whom was Jesus Christ. These initial revelations called for Handsome Lake to lead his people in a doctrine of: 1) confession of sins and a promise to cease from repeating those sins 2) strict temperance and 3) a series of rituals created to be "pleasing to the Creator"

Initially Handsome Lake described himself as simply a humble messenger of the Great Spirit. His prophesizing lost some believability and momentum when he shared the news, that on subsequent visits, the angels declared him divine and clairvoyant.

Over time Handsome Lake refined his gospel to include a series of values that went beyond the spiritual to offer broad guidelines for personal conduct and prescriptions for interpersonal interactions. Given the desperate and deteriorated state of the Iroquois Confederacy, many found the principles he extolled appealing. They included:
- Strict temperance
- Peace and Unity with your fellow Indian and the white man… Jesus spoke to the white man; Handsome Lake to the red man.…condemnation of the profit motive, promiscuity, gambling and dancing
- Land retention – no more land to be sold or transferred to the white man
- Schooling for all in English; mainly in Quaker schools… avoidance of total acculturation of white ways…learn white language and technology to improve standards of living and peacefully coexist with white society but retain Indian identity
- Revised domestic morality – focus on the sanctity of marriage, sin of divorce, supreme value of the nuclear family…a break from the matrilineal tradition where the clan's eldest female ruled… sons to obey fathers… mothers were not to interfere with the marriage plans of daughters

If Handsome Lake were running for elective office today, his platform would be heavily based on "family values". One proposed change that had to be delicately orchestrated concerned the specific roles of men and women. Traditionally women were responsible for the home and the raising of food while men's providence had been the forest, game food and war. In the past, little time was spent discussing the relative importance of each role; both were critical for the safety and prosperity of the clan.

Handsome Lake clearly broke with the long-held matriarchal tradition in advocating that the man be the "head" of the household. He taught that, with the loss of Iroquois hunting grounds, room must be made for the men of the tribe to continue as providers. He proposed that, as the family adapted to the ways of white farming, the work on farms must be shared between the genders with men taking on the main farming responsibility.

Ironically, the clan women were the most resistant to this radical change. The first of these "modern" men, were mocked and called "timid woman" by females resistant to sharing their traditional roles. Others accused these pioneering men of being transvestites.

Handsome Lake's teachings regarding the roles of men and women were contrary to centuries of embedded tradition. If men were to have greater responsibility and power, women by necessity, would have to forego some of their prior influence. While he stopped short of challenging the matrilineal principle, it was clear that he felt that the role of women and their female offspring must change. Not withstanding the perception that women should play a subservient role to men, the principles extolled by Handsome Lake were highly agreeable to a significant portion of a disillusioned population yearning to regain their dignity.

Handsome Lake's success, occurring between 1799 and 1815, was indeed remarkable. As the half brother of the very popular Chief Cornplanter, Handsome Lake had a degree of instant credibility. This provided some impetus to his selection as "Supreme Leader" of the Six Nations by the Buffalo Creek Council in 1801.

In 1802, Handsome Lake met with President Jefferson and requested that he pass legislation prohibiting the sale of alcohol to Indians. He also asked for the deed to the one hundred square mile Oil Springs Reservation for his exclusive use.

President Jefferson was impressed by Handsome Lake and his teachings. This endorsement brought him added credibility among greater numbers of the Confederacy. Following their meeting in Washington, Jefferson wrote to his "brother" Handsome Lake. Therein, Jefferson commends Handsome Lake's efforts in advocating temperance among his people and pledges his support of those efforts. While he also assures him that Iroquois land will be forever Iroquois land, he, not too subtly, suggests that it may make good sense for his people to sell their "excess" land and use the proceeds to improve the productivity of the lands they retained.

Thomas Jefferson: Indian Addresses

To Brother Handsome Lake
Washington, November 3, 1802
TO BROTHER HANDSOME LAKE: --

I have received the message in writing which you sent me through Captain Irvine, our confidential agent, placed near you for the purpose of communicating and transacting between us, whatever may be useful for both nations. I am happy to learn you have been so far favored by the Divine spirit as to be made sensible of those things which are for your good and that of your people, and of those which are hurtful to you; and particularly that you and they see the ruinous effects which the abuse of spirituous liquors have produced upon them. It has weakened their bodies, enervated their minds, exposed them to hunger, cold, nakedness, and poverty, kept them in perpetual broils, and reduced their population. I do not wonder then, brother, at your censures, not only on your own people, who have voluntarily gone into these fatal habits, but on all the nations of white people who have supplied their calls for this article. But these nations have done to you only what they do among themselves. They have sold what individuals wish to buy, leaving to every one to be the guardian of his own health and happiness. Spirituous liquors are not in themselves bad, they are often found to be an excellent medicine for the sick; it is the improper and intemperate use of them, by those in health, which makes them injurious. But as you find that your people cannot refrain from an ill use of them, I greatly applaud your resolution not to use them at all. We have too affectionate a concern for your happiness to place the paltry gain on the sale of these articles in competition with the injury they do you. And as it is the desire of your nation, that no spirits should be sent among them, I am authorized by the great council of the United States to prohibit them. I will sincerely cooperate with your wise men in any proper measures for this purpose, which shall be agreeable to them.

You remind me, brother, of what I said to you, when you visited me the last winter, that the lands you then held would remain yours, and shall never go from you but when you should be disposed to sell. This I now repeat, and will ever abide by. We, indeed, are always ready to buy land; but we will never ask but when you wish to sell; and our laws, in order to protect you against imposition, have forbidden individuals to purchase lands from you; and have rendered it necessary, when you desire to sell, even to a State, that an agent from the United States should attend the sale, see that your consent is freely given, a satisfactory price paid, and report to us what has been done, for our approbation. This was done in the late case of which you complain. The deputies of your nation came forward, in all the forms which we have been used to consider as evidence of the will of your nation. They proposed to sell to the State of New York certain parcels of land, of small extent, and detached from the body of your other lands; the State of New York was desirous to buy. I sent an agent, in whom we could trust, to see that your consent was free, and the sale fair. All was reported to be free and fair. The lands were your property. The right to sell is one of the rights of property. To forbid you the exercise of that right would be a wrong to your nation. Nor do I think, brother, that the sale of lands is, under all circumstances, injurious to your people. While they depended on hunting, the more extensive the forest around them, the more game they would yield. But going into a state of agriculture, it may be as advantageous to a society, as it is to an individual, who has more land than he can improve, to sell a part, and lay out the money in stocks and implements of agriculture, for the better improvement of the residue. A little land well stocked and improved, will yield more than a great deal without stock or improvement. I hope, therefore, that on further reflection, you will see this transaction in a more favorable light, both as it concerns the interest of your nation, and the exercise of that superintending care which I am sincerely anxious to employ for their subsistence and happiness. Go on then, brother, in the great reformation you have undertaken. Persuade our red brethren then to be sober, and to cultivate their lands; and their women to spin and weave for their families. You will soon see your women and children well fed and clothed, your men living happily in peace and plenty, and your numbers increasing from year to year. It will be a great glory to you to have been the instrument of so happy a change, and your children's children, from generation to generation, will repeat your name with love and gratitude forever. In all your enterprises for the good of your people, you may count with confidence on the aid and protection of the United States, and on the sincerity and zeal with which I am myself animated in the furthering of this humane work. You are our brethren of the same land; we wish your prosperity as brethren should do. Farewell.

Even though Handsome Lake made steady progress in converting native brethren to his Gawwiio (Longhouse Religion), all were not easily convinced. Some objected to the core principals of his revolutionary doctrine while others were distracted by the quickly evolving social, cultural and economic realities precipitated by the conclusion of the War of 1812. The end of conflict prompted an influx of white settlers who brought new tools and technologies as well as a seemingly insatiable thirst to acquire Iroquois land. They also brought theological competition to the Gawwiio in the form of Christian missionaries who were intent on saving the souls of the savage population.

When the ideas that Handsome Lake advocated showed immediate positive results, the popularity of his ministry spiked upward. The adoption of white farming techniques resulted in an agricultural renaissance for the Iroquois. Corn yields increased tenfold as a result of steel tipped ploughs, fertilization and crop rotation strategies.

Among the controversial aspects of the Longhouse Religion, was the continued persecution of those accused of witchcraft. Any evil that befell an individual, a clan or a tribe, that could not otherwise be explained, was blamed on those suspected of practicing witchcraft. Gawwiio lost some momentum when several "witches" were executed by followers in 1809. In protest of this practice, Chief Cornplanter and the allied Quakers chose to disassociate themselves from the Longhouse Religion.

One particular irony played out with regularity. While Handsome Lake espoused greater peace and harmony between the red man and the white man, the greater this interaction, the greater the opportunity for the Iroquois to be led astray by the unscrupulous among the white men.

Followers often relayed that it was Handsome Lake's influence that provided them the will power to finally stop drinking. Others simply referred to the overall heightened sense of inner strength and peacefulness. Quakers, reporting on their reservation visits in 1806, stated that they were stunned to find that most Indians were refusing liquor that was being offered.

Handsome Lake was least effective at Buffalo Creek where his old nemesis Red Jacket held court with considerable influence. The remaining pockets of resistance were on the smaller reservations along the Genesee River where the Seneca inhabitants were described as the "bad Indians". They were notoriously difficult to convert to the Gawwiio mainly because they resided in close proximity to the white men living on the adjoining land sold to Phelps and Gorham. The whites were accused of plying the natives with liquor and swindling them out of their limited possessions. The area had a reputation for lawlessness that was prompted by heavy drinking, brawling and assorted criminal behavior.

In 1806, Handsome Lake embarked on what he called "The Genesee Revival". He allotted three full days to confession. Despite his extra efforts, his success was limited to the chiefs and women of the clans. In his later years, he grew frustrated over his limited success in Buffalo Creek and the Genesee River area and decided to spend most of his time strengthening the conversions that had been achieved elsewhere.

Handsome Lake died at Onondaga on August 10, 1815 at age 80. The <u>Buffalo Gazette</u> was both brutally candid and laudatory in announcing his death …"Until fifty years old he was remarkable only for his stupidity and beastly drunkenness". They continued by relaying the story of his revelations of eighteen years earlier, wherein he was told "the Great Spirit is angry with you, and all the red men, and unless you immediately refrain from drunkenness, lying and stealing, you shall never enter the beautiful place which we will now show you." After describing Handsome Lake's visit to the gates of heaven, they concluded by describing his legacy… "The chief immediately abandoned his habits, visited the tribes, -related his story- which was believed, and the consequence has been, that from a filthy, lazy, drunken set of beings, they have become cleanly, industrious, sober, and happy."

While the Gawwiio had lost its one spiritual leader, his gospel continued to have a favorable impact on his people. Around 1820, Cornplanter, professed to a series of revelations that were similar to Handsome Lake's. The notable exception was that the Iroquois should not seek peace with the white man, but rather, avoid contact at all costs. He thereby joined in the doctrine long espoused by Red Jacket.

The Church of Handsome Lake continued to evolve through mid-century. In the 1840's, Handsome Lake's grandson, Jimmy Johnson led a second renaissance of the Church of Handsome Lake. While many of the aspects of the Gawwiio indeed complimented Christian ideology, the added appeal to the Iroquois followers was the distinct identification with the Indian tradition as opposed to the culture of the white community. The format of the contemporary doctrine of "Handsome Lakers" was set by the mid nineteenth-century and continues intact today.

12

Bringing Jesus to the Heathens

Evangelical Christians initiated extensive missionary work in the new world to bring the native heathens to Christianity. The Quakers had made modest conversion attempts in the last decade of the eighteenth century but it was the zealous Baptists that demonstrated staying power. They established their first mission in 1800 and were active for over 35 years. No issue since choosing allegiances at the beginning of the Revolutionary War proved to be as divisive within the Iroquois Confederacy.

Native people fell either into the Christian camp or what the missionaries chose to call pagans. Within the non-Christian contingency, the Iroquois tended to either follow the Gawwiio of Handsome Lake or align with the more simple doctrine of Seneca Chief Red Jacket. The latter vehemently contended that his followers were no less religious than the followers of Christianity. They were simply following a different God; their own Great Spirit. He contended that the main difference in ideologies was that the Iroquois God had not been chosen by the white man. Red Jacket summarized the Iroquois' simple religious beliefs in his epic 1805 speech. He described a religion wherein followers were dedicated to:

- being thankful for all of the Great Spirit's favors
- loving each other
- being united

Red Jacket once observed that the Iroquois never quarreled about their religion; there was unanimity. He rhetorically asked why, if the white man supposedly followed only a single unified religion, do they continually argue, debate and even fight regarding the apparent nuances of their religion?

Red Jacket was convinced that the missionaries were simply another arrow in the quiver of the white mans' conspiracy to make further inroads into tribal lands, impose their laws, their school systems and ultimately their rule of law upon his native people. He called the missionaries "black coats" who were diabolically attempting to win the hearts of his people. He was convinced that the missionaries' efforts were simply intended to pave the way for the land speculators who were intent on relieving his people of the land the Great Spirit had placed under their guardianship.

By the time Red Jacket was in his late teens, he became categorically opposed to any continued interaction with the missionaries or any of their white brethren intent on settling in Pleasant Valley. It was his belief that all contact with the white man should be eliminated and his Iroquois people revert solely to their native traditions.

When speaking out against the sale of Seneca land, Red Jacket stated:

"We stand as a small island in the bosom of the great waters...They rise, they press upon us and the waves will settle over us and we shall disappear forever. Who then lives to mourn us, white man? None."

Despite his elegant oratory in opposition to adopting the ways of the whites, Christianity steadily grew in popularity among his people. Red Jacket made a tactical error in combining his opposition to Christianity with all things white. As he lost the allegiance of converted Christians, he tended to lose their support on all fronts; including his opposition to his peoples' continued adoption of white customs and the sale of Iroquois lands. As time passed, the converted Christians represented a growing influential faction opposed to Red Jacket. So much so that, at one point, the aging chief was deposed. He appealed to the Tribal Council and, as would be expected, he defended his character and leadership with such conviction and persuasion, that he was reinstated as a Chief of the Seneca.

In 1805, Red Jacket delivered his most famous speech to a chief's council of the Iroquois Confederacy in response to a request by a New England missionary to ply his trade among the Seneca.

His remarks go well beyond a comparison of the religions of the White Man vs. the Red Man and the immediate question of whether or not to allow the missionary Mr. Cram free access to the Iroquois people. In just a few hundred words, he captures the essence of three hundred years of native peoples' attempts to peacefully accommodate the intrusions of the uninvited European masses to the Iroquois homeland.

He makes a compelling case for the abject hypocrisy of the white man who professed to have come to these shores from across the "great waters" so as to be allowed the freedom to practice their own religion. Now, after being befriended and fed by the native people, these same white men acted to deprive the native people of <u>their</u> own freedom to practice <u>their</u> traditional religion. He further asks why, if the white man's religion, written in a single book, is the only true religion, "did the Great Spirit not give our forefathers knowledge of that book"? Red Jacket contends that the Great Spirit, in fact, treats his red children, white children and Black children differently and therefore asks "why could he not give us different religions according to our own understanding"?

So cogent were his remarks, that his words are contained in Bartleby's List of the World's Famous Orations.

The World's Famous Orations.
America: I. (1761–1837). 1906.

Red Jacket on the Religion of the White Man and the Red
Red Jacket (c.1758–1830)
(1805)

"*FRIEND AND BROTHER:—It was the will of the Great Spirit that we should meet together this day. He orders all things and has given us a fine day for our council. He has taken His garment from before the sun and caused it to shine with brightness upon us. Our eyes are opened that we see clearly; our ears are unstopped that we have been able to hear distinctly the words you have spoken. For all these favors we thank the Great Spirit, and Him only.*

Brother, this council fire was kindled by you. It was at your request that we came together at this time. We have listened with attention to what you have said. You requested us to speak our minds freely. This gives us great joy; for we now consider that we stand upright before you and can speak what we think. All have heard your voice and all speak to you now as one man. Our minds are agreed.

Brother, you say you want an answer to your talk before you leave this place. It is right you should have one, as you are a great distance from home and we do not wish to detain you. But first we will look back a little and tell you what our fathers have told us and what we have heard from the white people.

Brother, listen to what we say. There was a time when our forefathers owned this great island. Their seats extended from the rising to the setting sun. The Great Spirit had made it for the use of Indians. He had created the buffalo, the deer, and other animals for food. He had made the bear and the beaver. Their skins served us for clothing. He had scattered them over the country and taught us how to take them. He had caused the earth to produce corn for bread. All this He had done for His red children because He loved them. If we had some disputes about our hunting-ground they were generally settled without the shedding of much blood.

But an evil day came upon us. Your forefathers crossed the great water and landed on this island. Their numbers were small. They found friends and not enemies. They told us they had fled from their own country for fear of wicked men and had come here to enjoy their religion. They asked for a small seat. We took pity on them, granted their request, and they sat down among us. We gave them corn and meat; they gave us poison in return.

The white people, brother, had now found our country. Tidings were carried back and more came among us. Yet we did not fear them. We took them to be friends. They called us brothers. We believed them and gave them a larger seat. At length their numbers had greatly increased. They wanted more land; they wanted our country. Our eyes were opened and our minds became uneasy. Ware took place. Indians were hired to fight against Indians, and many of our people were destroyed. They also brought strong liquor among us. It was strong and powerful, and has slain thousands.

Brother, our seats were once large and yours were small. You have now become a great people, and we have scarcely a place left to spread our blankets. You have got our country, but are not satisfied; you want to force your religion upon us.

Brother, continue to listen. You say that you are sent to instruct us how to worship the Great Spirit agreeably to His mind; and, if we do not take hold of the religion which you white people teach we shall be unhappy hereafter. You say that you are right and we are lost. How do we know this to be true? We understand that your religion is written in a Book. If it was intended for us, as well as you, why has not the Great Spirit given to us, and not only to us, but why did He not give to our forefathers the knowledge of that Book, with the means of understanding it rightly. We only know what you tell us about it. How shall we know when to believe, being so often deceived by the white people?

Brother, you say there is but one way to worship and serve the Great Spirit. If there is but one religion, why do you white people differ so much about it? Why not all agreed, as you can all read the Book?

Brother, we do not understand these things. We are told that your religion was given to your forefathers and has been handed down from father to son. We also have a religion which was given to our forefathers and has been handed down to us, their children. We worship in that way. It teaches us to be thankful for all the favors we receive, to love each other, and to be united. We never quarrel about religion.

Brother, the Great Spirit has made us all, but He has made a great difference between His white and His red children. He has given us different complexions and different customs. To you He has given the arts. To these He has not opened our eyes. We know these things to be true. Since He has made so great a difference between us in other things, why may we not conclude that He has given us a different religion according to our understanding? The Great Spirit does right. He knows what is best for His children; we are satisfied.

Brother, we do not wish to destroy your religion or take it from you. We only want to enjoy our own.

Brother, you say you have not come to get our land or our money, but to enlighten our minds. I will now tell you that I have been at your meetings and saw you collect money from the meeting. I can not tell what this money was intended for, but suppose that it was for your minister; and, if we should conform to your way of thinking, perhaps you may want some from us.

Brother, we are told that you have been preaching to the white people in this place. These people are our neighbors. We are acquainted with them. We will wait a little while and see what effect your preaching has upon them. If we find it does them good, makes them honest, and less disposed to cheat Indians, we will then consider again of what you have said.

Brother, you have now heard our answer to your talk, and this is all we have to say at present. As we are going to part, we will come and take you by the hand, and hope the Great Spirit will protect you on your journey and return you safe to your friends."

According to Iroquois custom, the traditional signal of disagreement with the words of a public speaker was a robust bout of audible flatulence immediately following the offending speakers concluding remarks. While Red Jacket surely "kept them awake" there is no record of such public display of disagreement with his messages.

13

The American War

It is a mystery why the United States assumes the naming rights to all military conflicts in which she partakes. The Vietnam War is known as the American War among the Vietnamese. The French and Indian War of 1754-1763 is only known as such within the textbooks given to American school children. Rather it is known as the War of Conquest in Ontario and Quebec and as The Seven Years' War in France, Great Britain and the rest of Canada. It is doubtful that the Iraqis refer to their conflicts with the U.S. as Iraqi Freedom or Enduring Freedom. Likewise, what we were taught to be the War of 1812 is known as the American War in Great Britain. It was also the war that produced Pittsford's first war heroes.

There was a great influx of pioneer families into the Genesee Valley between 1779 and the initiation of the war related embargos of 1809 and 1810. The rapid decline in commerce coupled with anxiety over personal safety on the frontier, caused some families to return to the comparable security of their former New England homes. Escalation of tensions with Great Britain caused many to assume that war was imminent. This resulted in a hunkering down to the safety and familiarity of established hometowns that were protected by trained, experienced militias. As the war approached, few were interested in complicating their lives by the uncertainties of pursuing a pioneering adventure.

Since prior to the Revolutionary War, each state was required to field and train a militia. Ontario County's first militia was established in 1790 and it was reported that "most of the officers were tavern keepers". As the population grew, Northfield could support its own regiment and enlisted Colonel Caleb Hopkins to command the 52nd Infantry Regiment.

As the War of 1812 became imminent, Cornplanter, wishing to further ingratiate himself with the U. S. Government, volunteered to muster and lead two hundred Seneca warriors in battle on the side of the Americans. Having chosen the losing side as an ally in the

American Revolution, he did not intend to make the same mistake again. His offer was declined.

In June of 1812, the U.S. issued a declaration of war on Great Britain. This action was prompted by a long series of disputes including the impressments of U.S soldiers into the British military, the continuing dispute over the American/Canadian border and longstanding disagreements regarding the Northwest Territories.

The lands of the Genesee River Valley had been relatively peaceful for the white man. Nearly all of the earlier hostilities had been directed at its dominant inhabitants; the Seneca Nation. The Huron Nation in French Canada sporadically conducted raids on Seneca villages but were ultimately defeated in the Beaver Wars of the 1650's. The year 1687 brought the French invasion led by Marquis DeNonville that ended in his hasty retreat. General John Sullivan 1788 campaign to permanently displace the remaining native people during the Revolutionary War dealt the native people a devastating blow.

The War of 1812 brought the battle to the home of the local white man; on land and sea. Just six months after the declaration of war, General George McClure led American troops in burning the contemporary capital of Canada at Niagara-On-The-Lake; then called Newark. The British responded in kind by burning the towns of Youngstown, Lewiston, Niagara Falls, Fort Schlosser and Buffalo. The tribes, located in present day Canada, were brutal warriors and allies of the British.

"...drunken, howling Indians pursued fleeing families eight miles east along Ridge Road, wielding scalping knives and tomahawks. All ages, all sexes were horribly mangled. Mills and dwellings along Ridge Road and the Lake Ontario shoreline were destroyed ...nearly 500 buildings were destroyed...on foot, old and young men, women and children flying from their beds, some not more than half dressed, without shoes or stockings, together with men on horseback, wagons, carts, sleighs and sleds overturning and crushing each other, stimulated by the horried yells of the 900 savages on the pursuit...formed a scene awful and terrific in the extreme".

In a continuing tit for tat, "militiamen and Indians plundered and burned Loyalist farms in Canada and raped the women".

"...when starving refugees from the holocaust on the Niagara frontier began streaming along Ridge Road and the Genesee Road seeking food and shelter and Batavia became the center for the war office...when British warships continued to anchor off Charlotte harbor...when cannonballs whizzed towards Nine Mile Point, the war had become a certain threat to the Genesee region. Buckskin clad men rallied to defend their homes and

all respected the leaders, Swift, Porter, McKinstry, Stone and Hopkins. Stone's dragoons, a cavalry troop raised by Captain Isaac White Stone in May, 1813, guarded the local settlements and the coastline".

Many assumed that the opposing navies would ultimately have a decisive battle on Lake Ontario that would influence the outcome of the war. One significant naval battle of the war took place at the mouth of the Genesee River but, victory was not so clear as to significantly influence the direction of the war. In fact, while there were numerous skirmishes with no clear victors and blustery shows of strength, the activities on the lake mainly consisted of a ship building competition between the British and American fleets. At the beginning of the conflict, the Americans had only a single fighting vessel (the Oneida) but did have a ship building facility at Sackets Harbor at the mouth of the Saint Lawrence River in the Thousand Islands. The attack by five British vessels on the Oneida as it sailed near Sackets Harbor was the catalyst that began the ship building race. The enemy's confidence was not enhanced by the fact that, despite the five to one advantage, they failed to sink the Oneida.

Commodore Isaac Chauncey was appointed to command the American navies in the Great Lakes. He initiated an accelerated building schedule centered on the shipyard at Sackets Harbor. In order to quickly equal the British fleet, he purchased or commandeered commercial ships and quickly had them outfitted as fighting vessels. Concurrently, he ordered the construction of ships designed expressly to defeat the British on the Great Lakes.

The British fleet was under the command of Commodore James Lucas Yeo. He wasted no time in attacking Sackets Harbor but did so with little resolve. Once met with resistance by the defenders, Yeo withdrew rather than risk loss of his own ships. In the meantime, the Americans set fire to two of their own ships to preclude them from falling into enemy hands. Once Yeo was clearly in retreat, they attempted to extinguish the fires but were successful in saving only one of the two ships.

In July, 1813 Chauncey's fleet encountered Yeo off the shores of Fort Niagara. As was typical of both sides overly cautious approach, they attempted to maneuver over the next several days into positions that provided advantages to their particular types of armament. In early August, two American ships sank in a squall. A few days later, two of Chauncey's ships were captured by American forces mainly due to an unanticipated shift in the prevailing winds.

On August 28, the opposing forces met again directly off the mouth of the Genesee River. The ensuing battle clearly favored the

Americans as Yeo's flagship, the Wolfe, sustained substantial damage. Yeo retreated into Burlington Bay. American historians are critical of Chauncey claiming he had not aggressively followed and destroyed the opposing fleet and thereby affected a turning point in control of the Great Lakes and, perhaps, hastened the war's conclusion.

Intensive shipbuilding by both sides continued over the winter of 1813 & 1814. While there was nominal equality in numbers of vessels, the Americans launchings were delayed by the late arrivals of armaments to Sackets Harbor. This left Commodore Yeo in an advantageous position as the spring of 1814 arrived. On May 14, he returned to the mouth of the Genesee with thirteen fighting ships.

Yeo's arrival was not a surprise to the local militia. In anticipation that the British intended to invade the port and capture the substantial stores of supplies warehoused there, Peter B. Porter, Brigadier General of western New York had ordered that two cannons be brought from Canandaigua to deter the enemy attack. The larger weapon, capable of launching 18 pound balls, required 17 oxen to drag it over the unimproved road between the two cities. The big gun was stored at Captain Stone's barn at State Street and South Avenue in Pittsford. Militia training in the operation of the cannon took place in the wagon yard at Stone's Tavern. By spring, the large cannon was in place at the mouth of the Genesee River in the Village of Charlotte. The smaller unit was at the Lower Falls near today's Lexington Avenue.

When Yeo arrived, a call to muster for the local militia yielded scant thirty-one able bodied men. Each was given a modest 24 rounds of ammunition. Captain Stone led his meager force from the back of a white horse.

> *"Led by Captain Stone, riding a white horse, this small force marched and counter marched, disappearing into the woods and then suddenly emerging over the crest of a small hill by Stutson Street, so as to impress the enemy and lead them to believe that a much larger force was assembled. Actually only Stone's handful of men were marching around the square formed by Stutson, Lake and Latta Road. At mid-morning, a boat came in from the British fleet and Captains Brown and Ely were sent by Stone with the warning 'Don't let them come into the river, don't let them pollute our soil'. So standing on the trunk of a large tree that had fallen into the lake, the two men tied a white handkerchief on a stick and the British boat drew along side."*

The British demanded surrender. Captain Stone's return message was clear: "Go back and tell them that the public property in the hands of those who will defend it...by God if they come ashore, they will wade in blood knee deep".

Subsequent British messengers further threatened that unless there was an immediate surrender, an army of soldiers and 400 Indians would be landing shortly. The American responded by stating that any British boats entering the river would be fired upon.

The British missed their opportunity. By the second night, Pittsford's Col. Caleb Hopkins had mustered between 600 and 800 additional militiamen to augment the mirage created by Captain Stone's thirty one soldiers. Yeo and the fleet decided not to test the feisty militiamen, lifted anchors and sailed away.

General Porter subsequently briefed the New York Governor: "We saved the town...The discovery that we had troops, without knowing their number, concealed in the ravine near the mouth of the river to cut off their retreat in case they entered it, together with the tone of the defiance with which we answered their demands...made them think it prudent to be off". Pittsford's Captain Isaac Stone's status as a war hero may have been short-lived but his deft tactical charade in intimidating the British to retreat was clearly clever military science.

This was the last appearance of the British fleet at the mouth of the Genesee and the last imminent threat by an invading foreign army in the Valley of the Genesee. Henceforth, Chauncey controlled most of Lake Ontario. This naval dominance was critical in permitting the Americans to capture the city of York (present day Toronto). In the ensuing months, the Americans captured five additional British ships. This substantially restricted the British ability to move troops and supplies throughout the region.

All was not perfect, however. Chauncey was directed to blockade the British Fleet at York to preclude them from providing support to the continuing war efforts. His efforts were impeded by a combination of foul weather and the existence of many small islands at the mouth of the Saint Lawrence River that could provide refuge. As a result, some British vessels managed to pass through the blockade and lend support to their forces in at the Battle of Crysler's Farm.

By July of 1814, Captain Stone's 52nd Regiment from Pittsford had grown to 138 men. Based on his leadership in deterring the British invasion at the Genesee River, Captain Stone was promoted to Lt. Colonel and his regiment was asked to help General Wadsworth in the continuing fighting on the Niagara frontier. His regiment participated in the capture of the British fort at Fort Erie. Col. Stone's stellar war record suffered immeasurable harm when some members of his regiment and a group of Indians were accused of burning the Village of St. David's to the ground. Stone had been asked to rid the village of enemy combatants and, in his mind, had done so. When he returned to the village and found it ablaze, he expressed surprise, dismay and no knowledge of who had torched the 30-40 log houses. Col. Stone requested a full inquiry into the matter. Before the investigation could take place, he was summarily dismissed from further military service by General Jacob Brown.

Col. Stone died that September while returning home to Pittsford from the Niagara frontier without the knowledge that the Treaty of Ghent would be signed in Paris on December 24, 1814. "Thus ended in tragedy the career of the Hero of Charlotte".

14

Red Jacket's Final Stand

As early as 1810 there were signs that many Iroquois were not satisfied with the inequity of their relegation to reservations which, collectively, represented only a small percentage of their original homelands. They began to communicate these concerns to the newly established government of the United States. Specifically they inquired as to the government's interest in relocating the Iroquois to lands further west. It is unclear how large a contingent is being quoted in the preamble to the Treaty of Buffalo Creek when it states... "WHEREAS, the six nations of New York Indians not long after the close of the war of the Revolution, became convinced from the rapid increase of the white settlements around, that the time was not far distant when their true interest must lead them to seek a new home among their red brethren in the West"

There were several false starts to what would eventually be the Treaty of Buffalo Creek. Red Jacket was the driving force in resisting the sale of any more reservation's lands to white developers. The Ogden Land Company had been lusting after the lands of the Buffalo Creek Reservation since the conclusion of the War of 1812. In 1819, they came very close to consummating an agreement promoted by Christian factions of the Seneca. The proposal provided the Seneca a cash settlement plus lands in Green Bay, Wisconsin for a new home. Red Jacket successfully vetoed the deal at the last minute.

By the early 1820's, Red Jacket was compelled to act on behalf of his people. He wrote to New York Governor Clinton requesting that all missionaries and teachers be removed from the Buffalo Creek Reservation. His petition stated:

> "The Governor must not think hard of me for speaking thus of the preachers. I have observed their progress and when I look back to see what has taken place of old, I perceive that whenever they came among the Indians, they were the forerunners of their dispersion; that they always excited enmities and quarrels among them; that they introduced the white people on their lands, by whom they are robbed and plundered

of their property; and that the Indians were sure to dwindle and decrease and be driven back, in proportion to the number of preachers that came among them. Each nation has its own customs and its own religion. The Indians have theirs - given to them by the Great Spirit - under which they were happy. It was not intended that they should embrace the religion of the whites and be destroyed by the attempt to make them think differently on that subject from their fathers."

The Governor acted favorably on Red Jacket's petition and encouraged the state legislature to pass a law requiring all non- native persons to leave Seneca lands. As a result, the missions and schools closed.

Red Jacket's efforts to isolate the Seneca and return to their long-held traditions, was constantly under attack. He was convinced that the Christian faction within the tribe was under the influence of the Indian agent who was intent on undermining his isolationist strategy. In 1822, an article appeared in the Niagara Journal (and several other publications), that accused Red Jacket of "drunkenness and lying". It was signed by five Christian tribe members and agent Jasper Parish and an H. Jones. Red Jacket's eloquent rebuttal, wherein he calls for the replacement of Agent Parish is printed in its entirety below.

RED JACKET'S SPEECH [Communicated.] -1822
Note: Red Jacket did not capitalize "Christian"

The Chiefs of the Seneca Nation of Indians lately held a Council in this village, (Batavia) and requested several of the citizens of this place to attend; when their celebrated chief and orator, Red Jacket delivered the following eloquent address. The publications which lately appeared in the Niagara Journal, and several other papers, signed by five Indians of the Christian party, Jasper Parish and H. Jones, it appears called forth from Red Jacket the following justification of himself and nation. He addressed himself particularly to Judge Ross, of this village, who happened to be present:--

My Brother and Friend--The Great Good Spirit who governs the world, and who knows our thoughts and actions, whether they are good or bad, has placed within the Indian bosom and the white man's bosom, a certain monitor which regulates our conduct, which prompts us to do good, and makes us sensible of our crimes when we do wrong, now tell me to speak to you.

I have lived many years, and have always been beloved and respected by my red brethren, for my love of peace and justice; a sincere honor and happiness, and an upright and honorable opposition to my change in those manners and customs which it first pleased the Good Spirit to give to us, his red children. I have from my youth up to the time that I *now address you, always been considered as the friend of the white man, and I say it without the fear of contradiction, (and the Great Good Spirit knows without vanity, or any desire to make the world believe that I have more influence with my red brethren, than I in reality have,) that I have at all times had it in my power, (for such is their belief in my honesty and attachment to their interest,) to control their passions and their feelings, so as to excite their love or indignation for their white brethren, or to abide by or breach the treaties made by us with the people of the United States. But I now feel hurt, and grieved at heart, to think I know that my character and reputation has been so wickedly and wantonly assailed-that it has been represented to be a compound on everything that is vile and wicked, and published in papers, which I am told are sent not only through the whole United States, but even over the great waters to Europe, and that too by parish and Jones, men that we have always loved until we found they were unfriendly to us; men who had every reason to love us, and be true to our interests. They were nursed and fed by us in the wilderness. We protected them in their infancy, we educated them like their white brethren, that they might not feel themselves or appear to their white brethren like the wild Indians of the forests; we gave them lands and made them rich, yes richer than any of their white brethren, and for what? Because we loved them, they were dear to us, yes, dear to us as the parent to the child that loves him. They were adopted parents, and to them we looked for counsel and advice, in all our difficulties.Property of.com*

But they have been grateful to us for all favors and presents? No, gratitude is a stranger to the white man's bosom. Like the cruel and ferocious Panther of the forest, when a whelp, it is feeble and helpless as the Puppy. The Indian takes it to his hut. He feeds and nurses it with the food he has provided for his children. It acquires strength, vigor and activity, and unmindful and ungrateful for what has been done for him, he falls upon and devours his benefactor and helpless infants.

But my friend let us see if we can find any excuse or justification for their conduct. They accuse me of drunkenness and lying, and say that I was drunk 2 days during the Great Indian Council held at Tonnawanta. I say this is false, and I again repeat it, that the whole of the facts which have been published by me and the Chiefs assembled at that Council, are true; whereas the statements made by Parish and Jones in the piece printed by them, are false, and I will prove it.

True it is, that I sometimes drink, and perhaps too much for my own good. But ought this to be published to the world? Is this a public act? Does it interfere with the treaties made between us and the people of the United States? No, it is only a private act. It concerns no one except myself and the Great Good Spirit, who, I know, will not approve, but knows of it. And here I wish to say that I myself know it is wrong. That in doing so, I set a bad example before my red brethren. But it is a habit which I unfortunately, with too many of my red brethren have caught from the white men, before we knew the fatal wicked and pernicious effects of this too delicious but strong water. But let not my Red Brethren follow my examples. Let my conduct in this respect be to them like the blaze emitted by an hundred dry hemlocks on the heights of the Allegany, to the wild beast of the forest warning them to fly far away,, and avoid danger and death. Examine then my public conduct through life, and see if you can find one blot or one stain to blacken my character. Look at the treaty made by me in behalf and for the Six Nations of Indians, with General Washington. Look at the treaty made between myself and Pickering at Canandaigua, examine them closely, and see if I have ever broken any agreement made by me in these treaties or any treaty made between the Indians and the President of the United States, wherein my name was signed to such treaty, or my faith was pledged for any tribe or any nation of the Six Nations of Indians, although I again repeat it. I have had at all times sufficient influence to persuade my red brethren to break them.

I have round my neck a silver plate, presented to me by General Washington, which he told me to preserve and wear so long as I felt friendly to him and the United States, as an evidence of his friendship for me. If I have ever violated any treaty or any agreement made by me, why has this not been taken from me. You see it here yet. I say I never have so done.

But as Parish and Jones, are not contented with what they have said about my private character, they say that the Indians are opposed to them because they are friendly to the christian religion. This is not true, because he has told me repeatedly that the "Black Goats did us more hurt than good, and that we ought to drive them away." When the Great Good Spirit made the world, he put in it the trees of the forests, the birds of the air, all kinds of animals, and fishes that live in the waters. To all these he gave their respective shapes, colours, natures, actions, &c. Although those are all fixed you see and are immovable. They cannot change, colour, nature or their actions or customs. He also at the same time made the White Man, the Red Man, and the Black Man. To the White Man he gave one way to worship him and certain customs; to the Red Man another, and his customs and way to live; and to the Black Man others still. Now I say we can't change our religion or custom, because they are fixed by the great good Spirit, and if we attempt to do it we shall offend our Great Spirit and he will punish us for it.

From the rising to the setting sun examine all the different tribes of Indians, and see in what a condition you find them. I have traveled far. I have been from the Atlantic to the shores of the Pacific, and I know the habits, customs and situation of almost every tribe and nation of

Indians. And I say that it is a fact, that whenever you find a tribe of Indians that have been 'christionized' and have changed their custom or habit, which the Great good Spirit gave them, you will see that they are a poor, worthless, lying, ragged, miserable and degraded set of beings; and instead of becoming white men, as they expected to have become by changing their customs and habits, they have formed connections with the blacks, and have become black men in their actions and conduct. I say, therefore, that the Great Spirit will not suffer his Red Children to change their religion or custom. But when they attempt to do it punishes them by turning them into Black Men. It is not because the White Men love the Indians that they want to make them christians, it is because they want to cheat them out of their property. The Black Coats that they send among us with honey on their tongue, have always proved themselves to be dishonest; they are an ignorant, idle set of creatures, incapable of getting a living amongst their white brethren, and are therefore sent amongst us to get a living. They bring along with them a worthless set of White Men who steal our horses and seduce our Squaws.

One thing more my Brother. Parish and Jones since they have become such good christians and pretend to do so much honesty, before they accuse me of being dishonest them clear themselves of the charges which we have brought against them, and not answer our statements which are true by abusing me. Let Jones return to the Indians the lands which he cheated Little Beard out of or at least give them to his Indian on, which he had by Little Beard's Squaw, after he had cheated his father. I have before stated, I am dissatisfied with the conduct of both Parish and Jones, and wish that Parish may be turned out of his office, and in saying this I am not alone, it is the voice of the whole Six Nations of Indians. We have put up with the treaties from these men for three years past. We have watched them narrowly and never have made any complaint until the whole matter had been submitted to a full council on the whole Six Nations of Indians held at Tonawanta. When the proceedings of that meeting were made known Parish instead of proving the accusations made by us as false as he ought to have done if it was not true, got four or five Indians who hold no place in our Councils to sign a false and abusive piece about the private reputation of the Chiefs who signed the proceedings of that Meeting and then published it to the World. He thought by this course, to frighten me into silence and subservience to his measures. But in this he is mistaken--so long as the Great Good Spirit will suffer me to live among his red children, I know it is my duty, (for a certain something within me tells me so) to watch over their interest, and as far as I am capable to protect them, from the cunning and avarice of the white men.

I have only one thing more to say, and it is this:--We wish the President would appoint as our agent in the room of Mr. Parish, (for we are determined that he shall no longer be our agent,) either James Gnash, Mr. Joseph Annin, Mr. John Z. Ross, or Ethan B. Allen, Esq. With the appointment of either of the above gentlemen we shall be satisfied, and wish to have it done immediately.

Source: *Republican Advocate*, Batavia: November 15-1822

Over the next seven years, the Ogden Land Company continued its efforts to convince the more pliable members of the Seneca Nation to see the merits in a cash-for-land agreement coupled with a new home some distance from the encroaching white settlers. In 1826, despite Red Jackets continued opposition, Ogden was able to secure agreement from the Senecas to sell eighty-one thousand acres contained in the Tonawanda, Allegheny and Buffalo Creek Reservations for fifty three cents per acre and a land grant in Wisconsin.

Unable to stop the majority vote by his Seneca, Red Jacket appealed to President John Quincy Adams to stop the sale. This infuriated the Ogden Land Company who orchestrated a smear campaign against their nemesis accusing him of "defaming the President", being anti-Indian education and disturbing the tribal council. Again, the Iroquois Christian faction was able to have Red Jacket removed from his role as chief.

Red Jacket was not deterred. His patience paid off in 1828 when President Adams, voided the agreement. While temporarily pleased with this turn of events, Red Jacket had grown weary of fighting both the white settlers and his own Seneca brothers. His disappointment was exacerbated when his eldest son was married in a Christian ceremony and his wife converted a few years later. Despite thirty years of marriage, his pride precluded their continued cohabitation. He subsequently reunited with her and, on his deathbed, acknowledged his error in abandoning her for her conversion to Christianity. He stated that he wished for her to continue to follow her chosen faith and characterized Christianity as a "good religion".

He died in 1830 before his effort to save Iroquois land for Iroquois homes was defeated yet again.

15

The Treaty of Buffalo Creek

In 1831, the U.S. Government signed a treaty with the Menomonie Indians of Wisconsin that transferred the ownership of 500,000 acres of Menomonie and Winnebago Indian lands near Green Bay to accommodate the relocation of the entire Iroquois Confederacy to these western lands. This move was to take place within a three year time period. While some New York State Iroquois did relocate to the Green Bay reservation, most were reluctant to do so. They grew to resent the white man's incessant pressure to force the native tribes further and further west. It became clear to them that the ultimate goal of the white settlers was to have all red brethren relocated to "Indian Lands" west of the Mississippi. Within a few years, the Iroquois proposed that the move to Green Bay be permanently aborted and that, in exchange for the Wisconsin lands, the U.S. provide suitable lands in "Indian territory". The government's "spin" on these discussions with the Presidents "red children" was contained in the preamble of The Treaty of Buffalo Creek. It states:

> *"And whereas, the President being anxious to promote the peace, prosperity and happiness of his red children, and being determined to carry out the humane policy of the Government in removing the Indians from the east to the west of the Mississippi, within the Indian territory, by bringing them to see and feel, by his justice and liberality, that it is their true policy and for their interest to do so without delay."*

Both sides assumed that a peaceful resolution to these concerns occurred in 1838 with the signing of the Treaty of Buffalo Creek. While it surely brought anguish to Red Jacket's spirit, the Seneca joined the Mohawk, Cayuga, Oneida, Onondaga and Tuscarora in agreeing to sell four New York State reservations (Buffalo Creek, Tonawanda, Cattaraugus and Allegany) to the Ogden Land Company. They also agreed to relinquish their title to the lands in Green Bay. In exchange, the Seneca would be provided land west of Missouri at the rate of 320 acres per tribe member, a specified amount of money for each of the reservations being relinquished and a total lump sum of $400,000. The latter stipend was to aid in the removal of their homes from the existing reservations, the purchase of domestic farm animals and tools and in their education in the "mechanical arts" and farming techniques.

Further they would have permanent assurance that their new home land would never be part of the United States. The latter guarantee was expressed in Article 15 as..."The lands secured to them by patent under this treaty shall never be included in any State or Territory of this Union." No wonder the subsequent references to the white man's "forked tongue."

The preamble of the Treaty of Buffalo Creek and selected portions of the treaty are contained in Exhibit # 2. It was stipulated that the Iroquois must relocate from the reservations of New York State and Green Bay within five years. The original treaty specified that Ogden Land Company would purchase all four of the reservations occupied by the Seneca Nation. This was altered in The Treaty of the Seneca of 1841 when it was agreed that only two of the four reservations would be sold to Ogden.

A major glitch occurred when, shortly after the signing, it was discovered that the Chiefs of the Tonowanda Band of Seneca had failed to sign the Treaty of Buffalo Creek or the Treaty of the Seneca. The Tonowanda Band of Seneca strongly preferred the lands of their forefathers and had no intention of moving to Indian Territory. They successfully repurchased the majority of their small reservation. The deal was consummated with the signing of the Treaty with the Seneca, Tonawanda Band in 1857. The Tonawanda Band of Seneca was all that remained of the once proud Seneca Tribe who once freely roamed all land west of Canandaigua Lake.

After the Treaty of Buffalo Creek, around two hundred Iroquois did move to the designated land in Kansas. They found the indigenous tribes unwelcoming, the climate less to their liking and the lands far less fertile. Nearly one-half perished in the first few years and the remaining one hundred who survived, returned to the reservations of far western New York State.

16

Northfield-Boyle-Smallwood to Pittsford

In the fifty years spanning the end of the eighteenth century and first several decades of the nineteenth, the Seneca Nation was losing its grip on its homelands, its sovereignty, its economic independence and its identity. During that half-century, the District of Northfield was morphing into seven towns and villages that survive today. Until the Treaty of Buffalo Creek was signed, the land largely west of the Genesee River was still legally in possession of the Seneca Nation. The former Seneca land east of the Genesee had been "sold" in their very first "land deal" to Phelps and Gorham on July 8, 1788 and was free for settlement and development.

This half-century was marked by steady development of the retail, commercial and residential areas of present day Pittsford. The village was located on the main wagon road between the mills at the Genesee Falls in "Rochesterville" and Canandaigua. Providing goods and services to those traveling this popular route proved to be lucrative business for the village's merchants, taverns and innkeepers. While fires destroyed some of the original structures, many of these first homes and buildings remain and are integral to the charm and character that endures.

The conclusion of hostilities with Great Britain opened the flood gates of pent-up interest in settling western New York and the Genesee River Valley. The sense that America would be forever independent of Britain and that western New York would not become part of Canada, brought confidence to those who were heretofore reluctant to immigrate to the new frontier. The area known as Northfield (incorporated in 1796) benefited from this renewed interest in starting a new life in the American "West".

Northfield consisted of 220 square miles and represented about one half of present-day Monroe County. Its borders were Lake Ontario on the north and the Genesee River on the west. The current eastern boundary was the present day Monroe County line and the southern border was the current town limits of present-day Pittsford, Henrietta and Perinton. Between 1800 and 1825, the area's population exploded. The number of inhabitants grew fifteen-fold from 1192 to 18,776 during this period.

The name Northfield lasted just 12 years. In 1808, the name was changed to Boyle. Two explanations are offered as to why the name was changed. First there was an existing town of Northfield in an eastern township in Richmond County, N.Y. that caused confusion. Secondly, while the area was, in fact "north" of Canandaigua, the area was not anything "field-like". Rather, the area was densely covered with both deciduous and coniferous forests. The only trails in the area had either been laboriously hacked out of the thick flora by white settlers or were ancient Indian paths or portage routes built between bodies of water; mainly to bypass the falls on the Genesee.

Thankfully, five years later in 1813, the area was re-christened Smallwood. In the interim, Perinton had been spun off as a separate entity in 1812. The Smallwood moniker was even shorter lived. In 1814 the area was divided; one section becoming Brighton and the other Pittsford. The village was renamed by Col. Caleb Hopkins, the popular town supervisor, whose heroic actions in the War of 1812 were described in an earlier chapter. Col. Hopkins' great-great-great grandfather sailed from Europe on the Mayflower. He named the town after his hometown of Pittsford, Vermont. Two years earlier, in 1812, Col Hopkins had bought a sizable farm and built his home in the village. The Hopkins Homestead still stands at 3151 Clover Street and his descendents continue to farm the property.

In 1818, the Town of Henrietta was sliced off and became an independent municipality. By the time that Monroe County was established in 1821, the District of Northfield had given birth to seven towns; Brighton, Henrietta, Penfield, Perinton, Irondequoit, Webster, Pittsford and an eastern section of what is now Rochester.

The book "Northfield on the Genesee" contains a chart that depicts the twenty-five year timeline associated with the successive division of the District of Northfield from a single jurisdiction containing the eastern half of the county to the seven towns and village that survive to this day. The information on that chart, improved for clarity, is shown below.

The Seven Villages Descended From Northfield

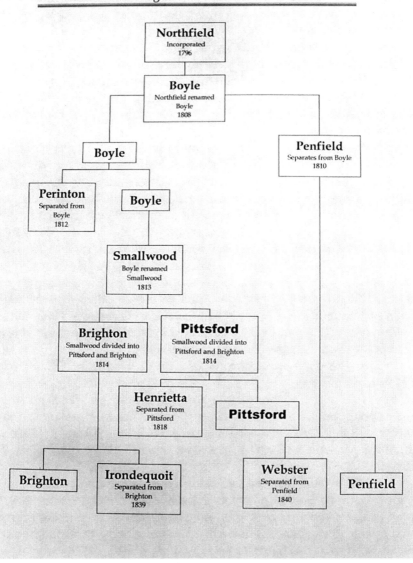

Chart by Sarah Bradbury

What is now known as the Four Corners of Pittsford, New York emerged as a result of the prevalent travel patterns of indigenous people seeking fresh water at Big Spring over a period of three to five thousand years. From this popular meeting place, these earliest inhabitants traveled north to Lake Ontario via present day North Main

Street and East Avenue. They headed south along today's South Main Street and Mendon Road towards Canandaigua and the Finger Lakes. Western travelers proceeded along a path that would become present-day Monroe Avenue.

In 1807, at the time that Pittsford was still Northfield, the original Phoenix Hotel was built. Many believe it was the first hotel and tavern in the village but records indicate that, in that same year, Glover Perrin opened a tavern across Main Street, adjacent to the current Town Hall site. The Phoenix was replaced in 1814 when the original facility was destroyed by fire.

"Beer is proof that God loves us and wants us to be happy" opined Benjamin Franklin. The first brewery in the area opened its doors in 1819 in Rochester on the east bank of the Genesee River. The Aqueduct Brewing Company changed ownership in 1878 and was rechristened Genesee Brewing Company. It remains at this location and has grown to become the nation's seventh largest domestic brewery. As the twenty first century dawned, the name was changed to High Falls Brewing Company and its product mix expanded to include a variety of boutique-style beers to satisfy the ostensibly "more sophisticated" taste of today's beer drinker. In 2008, a venture capitalist merged the assets of High Falls and Labatt USA to form North American Breweries. Much to the delight of loyal Pleasant Valley fans, the High Falls Brewing name was changed back to Genesee Brewing Company.

There are conflicting reports of Dewitt Clinton's 1810 visit to Pittsford. While scouting the path of the proposed Erie Canal, he spent at least one night in the village. Some maintain he was a guest at the Phoenix but Clinton himself mentions a "flea-haunted bed in the tavern of S. Felt". Mr. Felt's establishment was in the Village of Pittsford and "the Masonic emblem on the tavern sign was an enticement to travelers".

Growth in church attendance led to the establishment of the Second Baptist Church of Boyle in 1809. Originally the services were held every two weeks by a minister who traveled from Ogden Center. This required that he ford the Genesee. His dedication was clearly demonstrated on those Sundays when the river was too high to ford and he was forced south to traverse the bridge in Avon.

In 1814, there were nine churches established within the boundaries of Northfield. According to the book "Northfield on the Genesee"... "Baptist and Congregationalist doctrines appealed to the strong-willed, self-reliant types who could undertake the responsibilities of moving to an unsettled land". Locally, Penfield laid claim to having the first organized church but for some time before that, James K. Guernsey, a lay preacher, was credited with delivering the first sermon in Pittsford in Captain Nye's barn. One day, Reverend Guernsey purportedly attempted to redeem a silver dollar in a Canandaigua store that had been dropped in the collection plate by Israel Stone. To his surprise, the merchant determined that the coin was counterfeit and refused to honor it. Guernsey replied that he had been provided the coin for "preaching the gospel in the woods of Northfield". To which the merchant retorted "no doubt the money is as good as the sermon".

The Village of Pittsford enjoyed an economic boost in 1816 when the local entrepreneur Samuel Hildreth headquartered his new stagecoach line in the Village. The barns for Hildreth's forty horses were at the Phoenix Hotel. This network eventually dominated stage traffic in western New York State. His stages transported the mail from Canandaigua to Rochester displacing the contract that Samuel Felt had for carrying the mail via horseback since 1811.

In 1814, Mr. Hildreth, built his original home at the Pittsford Farms Dairy. He built it in the Federal style complete with a cellar kitchen.

On State Street opposite South Street, was located Mike King's Cider Mill and Dry House. The photo below depicts his crew taking a break from peeling, cutting and coring apples prior to oven-drying. The building's sign painter remains unknown but hopefully had secondary employment.

Mike King's Cider Mill. Courtesy of Paul M. Spiegel

The current Phoenix Hotel has occupied the southeast corner of the Four Corners since 1814. In 1816, Thomas Blair built a store on the land diagonally across the Four Corners to the northwest. The property changed hands several times over the next few decades but has remained a retail enterprise throughout its existence. The original building was destroyed by fire in 1866. It was replaced in 1870 by the Wiltsie and Crump Building; the beautiful brick structure that occupies the space today.

By the year 1818, the Phoenix Hotel had additional competition from the White Tavern (later named the National Hotel) located on State Street where the Star Market (turned library) was subsequently erected. Originally built as a stagecoach inn, the White Tavern competed for the patronage of the area's thirsty until 1941. The building was rechristened as The National Hotel in the early years of the twentieth century shortly before the wrecking ball made way for a used car lot.

The photo below shows a threesome of handsomely dressed townies at the bar in the Phoenix Hotel; usually described as the "top saloon" in town.

The Bar at the Phoenix Hotel. Courtesy of Paul M. Spiegel

Of the many hotels that were built to accommodate the growing center of commerce and trade, only the Phoenix Hotel and Brighton's Spring House, built in 1822, remain. The Phoenix Hotel, The National Hotel and the Spring House had springs mounted under their third floor ballrooms. Apparently a short-lived craze, the springs were intended to enhance the participants dance experience; perhaps not unlike adding modest resiliency to basketball courts. These spring-equipped floors remain at the Phoenix Building and the Spring House.

The Phoenix Hotel. Courtesy of Paul M. Spiegel

Three Pittsfords

There are three villages called Pittsford in the U.S.; all linked by the western flow of immigration. In addition to the Upstate New York village and the village in Vermont (population 1595) from whence both Caleb Hopkins and Samuel Hopkins immigrated, there is also a hamlet and township in south central Michigan (population 3140) by that name. Most villages ending with a "ford" were named based on an early settler's often arbitrary choice to ford a river or stream at that location. However, a topographical examination of each of the three Pittsfords yields no such bodies of water worthy of fording.

The original fording took place in Pitsford (one "t"), England presumably by a settler named Pits. It is a small village located seventy six miles northwest of London. A substantial reservoir (Pitsford Reservoir) confirms the existence of water needing to be forded. Immigrants from Pitsford, England first settled in the New England state of Vermont and christened their North American village Pittsford. When the village of Smallwood was split in 1814, Colonel Hopkins suggested his new home be called Pittsford, New York in fond remembrance of his Vermont hometown.

The momentum to settle the west continued with immigrants seeking a new and better life on the frontier. By 1836, a new township had been formed in southern Michigan. A significant number of the newly arrived residents had lived either in Pittsford, Vermont, or Pittsford, New York or both. Some restless souls immigrated from Pittsford, Vermont to Pittsford, New York and, finally to what would be called Pittsford, Michigan.

The first home in the Pittsford, Michigan area was built by the area's earliest tavern keeper, Samuel Cooley, who had immigrated from Pittsford, Vermont. Alpheus Pratt hosted the first township meeting in his home. While his association with Pittsford, New York is not clear, he suggested that the township be named after the Upstate New York village of that name. His recommendation was approved.

The publication "The Hamlet of Pittsford" produced by the Pittsford, Michigan Area School, contains an explanation of an earlier historical link between the New York and Michigan areas that eventually were both named Pittsford. This explanation extends back to the time of the French and Indian War. According to this account, the mighty Seneca Tribe from the Genesee Valley invaded and massacred the local indigenous people in the latter half of the seventeenth century. Survivors escaped to Wisconsin where they resettled.

"Rochesterville"

Rochester (originally "Rochesterville") was named for Nathaniel Rochester. In 1803, he and two fellow Revolutionary War officers, Charles Carroll and William Fitshugh, purchased one hundred acres along the shore of the Genesee River. They believed this property afforded great commercial opportunity by virtue of its proximity to inexpensive water power. The village was named Rochesterville in 1817. Over the next few years, additional land speculators merged their tracts to the original 100 acres. By 1823, the village had grown to over one thousand acres, had a population of 2500, was bisected by the new Erie Canal and had its name shortened to Rochester. The city center was established at the point where the Erie Canal aqueduct passed over the Genesee River. From this riparian intersection, a thriving city emerged.

The region's fertile soil yielded abundant grain crops. Flour mills powered by the Genesee River processed the grains of Pleasant Valley's farmlands and provided the economic engine that fueled growth and prosperity in the area. The efficient and affordable power of the Genesee River combined with low cost transportation on the Erie Canal was the ideal stimuli for a burgeoning economy. Rochester became the country's largest producer and shipper of flour...resulting in the moniker "The Flour City". Cheap, readily available power also served to lure other manufacturing and industrial enterprises to the area.

The robust economy meant jobs. The population skyrocketed as immigrants bypassed the older, sleepier communities of Canandaigua and Pittsford for "America's First Boomtown". In the seven years leading up to 1834, Rochester's population nearly quadrupled to 9200. The former village became the City of Rochester.

As Rochester prospered and its population grew to dwarf that of the adjoining communities, its commercial and economic impact began to spread throughout the Valley of the Genesee. While the older, well established villages of Canandaigua and Pittsford were able to survive and remain relatively prosperous, their rate of population growth was stymied. The availability of plentiful, affordable power in Rochester proved to be a compelling lure for entrepreneurs seeking to establish new businesses; businesses that would need ample numbers of employees. For this reason, from the mid- nineteenth century forward, Pittsford's fate and fortunes were inextricably linked to the Flour City.

17

"Follow the Drinkin' Gourd"

Tice Davids was a Kentucky slave. In 1830 he swam across a river adjoining his owner's property and began his escape to freedom. His dismayed "master" announced: "he must have used an underground road because he disappeared so quickly." News of his river escape spread through the slave community and others followed. Over time the underground road became known as the "Underground Railroad"

According to folklore, Peg Leg Joe was a conductor on the Underground Railroad and sang the words of a song titled "Follow the Drinkin' Gourd" as he led slaves to freedom in the North. The first verse was:

When the sun come back and the first quail calls,
Follow the Drinkin' Gourd
For the old man's waitin' for to carry you to freedom
If you follow the Drinkin' Gourd.

The "drinkin' gourd" was the vernacular used by fugitive slaves to describe the constellation Ursa Major seen in the northern sky over North America. Today that constellation is commonly known as the Big Dipper. Legend held that by following the Drinkin' Gourd, fugitive slaves could guide themselves true north to freedom.

Between the 1830's and the Civil War, a complex network of roads, rivers, lakes, footpaths, towpaths and safe houses emerged that aided an estimated 30,000 to 100,000 runaway slaves to find freedom. These escape routes were not restricted exclusively to a south to north direction. Some seeking freedom traveled further south to Mexico and Cuba although the largest number sought the safety of Canada. Many of these traveled north through Pennsylvania, entering New York State near Elmira, continued on to Lake Ontario where they could board boats bound for freedom in Canada. This "last 100 miles to freedom" is an important part of the heritage of the Finger Lakes, the Genesee Valley and Pittsford.

In his book titled <u>Underground Railroad Tales (With Routes Through the Finger Lakes)</u>, Emerson Klees details eight well documented passageways that wound through the Finger Lakes. Three passed through the Genesee Valley; one of these moved fugitive slaves, or "cargo" through Palmyra and one directly through Pittsford. See map.

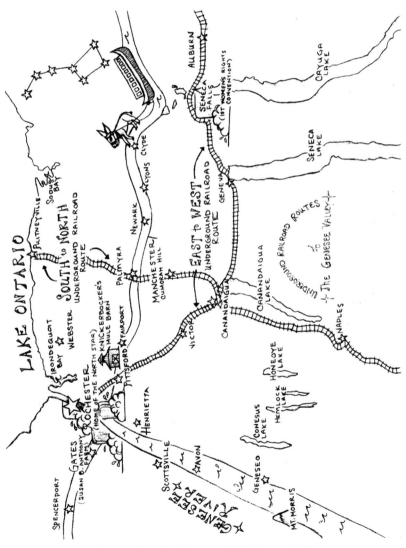

Underground Railroad Routes of the Genesee Valley.
Map by Alicia Ivelich

The Village of Bath served as an important junction for two routes through the area. One common passageway led from Bath to Naples through Honeoye Falls and into Rochester. An alternate route also emanated from Bath but after passing through Naples, veered northeast to Canandaigua, due north through Palmyra and straight to Lake Ontario at Pultneyville.

The main Underground Railroad route through Pittsford was a segment from Syracuse to Rochester following the current Routes 5 and 20. Under the cover of darkness, freedom-seekers traveled an east-to-west route that took them through Auburn, Seneca Falls[3], Geneva, Canandaigua, Victor, Pittsford and into Rochester.

While these are generally thought to represent the prevalent routes through the area, surely once runaway slaves reached the Genesee Valley, "agents" had to balance the availability of "stations" with the incoming "cargo". If there was a shortage of escape vessels on Lake Ontario, freedom seekers were moved to whichever station might be available within the Rochester, Brighton, Pittsford or Palmyra area. Similarly, freedom-seekers could easily be re-routed to Pittsford and Rochester if slave catchers were particularly active between Palmyra and Lake Ontario.

As runaway slaves entered the area, they accessed Canada via several optional routes. Some boarded boats docked on the shores of Lake Ontario, while others were taken upstream to the lake from Kelsey's Landing on the Genesee River. Ships flying the flag of a foreign country were particularly sought out because freedom was assured the moment a fugitive was on board. Once on the Lake, they sailed west along the northern shore and entered Canada at St. Catherine's. Others continued their trek to freedom by following the Erie Canal towpath west under the cover of darkness. Upon reaching the Niagara River, they crossed into Canada at Fort Erie. Once in Canada, escaped slaves were usually taken in by local residents; some with enthusiasm, others reluctantly. After the Civil War, most escaped slaves who had sought refuge north of the border, returned to the United States.

---

[3] It is interesting to imagine Seneca Falls of 1848; the very recently legally "freed" Frederick Douglas participating in the raucous first Women's Rights Convention and convincing the attendees to make voting rights the mainstay of their platform. This while runaway slaves waited in the village's haylofts and fruit cellars for the first moonless nights to slip away to their next station a few miles closer to freedom.

"The last 100 miles to freedom"

There is a limestone dome that lies below the streets, buildings, homes and flora of a substantial portion of the village of Pittsford. This subterranean dome has been eroded internally for thousands of years by the underground river that fed Big Spring. There are believed to be one or more substantial voids beneath the center of the Village. Some have postulated that these caverns and passageways were used to hide and move "cargo"[4] along the final 100 miles of the Underground Railroad

The Brighton-Pittsford Post has reported various first-hand accounts of the existence of tunnels and caverns under the village. The Lathrop House, located at 28 Monroe Avenue has been the subject of such anecdotes regarding the existence of both an entrance to the Pittsford Cavern (which may run under the Four Corners) and a tunnel that ran from that house to the Lutheran Church at the corner of Lincoln and Washington Streets.

In 1966, Mrs. Alan Drake described her 1906 visit to her relatives who lived at the Lathrop House. She and her cousin had heard about a safe hidden in the ground floor wall of the central chimney and decided to see if they could find it. The chimney was directly adjoining a dumbwaiter used to move food from the both the summer kitchen (located at the rear of the home) and adjoining, centrally located, winter kitchen. One door to the dumbwaiter opened into the winter kitchen; the other door into the summer kitchen.

The young girls had been given a clue that when the dumbwaiter was in the lowered position, it concealed the entrance to the safe. They raised the dumbwaiter while holding the door open and the safe, secured into a cavity in the chimney, was visible. The cousins also discovered that, when the dumbwaiter was in the raised position, "a passageway with steps going down" was exposed. They went down the stairs but, according to the account, the cousins were reluctant to go too far into the "spooky" cave.

The Lathrop House has been owned since 1974 by Douglas and Joyce Drake (no relation to the aforementioned Mrs. Alan Drake). They share a deep interest in the fascinating history of their home. Douglas Drake described additional enigmatic features of their home that serve to enhance the credibility of those that suggest it was a station on the

[4] A series of code word descriptors quickly evolved to describe the roles of those who facilitated the movement of slaves in their quest for freedom: "agents" generically described anyone who was a participant, "stations" were the temporary clandestine hiding places whether they be attics, basements, haylofts or tunnels and caves, "station masters" ran the stations, "conductors" physically accompanied escaping slaves (known as "cargo") from one station to the next and "stockholders" were those who contributed funds to buy food, clothing and other necessities.

Underground Railroad. Beneath the large front porch facing Monroe Avenue is a full height room measuring approximately ten by twenty feet. Traditional short cellar windows surround this room allowing some natural light to enter. The mystery lies in the fact that there is no entrance to this space. No interior entrance from adjoining rooms; no entrance from the outside.

Drake believes that he may have solved the riddle of this room-with- no-entrance. When replacing some wood flooring in the "winter kitchen", he uncovered and explored a spacious (perhaps three to four feet high) crawl space beneath the floor. When he reached the wall that separated the winter kitchen from the room-with-no-door beneath the front porch, he discovered clear indications of a former passageway connecting the two spaces. The arched entry had been completely filled with masonry material.

The dumbwaiter shaft was built into the wall between the summer and winter kitchens. Below the entrance to the dumbwaiter was both the winter kitchen crawl space leading to the room below the porch and the "passageway with steps going down" as described in Mrs. Allan Drake's adventure of 1906. So..."cargo" could have moved from the cavern or tunnel below the dumbwaiter, into the crawlspace beneath the winter kitchen, through the now-sealed entrance to the room beneath the porch. There, those "following the drinking gourd" could enjoy natural light while being hidden until dark when they were moved to the next "station".

Having read the accounts of the 1906 adventure of Mrs. Alan Drake and her cousin, Douglas Drake attempted to confirm or deny the existence of the stairs and passageway beneath the dumbwaiter. The dumbwaiter has long since been removed; its vertical shaft converted to accommodate heating and plumbing infrastructure for the home at the time it was modernized with indoor plumbing and central heating. The shaft remains, as does the pocket cut into the adjoining chimney that contained the safe concealed by the dumbwaiter.

Drake excavated the area below where the floor of the dumbwaiter had rested. He removed soft loam soil containing composted food scraps and chicken bones. He found it interesting that the soil composition used to fill the void below the dumbwaiter was so drastically different than the clay soil that was excavated when the house was built. This led him to conclude that whoever filled this space used material from the surrounding garden or compost heap; material accumulated long after the home was originally erected. If this space had been filled when the home was built, surely the convenient choice would have been to use the same clay soil that was removed to dig the lower level kitchens.

After digging to a depth of thirty inches, Drakes shovel struck concrete; the "passageway with steps" had been sealed.

Bryce Chase of Bryce and Don's Atlantic (service station once located across from the fire station) shared his experience while viewing the demolition of the Thomas Heaver house on Monroe Avenue in 1964. The home was being removed to accommodate the expansion of the fire station at the site. Chase reported that he and others dropped rocks into a circular hole that appeared in the course of the construction work. "When they hit the bottom, they bounced and rolled off in the direction of the fire hall to the east." When they dropped a five gallon can into the aperture and heard it roll a "long distance", they concluded that the underground chamber was substantial. Some speculated that the opening could have been the site of an abandoned dry well.

Chase declared his intention to fasten a harness around his midsection and use the winch on his tow truck to lower himself into the cavern for a better view. He unfortunately had to delay this adventure for two hours due to a prior appointment in Rochester. When he returned and began preparing to go spelunking, he discovered that the opening in the cavern crust had been patched and covered with concrete. The explanation for this action, provided at the time, was that there was fear of injury and the associated liability to the demolition contractor. Hence the last and most recent opportunity to confirm the existence of the Pittsford Cavern(s) was denied by the fear of litigation.

The most compelling anecdote regarding the existence of subterranean voids below the village appeared in the Brighton-Pittsford Post in 1978 when Paul Knickerbocker relayed a story that had been told to him by Tom Heaver in 1947. According to Knickerbocker, Heaver told him that while he was drilling a well at the home of Irving and Ida Crump at 14 Locust Street, he struck limestone at a depth of about 35 feet. Not easily deterred, Heaver set off two charges of dynamite. The second explosion broke through a limestone layer exposing a substantial cavern. Using a flashlight, he explored the cavern that ran south under Locust Street and as far as the Four Corners.

Mrs. Drake, Bryce Chase and Tom Heaver are now deceased. Paul Knickerbocker was close friends with Messrs. Chase and Weaver and was told directly about their cavern experiences. Both were upstanding citizens not prone to practical jokes or UFO sightings. Accordingly, Knickerbocker has "absolutely no doubt that the cavern exists"...."I was close friends with both Tom and Bryce; they had no reason not to tell the truth". Mr. Knickerbocker added that "when they were excavating to build the homes on Monroe Avenue, they pumped excess ground water into the cavern".

111

In discussing the possible existence of fugitive tunnels, Isabella Hart stated in her History of Pittsford …"theory is that an entrance near the canal went to the site of the Phoenix Building and Hargous-Briggs House with side tunnels branching off from the large tunnel."

During the time the village name was evolving from Boyle to Smallwood to Pittsford, a local merchant and whiskey-seller Augustus Elliot had his spacious home built at the address that is now 52 South Main Street. Elliot had profited handsomely from his village general store and even more so from supplying distilled spirits to U.S. forces during the War of 1812. His distillery was located across Main Street from his new home. Construction started in 1812 and was completed in 1815. When Elliot's planned nuptials to Sally Penfield failed to materialize, Elliot sold his home to Judge Ashley Sampson and promptly moved to Pennsylvania.

Prior to the opening of the Erie Canal, local home builders were largely dependent on the availability of indigenous construction materials. The freight cost associated with transporting bulky materials long distances often restricted their choices. It was Elliot's good fortune that Elihu Doud had discovered the perfect clay for brick making at the corner of Stone Road and South Main Street; an area then known as "Lusk Hallow". Doud provided most of the bricks for Pittsford's earliest homes.

During the most active years of the Underground Railroad, the home was owned by Judge Ashley Sampson. Behind the main home, stood a smoke house and, ironically, slave quarters. At the time, the expansive grounds extended to Locust Street and on to South Street; ample space for the home's vineyard and spacious gardens.

Ultimately Judge Sampson sold the home to James Guernsey, a local (apparently successful) preacher. Guernsey grew ginseng in sufficient quantities to develop a thriving export business in the herb. Title to the property passed to the families of David Haywood and Andrew Bancock before being acquired in 1851 by New York City's wealthy Hargous family. They used the property mainly to escape the heat of the City in summers. The Hargous family summered at the property for thirty-two years before selling it to James Vought in 1883. It then passed through a succession of owners (the families of Frank Emerson, Harry Culver and Lorraine Culver Truesdell) before William Briggs purchased the home in 1921. The home then passed to Theodore Briggs and J. Lenci before being purchased by Saint Louis Church in 1949. Prior to becoming the parish house, the Federal Style mansion was used as a school, a library and a convent. The home is known historically as the Hargous-Briggs House.

The attic of the Hargous–Briggs House contains fascinating indications that this was, in fact, a busy station on the Underground Railroad.[5] A wooden cage measuring eight by ten feet remains today. The cage door swings on hand-forged metal hinges; inside is a chain and shackle of the same vintage. It has been speculated for a long time that the cage and shackles were used as an elaborate charade in the event that the "station masters" could not move the "freight" before slave hunters or law enforcement officials arrived. The hoax consisted of shackling the runaway slaves inside the cage and professing to the slave hunters that they were only hours too late as the fugitives had just recently been captured and were awaiting transport back to their rightful owners.

The ground floor of the Hargous-Briggs House is divided into four square parlors that appear equal in size. Upon closer examination however, one discerns that the southern facing rooms are slightly smaller. Though these two rooms seem to share a common wall, in fact, they do not. Rather, hidden between the two parlors, lies a narrow passageway containing a set of stairs that extends from the basement to the third floor attic. When necessary, fugitive slaves could escape from the basement to the attic via these hidden stairs.

Barbara Briggs Trimble told of a hidden room used to hide "cargo" of the Underground Railroad. It was located on the ground floor between the living room and dining room. Access to this clandestine space was solely through a narrow staircase disguised behind an obscure linen closet in the second-story hallway.

Some have hypothesized that a substantial "bake oven" in the basement was used to harbor fugitive slaves. This "bake oven" was actually one of three cisterns used to hold the home's water supply. An apparent alternate subterranean escape route was also available. There is clear evidence of a bricked-in tunnel entrance facing the direction of the Erie Canal which was located several hundred yards to the north.

---

[5] Academics are quick to correctly clarify that the Underground Railroad had very little or nothing to do with a network of subterranean transportation routes or the railroad. When the Southern slave Tice Davids escaped across a river in 1830, his dismayed owner proclaimed that he "must have used an underground road, he disappeared so quickly". As the phrase was popularized, it transitioned to "Underground Railroad". Indeed nearly all of the "cargo" was moved above ground hidden in the backs of wagons (not on railroads); most often under the cover of darkness. This more accurate description however did not preclude creative "conductors" from utilizing whatever resources that might be available to them to minimize the likelihood of detection; including the use of basements, haylofts, chicken coops, dry wells, naturally occurring caverns or, for that matter, manmade tunnels. The transition from "underground road" to "underground railroad" was facilitated by the fact that railroads first began operating in the United States in 1831 and surely held much fascination to those witnessing its remarkable impact on transportation and commerce

Per the church's Father Jim Schwartz: "The door that supposedly leads to the caverns has long since been cemented closed." Did this tunnel enter the cavern that is reportedly under the intersection of State and Main at the Four Corners; did it lead directly to the towpath of the Erie Canal or did it allow freedom-seeking slaves to retreat south to other "stations" in homes along South Main Street?

How does one reconcile the fact that the owner of the Hargous –Briggs house, at the time, was the local judge; sworn to uphold the law? Surely Mr. Sampson was on the side of the law. Perhaps it does all make sense. Liberal northern judges were often sympathetic to the abolitionist movement. Judge Sampson was reasonably affluent and traveled among the more educated and like-minded villagers. This likely included the local clergy. It's not hard to imagine that if you could get a speeding ticket "fixed" through casual "connections" to local judges in the 1960's, that judges 100+ years earlier would look the other way to those following the high moral ground of facilitating the passage of freedom-seeking slaves through the village. Perhaps Judge Sampson's scam was perfect; what outsider would suspect unlawful deeds of a judge with shackled slaves in his attic. This, in a state, where slavery was legal until 1827.

A fascinating oral history exists regarding one local conductor on the Underground Railroad. Shelley Crump's father was the accomplished English stonemason Samuel Lee Crump. He visited America on his 1842 honeymoon and decided he liked what he saw. While visiting Rochester, he noticed a solicitation for proposals to build a cobblestone school in the nearby village of Pittsford. Few stonemasons at the time were familiar with the old-world art of building with cobblestones. Crump traveled to the village by foot and convincingly discussed his qualifications with the school's trustees. He was commissioned to build the stunning structure at 11 Church Street which is now the Masonic Temple. The original school built in 1842 was called the Stone Academy and is the oldest school remaining in the village.

Crump went on to build several cobblestone homes in the village. In 1870 he built the iconic brick Wiltsie and Crump building at the Four Corners. Samuel's son Shelley ran a very successful general store from that location for over fifty years. Samuel Crump's home and barn were located next door; the latter an important "station" on the Underground Railroad.

Over the years, Shelley Crump's granddaughter, Christine Crump Haynor shared stories told to her by her grandfather regarding his support of the abolitionist cause. Escaped slaves were hidden under tarpaulins in the back of horse-drawn wagons and driven into the family yard at midnight on prearranged dates. Crump and his wife prepared beds in the hayloft for the fugitives and provided meals. The following night they hid their charges in their own wagons and transported them to Lake Ontario where they escaped to Canada.

Slave owning was not restricted to the Southern United States. Austin Steward was "owned" by a "master" in Bath, Steuben County, New York. Steward had the audacity to smuggle books, pencils and paper to his quarters. His master became aware of these transgressions and, according to Steward: "...if he saw me with a book or a paper in my hand, oh, how he would swear at me, sending me off in a hurry, about some employment. Still I persevered."

His owner made an error in 1815 that would have lasting impact. He hired Steward out as a favor to a friend. By strict interpretation of the laws at the time, this gave Austin the legal right to claim his freedom. Stewart was one of the first slaves to believe in the possibility of freedom. Anticipating that his master would stubbornly resist the loss of his "property", he fled fifty miles to Manchester in Ontario County and then onto Canandaigua which, at the time, was the area's largest city. The Comstock family, who were one of the areas first settlers, took him in and stubbornly resisted attempts by his former master to reclaim his "property". They did so despite the fact that slavery was still legal in New York State at the time.

Slavery was perhaps no more "humane" in New York State than in the Southern States. Steward commented: "Everywhere that slavery exists, it is nothing but slavery. I found it just as hard to be beaten over the head with a piece of iron in New York as it was in Virginia."

Steward traveled through Pittsford en route to making a delivery for the Comstocks in Rochesterville in 1816. Likely water stops included Irondequoit Creek and Big Spring. He later described Rochesterville: "It was a very small and forbidding looking place at first sight, with few inhabitants, and surrounded by a dense forest."

Like many early abolitionists, the Comstocks were Quakers. Despite the fact that Steward was already an adult, his host family provided strong encouragement to him to learn to read and write. Clearly gifted, he went on to become a successful business person, author and teacher.

Presumably with funding from his Canandaigua sponsors, Steward moved to Rochester in 1816 and opened a meat market; thereby becoming Pleasant Valley's first entrepreneur slave. This displeased the locals who quickly demonstrated their distaste for competing against a freed slave by repeatedly tearing down his sign. This prompted a letter from Edwin Scrantom who was the son of Rochester's first mayor. He said: "I remember your commencement in business and the outrage and indignity offered you in Rochester by white competitors on no other ground than that of color. I saw your bitter tears."

Some former slaves formed "colonies" in Canada. Austin Steward left Rochester to help lead Wilburforce Colony, near London, Ontario, Canada in the early 1830's. In 1836, he returned to open a grocery which was subsequently destroyed by fire. This prompted his move back to Canandaigua where he taught school to Black children.

Austin Steward was a civil rights pioneer; speaking out against slavery and facilitating the passage of escaped slaves through the region. In 1857, his autobiography, Twenty Two Years a Slave and Forty Years a Freeman was published. One hundred and fifty years later, his work remains a poignant classic.

In the Southern State of Maryland in 1817, Captain Aaron Anthony owned, what was considered a modest holding of, two or three farms and about thirty slaves. Before word spread of Governor Clinton's authorizing the digging of the Erie Canal, one of those slaves, Harriet Bailey was with child. Local rumor held that Captain Anthony had fathered the male child named Frederick Bailey born in 1818. As was common at the time, slaves only guessed their age and masters occasionally "helped" by narrowing the range by recalling a particular season or event coincident with their birth. They may suggest that a particular slave was born around harvest time, planting time or when the cherry blossoms were at their prime in a given year. Or...they might recall that he or she was born in the "year of the great flood" or year of the last drought. As close as Frederick Baily came to knowing his date of birth was when Captain Anthony (his father?) told him in the year 1835 that he thought he was "about seventeen years old".

Following tradition, Harriet Baily was separated from her child before he reached his first birthday. She was relocated to another of the master's farms, twelve miles away, near Lee's Mill. Theoretically this separation was to dull the affection between child and mother and to facilitate peace and calm among the slaves. Frederick and other children who were too young to work the fields were tended by an elderly female slave too old to be productively engaged in farm labor. It was his good fortune that Frederick's child-care provider was his grandmother Betsey Baily.

Before she died in 1825, Harriet saw young Frederick only four or five times and never in the light of day. After toiling in the fields for a full day, she walked the twelve miles to Captain Anthony's other farm where she would put young Fredrick to bed before returning just before dawn to her assigned workplace. Her round trip journey was just over two miles short of walking a marathon to spend a few minutes with her child. The truth of Frederick's paternity died with her.

Frederick later recounted the news of his mother's death..."Never having enjoyed, to any considerable extent, her soothing presence, her tender and watchful care, I received the tidings of her death with much the same emotions I should have probably felt at the death of a stranger".

Too young for productive labor, Frederick's early years were spent in an uneventful existence, playing in the woods under the watchful eye of his grandmother. As he approached adolescence, Frederick's grandmother delivered him as directed to the Lloyd Plantation, which was also managed by Captain Anthony, and was located near the eastern side of Chesapeake Bay. Here he joined his older brother and two sisters and began his life as a slave.

It was a bleak life. The sole nourishment for slave children was cornmeal mush dumped unceremoniously into a pig's trough. Each child was furnished a single long linen shirt as their sole clothing.

Today, Captain Anthony would be termed a child rapist/molester and be forced to register as a sex offender. In 1825, when Frederick was a boy of seven, his fifteen year old Aunt Hester repeatedly rebuffed the sexual advances of Captain Anthony. Late one night, Frederick was awakened to her screams and peered through the cracks in the slave quarters to the adjoining room. There he witnessed Anthony exacting painful punishment with the lashes of an ox-hide whip. Hester was stripped to the waist, bound at the wrists with her hands held above her head by a rope secured to the ceiling. Blood streamed down her back as Anthony cursed her recalcitrance with every blow. Little Frederick cowered in fear lest he be discovered. This was but the first of a long series of atrocities that became indelibly etched in his young mind.

Slaves of mixed-race endured greater challenges and indignities than those of pure-race, primarily at the instigation of the mistress of the plantation. She had the gnawing anguish of contemplating the possibility that the mixed race slaves were a product of the master's loins. She distained his fornication with slave women as manifested in the mixed-race offspring. Accordingly, mixed-race slaves were more frequently sold at the earliest age so as to mitigate this festering irritation. Ironically this was often a better alternative for the slave child. The remaining option was to become the literal "whipping boy" of a master who was intent on proving that he held no affection for his illegitimate offspring. More than one anecdote described a master enlisting a white son to whip his mixed race half-brother while standing by nonchalantly so as not to raise suspicion that he held any affection for the victim.

Frederick's charm emerged at an early age and he came to the attention of Lucretia Auld, the newly married daughter of Captain

Anthony and, possibly, his own much older half sister. So impressed was she, that, in 1826, she became his sponsor. She arranged for him to leave the fields and move to her brother-in-law's home near Baltimore where his duties would be to run errands and provide child care. As a parting gift to the eight year old, she gave him his first pair of pants.

At about this time, an unrelated Anthony family celebrated the birth of their daughter Susan in Adams. Massachusetts. It was February 20, 1820 and a far different world than that of Frederick Baily. When Susan was six year old, Daniel and Lucy Anthony moved with their daughter to the Hudson River Valley of New York State. There, Daniel organized a school in their home to educate the neighborhood children; including his own. He felt the need to do so after the local teacher refused to teach his daughter Susan, long division "because she was a girl". Anthony could do so because he was free, white and felt strongly that his daughter should have the same opportunities afforded boys.

Nearly two centuries later, Gertrude Stein and Virgil Thomson would write an opera titled "The Mother of Us All" that artistically portrayed the life of Susan B. Anthony. Precocious Susan began teaching school herself at age sixteen but felt ill-prepared. Her Quaker father was committed to his daughter's education and enrolled her in a Quaker boarding school in Philadelphia. Her education was disrupted shortly thereafter when the family's finances were devastated by the "Panic of 1837". In order to help support the family financially, Susan began a teaching career in 1839. She excelled; eventually becoming Female Department Headmistress at Canajoharie Academy.

18

The Erie Canal

Fifteen Miles on the Erie Canal[6]
By: Thomas S. Allen

I've got an old mule and her name is Sal
Fifteen miles on the Erie Canal
She's a good old worker and a good old pal
Fifteen miles on the Erie Canal
We've hauled some barges in our day
Filled with lumber, coal, and hay
And every inch of the way we know
From Albany to Buffalo

Chorus:
Low bridge, everybody down
Low bridge for we're coming to a town
And you'll always know your neighbor
And you'll always know your pal
If you've ever navigated on the Erie Canal

We'd better get along on our way, old gal
Fifteen miles on the Erie Canal
'Cause you bet your life I'd never part with Sal
Fifteen miles on the Erie Canal

---

[6] Thomas A. Allen wrote this song in 1905 to commemorate travel on the Erie Canal during the period of 1825 to 1880 when barges and Erie Canal Boats were powered exclusively by mules. The well known song has had a series of titles including Low Bridge Everybody Down, Low Bridge, The Erie Canal Song, Fifteen Miles on the Erie Canal, Fifteen Years on The Erie Canal and Mule Named Sal.
In the late twentieth, early twenty first centuries, the nostalgic classic was recorded by some of the country's most popular folk musicians. These included Glenn Yarborough, Pete Seeger and the Weavers and The Kingston Trio. The country western group Sons of the Pioneers also re-recorded the song. Most recently it was included in Bruce Springsteen's 2006 album titled We Shall Overcome: The Seeger Sessions.

Git up there mule, here comes a lock
We'll make Rome 'bout six o'clock
One more trip and back we'll go
Right back home to Buffalo

Chorus

Oh, where would I be if I lost my pal?
Fifteen miles on the Erie Canal
Oh, I'd like to see a mule as good as Sal
Fifteen miles on the Erie Canal
A friend of mine once got her sore
Now he's got a busted jaw
Cause she let fly with her iron toe
And kicked him in to Buffalo

Chorus

Don't have to call when I want my Sal
Fifteen miles on the Erie Canal
She trots from her stall like a good old gal
Fifteen miles on the Erie Canal
I eat my meals with Sal each day
I eat beef and she eats hay
And she ain't so slow if you want to know
She put the "Buff" in Buffalo

Chorus

"It's the Water"...again. The completion of the Erie Canal in 1825 was the catalyst for massive population growth in Upstate New York. The 363 miles of waterway connected Albany to Buffalo and, more importantly, the Hudson River to Lake Erie and accordingly, the Atlantic Ocean to the Great Lakes. It caused the Village of Pittsford to emerge as a busy shipping port and allowed local farmers, millers, brewers and food processors to sell their goods to customers in a drastically expanded geographical area. The efficiency of horse or mule drayed barges was so superior to overland methods, that shipping costs were reduced by ninety percent. Within the first ten days that the canal opened, Rochester flour mills shipped 40,000 barrels of flour to the formerly untapped markets of Albany and New York City.

Low cost barge transportation allowed local farmers to ship less perishable grains to eastern markets and effectively compete with farmers located in closer proximity to these populated areas. Rochester, with cheap power provided by the falls of the Genesee, soon became the center for commercial and industrial growth in the region. Grain crops from western New York were transported to Rochester to be converted to flour in the mills powered by the mighty Genesee. Rochester became known as The Flour City.

Upon completion of the canal, the cost of moving a ton of flour from Pittsford's mills to the port of New York City was reduced from $120 to $6. The transportation time was reduced by 75%; from twenty days to five days. Prior to the completion of the Erie Canal, Boston, Baltimore, Philadelphia and New Orleans all processed more freight traffic than New York City. Within twenty five years of the Erie's completion, New York was the most active port in the United States. The total cargo passing through its port was greater than the combined traffic of Boston, New Orleans and Baltimore.

Jessie Hawley hatched the idea of the Erie Canal while sitting in the Canandaigua debtors' prison. He had gone broke, trying to sell grain and produce from the plains of Upstate New York to the Eastern Seaboard. While there was considerable commerce across the breadth of the state in compact but expensive products such as furs, the higher prices on these items easily absorbed the higher shipping expenses of using pack animals. This was not the case with bulky, relatively inexpensive agricultural products. Hawley was certain the only answer was water transportation.

President Jefferson considered the massive engineering challenges too daunting and thought the idea was folly. Undeterred, Hawley successfully enlisted the support of Joseph Ellicott who was the agent for the Holland Land Company in Batavia. Using Ellicott's influence, Hawley ultimately convinced Governor DeWitt Clinton of the merits of his proposal. The Governor authorized construction that began in 1817 at Rome, New York.

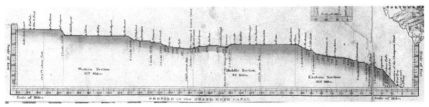

Erie Canal Maps (c. 1853) – Showing 600 foot rise in elevation.
Images are in the public domain.

Considered a significant engineering marvel at the time, the Erie Canal effectively opened what was then known as the wilderness and

121

now known as the Midwest to further settlement. A grand celebration took place to mark "the wedding of the waters"; the connecting of the Great Lakes with the Hudson River and the commercial capital of New York City. As cannons fired, Governor DeWitt Clinton toasted the 1825 event aboard his boat Seneca Chief as it bobbed in the still waters of the Erie Canal.

Originally the Erie Canal was only four feet deep and 40 feet wide. The major engineering challenge was how to accommodate the 600 foot rise in elevation between The Hudson River and Lake Erie. (See above map) This was accomplished through a series of 77 locks along its length; each lock measuring 90 feet long, 15 feet wide and facilitating an elevation rise of up to 12 feet.

The photo below depicts the well maintained towpath as it passes under Pittsford's State Street Bridge in the early years of the Erie Canal.

Erie Canal Towpath & State Street Bridge in Pittsford.
Courtesy of Paul M. Spiegel

Pittsford's dray mule concession was located in a barn located on Schoen Place. The building has endured many iterations since the early nineteenth century. Presently it is the home of Mustard's Eatery and Bar.

The business model used to provide animal power to haul barges and packet boats on the Erie Canal now seems anachronistic. Fellow concessionaires worked on the basis of a handshake in trading, exchanging and tending each other's mule herds. Barges entering the village pulled by tired mules were exchanged for a fresh team. The exhausted pair were fed, watered, sheltered and rested for a few days until they were adequately revived to haul a barge in the opposing direction; presumably back to their "home" barn and owner. It was a tough business. The system was dependent on cooperating concessionaires taking good care of each other's mules while in their guardianship. Despite what seemed a high-risk business proposition, only occasionally did owners lose a mule that was sent off in the wrong direction or receive an older, lame or inferior steed in place of their own.

The Erie Canal was ultimately credited with initiating a period of vast economic expansion that effectively tied the growing industrial and agrarian infrastructures of the Great Lakes to the commercial interests and growing populations of the East. It inspired massive migration from New England and Europe to both western New York and the Great Lakes Region. The canal's impact on the long-term demographics of Upstate New York was substantial. Three quarters of the population of Upstate New York still resides no further than twenty five miles from the trade route established by the original Erie Canal.

19

Pleasant Valley's Fred Baily?

"At that moment – from whence came the spirit I don't know – I resolved to fight"

Frederick Baily

Slave Frederick Baily's working and living conditions dramatically improved under the guardianship of his benevolent mistress Sophia Auld. At his request, she agreed to teach him to read and he made speedy progress. This proved to be short-lived however, as Sophia's husband Hugh became furious when he learned of her breach of tradition and good sense. Prevalent, contemporary wisdom was that a literate slave was no longer a good slave. He would have the propensity to disobey his masters and the capability to forge his own freedom papers and escape to the North.

Not to be deterred from his newly discovered joy of learning, Bailey befriended poor white children as he was running his household errands and enlisted them as surrogate teachers. He surreptitiously read books and newspapers with the constant fear of being caught. Through his tenacious will, he became an adept reader. At age thirteen, a copy of <u>The Columbian Orator</u>, containing a series of speeches on freedom, ignited his passion to end slavery. He continued to digest the contents of local newspapers in his thirst to learn more about abolitionist's activities and his dream of emancipation.

While Bailey was still a teenager, Aaron Anthony died and within a year so did his benefactor Lucretia Auld. As "property", Frederick Baily was juggled about like a favorite piece of furniture. He ended up as a field hand on the farm owned by Lucretia's brother Thomas. Thomas Auld was a mean spirited racist who starved and beat his slaves. Bailey received an ample share of his wrath. When he attempted to organize a Sunday religious service for slaves, his belligerent master deemed him in need of "breaking". This chore was entrusted to his neighbor Edward Covey, a less affluent farmer, well known for his ability to break the spirit of the most recalcitrant slaves.

Bailey was "loaned" to Covey. Soon after his arrival, he was erroneously accused of mismanaging a team of oxen. This provided Master Covey the excuse he was seeking to make an example of young Frederick Baily. He initiated a month of nearly continuous beatings which culminated in Frederick's collapse while working the fields. Covey continued to beat and kick the "broken" slave.

While Frederick Baily's body may have been "broken" in Edward Covey's field, the final beating seemed to hyper-activate his will to survive. This intense burst of inner strength was prompted by the current desperation in his life coupled with the glimpse of freedom enjoyed by freed Black slaves that he had witnessed in Baltimore. The next time Covey attempted to tie him to a post for a beating, Bailey later wrote: "At that moment – from whence came the spirit I don't know – I resolved to fight. I seized Covey hard by the throat, and as I did so, I rose." Covey and Bailey fought for nearly two hours before Covey gave up. While Bailey's likely fate would have been death for attempting to harm his master, Covey was too proud to admit defeat at the hands of a sixteen year old slave. Frederick later recalled this as his personal "resurrection".

> "It rekindled the few expiring embers of freedom, and revived within me a sense of my own manhood. It recalled the departed self-confidence, and inspired me again with a determination to be free…He can only understand the deep satisfaction which I experienced, who has himself repelled by force the bloody arm of slavery. I felt as I never felt before. It was a glorious resurrection, from the tomb of slavery to the heaven of freedom. My long-crushed spirit rose, cowardice departed, bold defiance took its place, and I now resolved that, however long I might remain a slave in form, the day had passed forever when I could be a slave in fact"

In order to distance himself from the visible reminder of his humiliation, Covey sold Frederick Bailey to neighboring farmer William Freeland in 1835. Within a year, Frederick had organized an illegal school for slaves. They met secretly at night. Their focus soon turned to planning their escape to freedom via the free state of Pennsylvania. One of the conspirators divulged the plot to his master and the entire group was arrested and jailed. To Bailey's surprise one of the Auld brothers arranged for his release and he was sent back to Baltimore. Upon arrival, Hugh Auld hired him out to a local shipbuilder to learn the trade of caulking (squeezing flexible caulk between the seams of a ship's planks to prevent leaks). There Bailey was badgered and, ultimately attacked by a group of whites who viewed the work he performed as a threat to their own employment. Hugh Auld considered filing charges against the antagonists, but at the time, the southern courts would not allow a black person to testify against a white. He decided to drop his plan to pursue some small semblance of justice.

Much of Baily's free time was spent with a group of educated free Blacks and their East Baltimore Mental Improvement Society. Here he quickly learned debating skills and became smitten with a free Black woman member by the name of Anna Murray.

Frederick Baily became a skilled caulker and was paid at the top of the wage scale. He resented having to relinquish each week's paycheck to Hugh Auld. Despite his master's commitment to free him at age 25, Frederick became equally committed to shortening that timeframe. He vowed to escape, but needed traveling money.

Frederick Baily negotiated an agreement with Hugh Auld whereby Bailey would give Auld a fixed amount from his earnings each week and whatever Frederick could earn above that amount would be his to keep. Bailey became frustrated when his saving did not grow at the pace of his impatience to be free. His yearning was so great that he resorted to borrowing money from Anna Murray. It was time to set himself free.

He boarded a train bound for Philadelphia. When the conductor arrived in the "negro car" and asked for papers and tickets, Bailey presented the borrowed documents of a sailor friend that proclaimed him to be a free seaman. From Wilmington, Delaware, he took a ferry to Philadelphia and embarked on the next train to New York City. On September 4, 1838 Frederick Baily was free! He attempted to describe his exhilaration...

"The flight was a bold and perilous one, but here I am, in the great city of New York, safe and sound, with out the loss of blood or bone. A free state around me, a free earth under my feet! What a moment this was to me! A whole year was pressed into a single day. A world upon my agitated vision. It was a moment of joyous excitement which no words can describe. Sensations are too intense and too rapid for words. Joy and gladness, like the rainbow of promise, defy alike the pen and pencil..."

Free but not free from slave catchers who roamed the city. He did not know whom to trust. He confided in a "fellow sailor" who took him to David Ruggles of the New York Vigilance Committee. Unbeknownst to Bailey, David Ruggles was the station master on the first link in the Underground Railroad. Feeling temporarily safe, he asked Anna Murray to join him in New York. They were married on September 15 of that year and moved to New Bedford, Massachusetts where he understood that he could obtain work as a ship's caulker and be relatively safe from slave catchers.

20

"Failure Is Impossible"

"Where, under our Declaration of Independence, does the Saxon man get his power to deprive all women and Negroes of their inalienable rights?"
Susan B. Anthony
Speech at Ninth National Women's Rights
Convention of 1859

When Frederick Baily moved to New Bedford, his comparatively affluent Black landlord was reading Sir Walter Scott's The Lady of the Lake. Seeking a new identity, Bailey borrowed a character's name from the book. He felt the name "Douglass" had a distinguished ring to it. Frederick Baily became Frederick Douglass!

Among Douglass' enlightenments while in New Bedford were his observations that many of the fellow freed slaves lived a better life than his two former slave masters; Thomas Auld and Edward Covey. He began to recognize the gross inherent inefficiencies in the adversarial master/slave relationship. He marveled at how much more productive a small number of willing free Black men choosing to work were compared to a far greater number of slaves forced to labor in the fields of the South.

Douglass was free but far from equal. In startling contrast to the South, Massachusetts public schools were open to Blacks. Likewise churches but seating for Blacks was exclusively in the Black section. Skilled jobs, even in the shipyards, were available to Blacks only if no whites were willing to take them. As a result, Douglass was not able to demonstrate his caulking skills and was relegated to low paid, unskilled manual labor.

Within a few months of moving to New Bedford, Douglass began reading the Liberator, an antislavery paper edited by William Garrison, the leader of the American Anti-Slavery Society. Douglass wrote "The paper became my meat and drink...my soul was set all on fire." The white Garrison soon became his mentor and for ten years, Douglass traveled through the Northern States preaching their doctrine of non-violent protest against the southern slave owners. While both opposed slave uprisings, they agreed that slavery must end.

Douglass' speeches had great impact. The audiences' attention was always seized when he was introduced as a "piece of property". He typically recalled anecdotes of his life as a southern slave but was cautious to avoid specific details so as not to be identified as the missing "property" of Thomas Auld. To reveal such information held the inherent risk of becoming the focus of fugitive slave hunters.

Douglas spent considerable time opposing a group of White Southerners in their initiative to require freed Blacks to move to Liberia and join a group of freed slaves that had established a settlement there in 1822. Concurrently, southern slave owners were conducting their own public relations campaign that depicted happy, well-fed and finely clothed slaves working half days in the sun and enjoying unprecedented job security. Unbelievably, this fiction found some support in the North and abolitionist meetings were regularly disrupted by angry white mobs.

So popular was Douglass on the lecture circuit that he was encouraged to publish his life story. He did so in 1844 – 1845. He insisted on naming names and provided specific details of his abuse at the hands of his former masters despite advice to the contrary from many of his friends. Five thousand copies of the <u>Narrative of the life of Frederick Douglass, an American Slave</u> were sold and it became a best seller. Now Thomas Auld could reclaim his "property".

Exposed, he traveled to England in the summer of 1845. The English had freed all slaves within their colonies in 1838 and the vigor of the anti-slavery movement remained. He was very popular on the lecture circuit throughout the British Isles. While he missed Anna and his family and pined for his homeland, he was reluctant to come back to America due to the constant threat of his recapture and return to slavery. Two English friends sent $710.96 to the Auld brothers and on December 5, 1846, Hugh Auld signed the papers that made Frederick Douglass a <u>legally</u> free man for the first time. In the spring of 1847, Douglass returned to America.

While Susan B. Anthony was teaching in Canajoharie in 1845, her father, Daniel Anthony bought a small farm just west of Rochester in the town of Gates. While tending the farm, he worked part-time trying to build a business as an insurance agent. He eventually tired of his dual career and, in 1845, asked Susan to move to Gates and run the farm so he could focus on growing his business for New York Life Insurance Company. She had grown tired of teaching and aspired to have a far greater impact on the world. She accepted his offer.

Daniel Anthony had been a longtime abolitionist and the family farm became a regular meeting place for Frederick Douglass and his antislavery friends. Susan Anthony's initial interest in human rights was sparked by exposure to these frequent spirited discussions at her home. Her friendship with Douglass was kindled at these meetings but was nourished by an intense common commitment to freedom and equal rights for all people regardless of race or gender.

Anthony's initial efforts at reform were focused on the temperance and abolitionist movements. In fact, she was not certain that she agreed totally with the women's right cause. In 1848, she joined the Daughters of Temperance but was refused the right to speak at their convention solely due to her gender. Inspired by this injustice, she started her own organization; the Women's New York State Temperance Society.

Ms. Anthony did not attend the first Women's Rights Convention held in Seneca Falls in 1848. She did attend an abolitionist gathering in that same city in 1851. There she became convinced that women could not effect real change until such time as they had the right to vote. She began her incredible career as a leader and reformer when she attended her first women's rights convention in Syracuse in 1852.

Two years later, Anthony was the driving force leading a campaign to take a seminal first step in bringing equality to women. She secured 10,000 signatures advocating the rights of women to have equal guardianship rights of their children and to maintain total control over the wages they earned. In the later half of the 1850's she led efforts to: insure that women delegates were seated in the "Whole World's Temperance Convention", assisted Rochester seamstresses in demanding equitable wages and helped female teachers fully participate in the formerly male dominated New York Teacher's Association annual meeting.

It is fascinating to compare the struggles for gender equality that Susan B. Anthony led in the nineteenth century to the inalienable rights afforded women of the Iroquois Confederacy from the sixteenth century forward. Anthony not only fought for women's right to vote but also their rights to own land and property, the right to attend college, the right to retain ownership of her own wages (a wife's earnings automatically became the property of the male head of household) and equal rights of child custody in the event of divorce (fathers were automatically awarded custody).

The constitution of the Iroquois Confederacy (Haudenosaunee) clearly defined very specific rights of females of member tribes. Some could legitimately contend that these rights were equally unfair to men. Iroquois women retained their rights to separate property that they brought to a marriage and land "ownership" was clearly the exclusive right of women. They alone decided which clan would cultivate each tract of land and could expand or reduce these assigned areas at their sole discretion. While women could not be chiefs, they alone selected the candidates who could be awarded such responsibilities and acted to displace chiefs that failed to perform up to their standards. Female Iroquois chose marriage partners for their children, arbitrated the marital disputes of their offspring and decided whether separation and divorce would be allowed. Iroquois children inherited property only from their mothers because, they alone, held property.

It is reasonable to contend that the rights among the genders was grossly imbalanced in both societies; the white American immigrants from Great Britain and Europe favoring males and the Iroquois Confederacy of Native Americans showed equal favoritism toward its female members. The significant difference was that white female immigrants strongly coveted and fought diligently for equal rights. When Handsome Lake advocated that male tribe members begin sharing some heretofore female roles, there was considerable pushback. Most male Iroquois preferred their historical role as hunter, fisherman, warrior and resisted attempts to further engage them in traditionally female activities of child-care and farming.

After arriving back in America, friends in England convinced Frederick Douglass to create and publish his own abolitionist newspaper. Not wanting to compete with the Liberator, edited by his friend Garrison, he decided to move his family west to the boomtown of Rochester, New York.

"Right is of no sex – Truth is of no color – God is the Father of us all, and we are all Brethren"...so proclaimed the masthead of Douglass' inaugural weekly newspaper, The North Star on December 3, 1847. Surely Susan B. Anthony was thrilled by such words but mixed reviews followed by others. Many abolitionist friends praised his efforts but the New York Herald urged readers to toss Douglass's presses into Lake Ontario. Over time, Rochestarians began to take special pride in being home to Douglass and his groundbreaking publication. In 1851, The North Star was renamed Frederick Douglass' Paper in hopes of boosting circulation based on its editor's growing popularity. It is doubtful that the name change was prompted by any pressure Douglass felt from those objecting to the "North Star" name as a not-so-subtle reference to the astronomical navigational aid used by freedom-seeking slaves intent to "Follow the Drinking Gourd".

Long before the term "Black Pride" was coined, his paper was a beacon of hope and served as the nation's primary communication vehicle to share testimonials of the successes of the nation's Black population. It was the nation's best known Black newspaper and its publisher was the most respected Black leader in the country.

Frederick Douglass attended the first women's rights convention in 1848; four years before Susan B. Anthony took up the cause of women's suffrage. At that convention, Douglass convinced the reluctant participants to make voting rights, an integral part of their platform. Knowledge of this contribution no doubt helped to cement the decades-long productive relationship Anthony and Douglass shared as abolitionists and advocates for equal rights for women.

In 1850 the second and far more harsh Fugitive Slave Act was passed by congress. This is sometime known as "The Compromise of 1850" because it was a result of northern congressmen agreeing to allow California to enter the Union as a free state in exchange for the passage of this tougher law. It was meant to appease the southern slave owners by putting teeth in the earlier law that, while in effect since 1793, was largely ignored in the Northern States. The revised and strengthened law allowed for $1000 fines and prison sentences for those who aided escaped slaves or in any way impeded their capture.

The passage of this act prompted a quantum leap in "traffic" on the Underground Railroad. So ominous was the wording, some freed slaves living in the North chose to flee to Canada. One hundred and fourteen members of a Rochester Baptist Church were among those who chose to seek refuge across the border.

Prompted by his notoriety, Frederick Douglass often found runaway slaves on the doorstep of the building that housed his newspaper. They were desperately seeking refuge from slave hunters and safe passage to Canada. His home became a busy station on the Underground Railroad and Douglass was considered the superintendent of the greater Rochester system. As such, his duties included those very active segments in Pittsford. Douglass is credited with directly assisting with the transportation of hundreds of slaves through the area. He proudly professed that not a single of his charges was captured while under his supervision.

An oft repeated anecdote involved three fugitive slaves harbored by Douglass. They were vigorously pursued by the authorities because they had shot and killed a slave hunter attempting their capture in Pennsylvania. Douglass dressed them in women's clothing and personally drove them in his carriage to a dock on the Genesee River where a boat awaited their escape to Canada. Just prior to embarking, one of the fugitives, a Reverend Parker, awarded Douglass the pistol used to dispatch the slave hunter.

Douglass grew impatient with the glacial pace of initiatives to end slavery. He began to question the merits of his own long-held doctrines of non-violence. He challenged the position of his longtime mentor Garrison who opposed using politics to effect change and began urging his readers to fight for the end of slavery through political reform.

Though proud of their liberal leanings, Rochester Public Schools were not open to Douglass' children or any Blacks. He enrolled his oldest child in a private school but, to his chagrin, she was taught separately from the white students. By 1857, inspired by the progressive policies of his former home state of Massachusetts, Douglass successfully led the effort to integrate Rochester's public schools.

In 1859, Douglass met with John Brown who urged him to join his planned attack on Northern Virginia's Harpers Ferry. While Douglass shared Brown's disgust for slavery, he declined to participate on the basis that the abolition movement's overall progress and growing popular support would be hampered by an armed attack on federal property. On October 16, John Brown and his band captured the armory and demanded freedom for slaves. Colonel Robert E Lee made quick work of the group. Brown was tried, convicted of treason and hanged.

Unfortunately, letters discovered at Harpers Ferry implicated Douglass in the conspiracy. The "station master" himself, had little choice but to hop on board the Underground Railroad and flee to Canada. His own contentions of innocence were offset by accusations that Douglass had committed to bring reinforcements to Harpers Ferry. Regardless he praised Brown as a "noble old hero".

In November of 1859, Douglass returned to England. When word spread that he was now a fugitive from the U.S., the enthusiasm for his mission and message grew exponentially. Prior to commencing his planned lecture tour to France, he learned of the death of his youngest child. He returned broken-hearted to Rochester.

While she led a sustained and consistent effort for women's rights, as the Civil War appeared eminent, Susan B. Anthony spent a progressively greater amount of time working for the abolitionist movement. She was selected to become the primary New York State agent representing the American Anti-Slavery Society in 1856.

In 1860, just prior to the beginning of the Civil War, Rochester's Black community had diminished to less than 1% of the total population – i.e. 567 Blacks among a total of 100,081 residents. As the presidential election of 1860 approached, Frederick Douglass emulated the Italians in WW II; switching his allegiance as the tide swung back and forth between candidates. Perhaps he was simply a pragmatist intent on making certain that the best interests of his constituents were represented with the likely winner. The platforms aligned as follows:

- Proslavery Democrats – Vice President John Breckinridge

- Moderate Democrats – Senator Stephan Douglas of Illinois
- Constitutional Union Party (Strong antislavery) – Gerrit Smith
- Republicans (Only opposed to the spread of slavery into new territories) – Abraham Lincoln

Douglass vigorously supported and campaigned for Smith until it became clear that he was not garnering sufficient popular support to be elected. He then swung his allegiance behind Lincoln. The Democrats split the vote giving neither of them more than Lincoln even though collectively, they easily surpassed his vote total.

In early1861, six more states seceded from the Union. Hoping to reconcile the nation, Lincoln pledged to uphold the Fugitive Slave Act and to allow slavery to continue in those states where it already existed. While Lincoln would ultimately be given credit for emancipating the southern slaves, this was not his priority as the union was beginning to dissolve. His sole focus was on preserving the Union. The leadership in the South was intent on succession and retaining their rights to own slaves.

Lincoln's lack of resolve in putting an end to slavery only served to invigorate Douglass. With renewed passion, he went on the lecture circuit demanding freedom for all slaves and the right for freed slaves to join the Union Army. By 1862, Lincoln had come to the epiphanic conclusion that Pleasant Valley's Frederick Douglass' demands represented the singular righteous path for the nation. On New Years Eve, he issued the Emancipation Proclamation.

In early 1864, Lincoln asked Douglass to create an evacuation plan for southern slaves in the event that the war could not be won. This contingency plan was never deployed because, by the end of 1864, the Confederacy had exhausted both its food and money.

As a Union victory became evident, General Grant depended heavily on his military secretary Lt. Col. Ely Parker to prepare and write the proposed terms of surrender to be presented to General Lee. Col. Parker was a bright, articulate, highly educated lawyer and accomplished engineer who ultimately was promoted to the rank of General. President Grant later appointed him to be Commissioner of Indian Affairs in the Department of the Interior. He was also a proud full-blooded Seneca Chief by the name of Ha-sa-no-an-da who was born on the Tonawanda Reservation in 1828, whose mother was the great granddaughter of Handsome Lake and Red Jacket's grandniece.

On April 9, 1865, the war was over. Four days later, on April 13, Col. Parker had his last staff meeting with President Lincoln. He was joined by General Grant and the General's staff. Immediately following the meeting, Col. Parker departed for his homeland in western New York State. President and Mrs. Lincoln sought respite at the Ford Theatre where he was the first American president to be assassinated.

After the Civil War, the 14th and 15th Amendments granted the right to vote to freed male slaves. Susan B. Anthony opposed their passage because females were specifically excluded from the legislation. This was the first disagreement she had with her close ally and friend Frederick Douglass. Anthony was discouraged that Black men were solely pursuing their self-interests without regard to the women of any race.

With slavery abolished, Anthony focused her time exclusively on women's rights. She co-founded the newspaper named The Revolution with longtime friend and fellow suffragette Elizabeth Cody Stanton. The publication's sole mission was to champion the cause of equal rights for women. The first issue was published in 1868. In addition to women's suffrage, the newspaper advocated equal pay for women, higher education opportunities and equity in divorce laws.

In 1869 she co-founded the National Woman Suffrage Association with Elizabeth Cody Stanton and spent the next thirty years aggressively advocating for women's right to vote. She grew frustrated by the slow progress and in 1872 registered to vote in the upcoming presidential election. Anthony was arrested after voting; tried and convicted in the District Court in Canandaigua. She vowed never to pay her $100 fine. She fulfilled that pledge.

Susan B. Anthony's reach became global in 1888 when she founded the International Council of Women. She traveled to London in 1899 and Berlin in 1904 as head of the American delegation to their conventions. At this time, she was concurrently raising money to facilitate the admission of women to the University of Rochester. Through her efforts, women were admitted in 1900.

In 1877, Frederick Douglass paid a visit to Thomas Auld, his former master/owner. The two left on good terms after Auld offered both justification and contrition for his earlier actions as a slave owner.

Frederick Douglass (c.1879). This image is in the public domain.

Anna Douglas died in 1882 and two years later, Frederick married a white woman named Helen Pitts who was twenty years his junior. To those who criticized his decision to choose a mate of a different race, he responded saying that "in his first marriage he had honored his mother's race and in his second marriage, his father's". Frederick Douglass died of a heart attack on February 20, 1895 and is buried in Rochester.

While speaking at a suffrage convention in Baltimore in 1906, Susan B. Anthony coined her signature dictum "Failure is Impossible". She did not live to see women granted the right to vote. She died at her home at 17 Madison Street in Rochester in March of that year and is buried in Mount Hope Cemetery. Her dream was not realized until fourteen years later with the passage of the 19th Amendment. The amendment states: "the right of citizens of the United States to vote shall not be denied or abridged by the United States or by any state on account of sex."

21

From Agrarian Hub to the "Burbs"

In 1834 the Rochester and Auburn Railroad built tracks through the Village of Pittsford and opened, what would become, a busy freight and passenger depot. Much like the Erie Canal, this new transportation option provided Pittsford a significant favorable economic bump. Again, the practical economic reach of local farmers was dramatically expanded as train shipments allowed for the prompt delivery of locally grown crops and produce to more distant markets. The speed of rail transportation allowed Pittsford farmers to broaden their mix of crops to include perishable fruits and vegetables that could be whisked to a broader geographic market. Pittsford remained a local shipping center through the 1950's until truck transportation displaced the rails as the most cost effective shipping method for bulky products. The Renaissance Delmonte Lodge now adjoins the site of the thoughtfully restored old Rochester and Auburn and later New York Central Depot.

Beginning in the 1850's, the Rochester affluent began building "country estates" in Pittsford. This signaled the area's gradual transition from a hearty agrarian based community to one characterized by suburban sprawl. Land was plentiful and local sawmills provided ample quantities of modern building materials.

While the indigenous Iroquois and the white frontier settlers were each erecting their own definition of modern homes only a few miles from one another, the elements of their respective building techniques were centuries apart. The white settlers were abandoning the traditional frontier log cabin for the comforts afforded by the use of precision milled framing lumber, finely crafted siding and wood shingles. At the same time, the Iroquois looked longingly at the privacy and relative luxury afforded by the white man's log cabin.

The Iroquois had been building their simple but drafty communal longhouses for centuries. The method of bending the tops of vertically erected poles to form the sloped roofs of their longhouses was fast, efficient, utilized plentifully available resources and required no special tools. But....they shared an eighty foot long structure with a dozen or more clan families, the roof's smoke holes also allowed rain and snow to enter and, by nature, the walls provided only modest protection from winter winds.

Two factors prompted a baby step of acculturation. By this time, local Seneca who subscribed to Handsome Lake's doctrine of selectively adopting certain aspects of the white man's culture began to yearn for the creature comforts that could be enjoyed by emulating the white settler's building methods. Secondly, they now had access to the tools necessary to fabricate timbers used in this construction style, namely the steel tipped hatchet. With this tool, it became practical to cut more precise notches in log ends to allow their proper nesting and fastening. As a result, they largely abandoned the traditional longhouse as the preferred form of housing and began building the log cabin style that Israel Stone first erected at Big Spring in 1789.

In support of the burgeoning population and diverse business community emerging in the Village of Pittsford, a young German immigrant named Thomas Spiegel built a substantial blacksmith and wagon shop on the northeast corner of the Four Corners in 1860. While an anachronism today, the local blacksmith was the contemporary equivalent of the high-tech entrepreneur. During the two hundred years preceding the invention and commercialization of the automobile, the "smithy" was revered like the village doctor or preacher. His contribution to the well-being of his neighbors went well beyond the traditional role of shoeing horses and oxen. He built and repaired plows, miscellaneous farm equipment and critical household cooking equipment. He was the primary source of hand- cut nails used to construct the community's barns, fences and homes. Blacksmiths' services centered on fashioning necessary tools from iron using only fire, anvil and hammer were so integral to early nineteenth century life, that they were considered local heroes.

Samuel Bennett was the first smithy in the village. The local villagers were so anxious to access his services that, prior to building a suitable shop, he set up his anvil and business in the village center under the shade of a large tree. In addition to Tom Spiegel, several others offered blacksmith services to villagers in the early twentieth century. They included John Utz at 10 South Street and Alfred D. "Laddie" Smith who worked from his home at 32 South Main Street.

Spiegel's building abutted the residence of the local tailor who had built his combination home/tailor shop just east of the Four Corners in 1855. The latter would, over time, morph into a series of popular taverns[7] including Tallo's Town Tavern and present day Thirsty's at 8 State Street.

Spiegel added interesting variety to the architecture of the village center with his imposing structure topped with the mansard roof shown below.

Spiegel's Wagon Shop. Courtesy of Paul M. Spiegel

As reflected in the image, Spiegel catered not only to those seeking "carriages and surreys" but also "cutters and sleighs". The Pittsford Athletic Club had its meeting room on the second floor for many years. Spiegel's Wagon Shop prospered for about fifty years but in 1910, feeling the intense competition from horseless carriages, Mr. Spiegel closed his business. Lem Lusk subsequently established an auto repair enterprise at the site but the building suffered significant damage in a fire and had to be demolished in 1916. Shortly thereafter the first of a succession of gasoline service stations was erected on the site.

---

[7] The succession of taverns began in the 1930's with Scoop and Hazel's. Warriners Town Tavern emerged in the 1940's, Windy's in the 50's and Tallo's in the early 1960's. Thirstys opened in 1971.

State Street - Parker Building, Wiltsie & Crump,
Spiegel's Wagon Shop
Courtesy of Paul M. Spiegel

The photo above was taken from State Street facing west. The unpaved central intersection was clearly built to be friendly to the feet of the horse and oxen traffic prevalent at the time. Spiegel's Wagon Shop is on the right, Wiltsie and Crump's store in the background to the right and the Parker Building is to the left.

Note the small, grassy truncated triangular park that existed between the Phoenix Hotel and State Street for a hundred years. It was removed in the 1920's; about a decade before the service station was added in front of the hotel and State Street was widened.

The Phoenix Hotel remained a hostelry under its original name for one hundred and fourteen years. In 1921 it was purchased by H.L. and G. L. Tyler and renamed Tyler's Inn. They enclosed the porch on the State Street side of the building and painted the entire structure white. At some point in the next twelve years, the establishment was re-christened The Pittsford Inn.

Over the decades, the old Phoenix Hotel (aka Pittsford Inn/The P.I.) grew verandas on two sides which were eventually fully enclosed. The porch was later removed to allow for the development of the small patch of land between the hotel and State Street. The adjoining horse stable was long gone when the Flying A service station was erected on the site to satisfy the villager's growing thirst for petroleum.

In 1867, James Wiltsie acquired the property that would be eventually known as Wiltsie and Crump. Mr. Shelley Crump, a valued employee of the former owner and son of Samuel Crump, a local stonemason and conductor on the Underground Railroad, agreed to continue his employment under the new ownership. A few years later in 1872, Wiltsie offered a partnership to Mr. Crump. Fifteen years hence, Mr. Crump bought Mr. Wiltsie's interest in the store and he retained full ownership until his death in 1926.

In the early years, the rear of the building was a popular place to tether a horse while conducting business in the village. In the new century's second decade, Shelley Crump was the first to offer gasoline to fill the tanks of the newly motoring public. His sons Claude and Samuel continued to run what was thought to be one of the longest continuing general stores in the county until 1937.

Sometime after the Crump's relinquished ownership of the store, a Harts Market opened for business. Harts later became Star Market. Since then, a succession of banks, insurance companies and, more recently, drug stores have occupied the building.

The main northern portion of The Parker Building dates to 1826 when Messrs. Clapp and Lathrop opened a general store on the site. The original building extended from Monroe Avenue to the present day center doorway which led to the apartments above the store. Mr. Lathrop bought out Mr. Clapp's interest and acquired the adjoining property to the south which extended to the Town Hall. He built the remaining half of the building in 1837 but left a vacant space between the southern addition and the Town Hall. This space would later contain the Central Pharmacy. For a period of thirty three years, beginning in 1865, Henry A. Parker operated a combination general store, furnace and tin shop in the main northern section. Subsequent owners operated some variation of general store in the building; usually in the northern portion of the building.

The opening of the Erie Canal created many additional opportunities for the Village and its residents; both as employees and entrepreneurs. Pittsford became an important shipping port for locally grown farm produce and for those that processed the bounty of local farms: the millers, distillers, cider-makers and fruit-dryers. This prompted substantial development along both sides of the waterway. The original canal was far more narrow than today's version. Accordingly, some of the original businesses that hugged the southern banks of the canal were lost when the canal was widened and deepened.

In the 1860's Jarvis Lord, a wealthy local farmer, general contractor, Erie Canal contractor and politician purchased the property which is now the Pittsford Farms Dairy and remodeled the original home in the

Italianate style. He added the wrap around porch, tall windows, cast iron fence, fountains, statuary and barns to form one of the area's first country estates.

The property became known as Pittsford Farms in 1888 when it was purchased by Frank and Estelle Hawley. The plural "farms" was a product of their combining three smaller properties into a single farming and dairy operation. They invested an additional $250,000 in acquiring adjoining acreage, building new and improved barns and establishing a highly regarded breeding facility for Jersey cattle. Today Pittsford Farms Dairy represents Pittsford's oldest continuous running enterprise. Environmentally focused patrons appreciate the fact that they can still return glass milk bottles to the farm to be sterilized and reused.

Frank Hawley mysteriously disappeared in 1898 and, like Jimmy Hoffa, was never seen again. Estelle carried on and began a breeding farm for Shetland ponies which ultimately gained an international reputation.

Like most immigrants to the area, Daniel Rand grew up in New England. In Connecticut, he worked for his sister who owned a blasting powder factory. In 1863, he came to Pleasant Valley seeking a location to open his own manufacturing facility. He was befriended by Mortimer Wadhams who owned a grist mill at Railroad Mills on Irondequoit Creek. Together they concluded that an adjacent site provided everything needed for a powder mill; fresh water, low cost transportation on the Erie Canal and seclusion. The latter being a safety precaution in the event of an accidental explosion.

Rand and Wadhams formed a partnership and began producing blasting powder for use in the stone quarries of western New York and coal mines of Pennsylvania. Soon they enjoyed robust demand supplying gun powder for the Union Army in the Civil War.

Explosions and the potential for injuries to employees were a constant concern and Rand was diligent in taking suitable precautions. In order to localize any accident, he built several separate buildings each one responsible for a different step in the manufacturing process. To minimize the chances of errant sparks, he used wooden pegs in constructing the structures. Materials were moved from one building to the next on small wooden rail cars which used spark free wooden wheels. Daniel married his partner's daughter and built a home and machine shop high on a hill a substantial distance from the explosives.

Despite their safety precautions, a massive early morning explosion rocked the powder mill in 1887. The blast was heard in Avon; the tremor as far away as Canandaigua and Honeoye Falls. Fortunately, the mill workers were having their breakfast at the time and there were no injuries.

After Daniel's death, his son and wife ran the powder mill until 1910. They decided to close the business at that time after another series of explosions. Monroe County acquired the property in 1930. Powder Mill Park continues to serve the area's hikers and picnickers.

As the demand for suburban living increased, prices on farmland in close proximity to the jobs and retail services of the village began increasing in value. Much of it was sold to eager homebuilders. With considerable foresight, the Town of Pittsford purchased the future development rights to most of the Pittsford Farms Dairy and placed the property into the town's agricultural conservation easement. This assured that a large portion of the farm would remain dedicated to the village's agricultural roots and its home and barns remain an important element of the village's unique charm.

The ballot measure of March 5, 1889 called for raising the princely sum of $7,000 "for the purpose of purchasing a site, and building a Town Hall". This measure passed. Much to the good fortune of the local populace, the site due south of the Parker Building on South Main Street was available for purchase. There must not have been any shortage of materials or labor, for in the following year, the corner stone was set for the original (and current) Pittsford Town Hall.

The Town's business has been conducted in this structure ever since. Originally, the building contained just two small offices; one on each side of the entrance. The remainder of the building was a two story open hall well-suited to function as the venue for the town's first high school basketball team of 1906-1907. Due to a shortage of available alternate facilities, the building also served the community as movie theatre and performing arts center. A jail cell, to temporarily hold excessive revelers from one of the town's six taverns, was located in the basement.

22

Temple of Fine Tailoring

"A quality garment looks new when it's old and feels old when it's new"
Jeremiah Hickey, Co-founder,
Hickey Freeman Company

The late nineteenth century was a period of dramatic change to the economy of Rochester and Pleasant Valley. There began a slow transition away from the area's traditional agrarian base. The bountiful grain harvest of the area combined with the latent power of the mighty Genesee had prompted local entrepreneurs to capitalize on these resources by developing thriving flour milling operations that put Rochester on the map. The presence of 500,000 grazing sheep in the Valley of the Genesee provided ample raw materials for Rochester's growing number of woolen mills. These mills, in turn, supplied locally produced fabric to a burgeoning local clothing industry.

Jacob Freeman and Jeremiah Hickey became close friends while working at Wile, Brickner and Wile; a Rochester producer of fine men's clothing. When, in 1899, both were offered opportunities that required them to move away from their native Rochester, they decided to reject the promotions and strike out on their own. With two additional colleagues and a combined $25,000 investment, the four formed Hickey, Freeman and Mahon Company. A year later, Thomas Mahon left the company and the firm was re-christened Hickey and Freeman Company. Eight years later, it became simply Hickey Freeman Company.

At the time, ready-to-wear clothing manufacturers typically retained the services of a cadre of independent tailors to turn out fine clothing on a piece-rate basis. Aspiring to become the premiere purveyor of the finest quality men's suits, Hickey and Freeman recognized the inherent quality control challenges of hiring a stable of tailors whose skill levels varied greatly depending on individual experience and process preference. They correctly assessed that one tailor may be particularly gifted at stitching a collar or attaching a sleeve but far less adept at rolling a lapel.

Hickey and Freeman turned the handmade clothing industry upside down. They opened a 77,000 square foot building where every suit was hand stitched in a single building by tailors who performed only the specialized task for which they were particularly well-trained and skilled. The person most skilled in each specialty performed exclusively that task before passing the garment to the next tailor who was equally expert in the next phase of creating the finest of hand-sewn men's suits. With spacious work areas, clean restrooms, ample fresh air, and abundant natural light the Hickey Freeman factory became known as the "Temple of Fine Tailoring". This reputation allowed the company to attract the best tailors and seamstresses from throughout the U.S. and abroad.

Seven decades before 20th century manufacturers realized that Americans would, in fact, pay premium prices for products of premium quality, Hickey and Freeman had the company motto "Keep the Quality Up" liberally displayed throughout the factory floor and etched into the entryway of the company headquarters.

Jeremiah's Hickey's son Walter led the company into the nineteen sixties and his grandson Walter remains at the helm today. Jeremiah's daughter Margaret was a longtime Pittsford resident and the wife of John C. Menihan whose stunning paintings of Pittsford are on the cover of this book. Their children recall grandfather "Jerry" and his tutorial on fine tailoring… "a quality garment looks new when it's old and feels old when it's new".

This singular focus on quality has served the company well. As the oldest maker of handmade fine men's clothing in the United States, many would contend the brand has earned near iconic status. Hickey Freeman continues to thrive today (as a subsidiary first of Hart, Schaffner and, more recently, Hartmarx Corporation) and proudly counts among its past and current loyal customers Dwight D. Eisenhower, Lyndon Baines Johnson, George H.W. Bush, Hubert Humphrey, Walter Mondale and Al Gore.

23

Birth of the Imaging Industry

"Make the camera as convenient as the pencil"

George Eastman

The birth of the "Imaging" industry occurred in Rochester, N.Y. in the year 1880. Quite by coincidence, in that year: 1) George Eastman began manufacturing his photographic plates using his revolutionary dry emulsion 2) John Bausch and Henry Lomb began offering photographic lenses and 3) Rochester Optical Company introduced its first cameras.

By 1903, Rochester Optical had merged with five other camera companies but failed to achieve profitability. George Eastman acquired the company for $330,000 and it became the Rochester Optical Division of Eastman Kodak.

When John J. Bausch opened his optician's shop in Rochester in 1853, business was not initially brisk. Although many people had heard of eye glasses, few had ever seen the recent invention.

Mr. Bausch emigrated from Germany in 1850 at age 20. He was a gifted optician and held the rights to a unique process to make vulcanized rubber eyeglass frames. But Mr. Bausch preferred to use his time in demonstrating his exceptional skills in crafting complicated optical products. Not long after starting his venture, he found himself in a cash flow crunch and borrowed $60 from fellow German immigrant Henry Lomb, owner of a successful cabinet business. Bausch pledged at the time to make Lomb a partner if the business survived and prospered.

John J. Bausch and Henry Lomb.
Courtesy of Bausch & Lomb Incorporated

When Lomb returned as a Captain from serving in the Civil War in 1863, Bausch made good on his pledge and the Bausch and Lomb Company was formed. Lomb apprenticed under Bausch and in 1866 moved to New York City to lead sales efforts in the contemporary center of American commerce. Eyeglass sales flourished after the Civil War and the company expanded quickly to meet the demand.

Despite the financial success of the eyeglass business, in 1875 Bausch's eldest son Edward, urged his father to diversify into corollary emerging technologies; namely microscopes. That business was equally successful and by 1903, the partners had profitably delivered 44,000 microscopes in addition to the twenty million eyeglass lenses sold that year. This success provided the confidence to further broaden their product line.

In 1883, Bausch and Lomb introduced photographic lenses, and five years later, camera shutters and binoculars. Most of these products were proprietary, protected by patents and, therefore, very profitable. During World War l, sales of their technologically unique sunglasses, sold mainly to the military, were an important additional source of profitable revenue.

Henry's son Adolph Lomb built a fine home on the family farm in Pittsford in 1911. The "fireproof" structure was built at the corner of Sutherland Street and West Jefferson Road and used as a second home in summers and on weekends. Adolph died at a young age and his mother sold the home and farm to Nazareth College for their new campus. Nazareth in turn sold forty six acres to the Pittsford Central School District in 1946. Initially the Lomb House was used as a school building but later remodeled into administrative offices for the district.

Rochester began emerging from its flour milling roots to become known as Kodak Town in the late nineteenth century. In 1888 George Eastman made his first photographic plates. That same year, Kodak opened for business and promoted their Kodak Number One Box Camera. Within sixty years, various studies indicated that between twenty percent and one-third of the area's residents were dependent on Eastman Kodak or one of its many local suppliers for a paycheck.

George Eastman was the Henry Ford of the photography business. Henry Ford did not invent the automobile but rather, made it affordable to the masses. Similarly, George Eastman brought picture taking to the common people. While Henry Ford was still learning machining trades, George Eastman was establishing the model for interchangeable parts, assembly lines and mass production that would revolutionize the world's manufacturing plants.

George Eastman was born in Waterville, New York on July 12, 1854. His father was a friend of Booker T. Washington and a "conductor" on the Underground Railroad. When George was five years old, his father sold his nursery business and moved the family to Rochester where he taught penmanship. He recognized a need in the community for advanced business education and founded Eastman Commercial College. Profits from the enterprise provided for a relatively affluent lifestyle.

When the senior Eastman died unexpectedly, the college floundered financially and the family was placed under significant financial hardship. While George's mother continued to receive modest residuals from the college's profits, the family found it necessary to move to a rented house in a less expensive neighborhood. The widowed Mrs. Eastman took in boarders to help keep the family financially afloat.

When George was sixteen, a new family of tenants came to live in the Eastman home. The family of five was headed by thirty two year old Henry Strong. Henry had dropped out of school at age sixteen and shipped out as an itinerant sailor. He jumped ship in France and eventually returned to America to help his cousin start a business in St. Louis. The business promptly failed and the capricious Strong decided to climb Pikes Peak; in the height of winter. After serving as a paymaster in the Civil War, he returned to Rochester to settle down, marry and help run the family buggy whip business; Strong-Woodbury Whip Company. Strong and Eastman quickly became close friends; a friendship that would endure and flourish for decades.

There are conflicting accounts of the magnitude of the Eastman family's financial woes. Over the years, it made compelling story-telling to describe young George Eastman overcoming great obstacles at a young age to support his widowed mother, his disabled sister and a second older sister. According to this popular version of the story, young Eastman persevered, despite these significant hardships, to become the consummate success story.

Perhaps a more balanced report described how his mother, by her frugal spending habits, was able to send George to the best private boy's school in Rochester. While he did quit at age fourteen, some people suggested that this action was more a reflection of his desire for independence and adventure than for dire economic necessity. Expectations regarding George's ability to support the family were modest. One of his high school teachers characterized him as "not especially gifted".

Mr. Eastman did not attempt to quell renditions that described his more humble beginnings. Perhaps truth lies somewhere in the middle.

Young Eastman quickly secured work as a messenger boy at a local insurance company. Within a year, he was hired by a competing company as an office boy responsible for filing policies. His drive and ambition were recognized by management and soon he was writing policies. His weekly salary of $5 was inadequate to support his widowed mother and sisters, so George began studying accounting in the evenings. In order to supplement his wages at the insurance company, Eastman worked part time as a Rochester Firefighter. Profound work ethic defined his character throughout his life.

He was subsequently hired by Rochester Savings Bank at the princely (at the time) salary of $700 per year. Eastman was promptly promoted to an assistant bookkeeper post with a salary of $1000 annually. Because annual salaries of $400 were considered an average working wage at the time, his family was confident that Eastman was destined for a bright and prosperous career in banking.

As he approached his twenty-fifth birthday, George planned a vacation to Santo Domingo. A work colleague suggested he visually record the adventure to share with friends upon his return and, in doing so, perhaps altered the course of history.

Photography at the time was largely the domain of professionals. This was due to the expensive, messy, time-consuming process of developing film. Undeterred, George paid $5 to be taught the skills necessary to take photographs and process film. His first photograph, taken in October of 1877, captured the Erie Canal aqueduct as it passed over the Genesee River in Rochester.

He purchased a camera and equipment to permanently record his vacation adventure in photographs. He described the equipment package as a "packhorse load". The camera was the relatively straightforward piece of equipment; the paraphernalia and multiple chemicals to process the "wet plates" were the bulky, clumsy components. Current technology required that the exposed wet plates be immediately processed before they were allowed to dry. This required Eastman to pack a tent to serve as an onsite processing lab. Within the tent, he erected a foldable table on which to apply the wet emulsion and developed the exposed plates.

There is no record of Eastman having an "aha moment"; a sudden revelation that the current state of the photographic process was a very big problem awaiting an equally big solution. He was fascinated by photography and gradually became obsessed with simplifying the process. A visionary was born.

Eastman learned of British inventors who had developed an emulsion that remained light sensitive even after drying. He scoured British scientific journals and magazines and experimented with formulas that he found. Hewlett and Packard worked in a Palo Alto, California garage nights and weekends developing their breakthrough technology. George Eastman worked at the bank during the day and perfected his emulsions in his mother's kitchen at night and on weekends. It took three years. By 1879, he had not only perfected a superior dry process emulsion that allowed photographers to develop the exposed plates at their leisure but also invented and patented a machine to efficiently manufacture the dry plates.

His patent attorney was George Seldon. In addition to being a respected attorney, Seldon was an accomplished photographer and mentor to Eastman. Coincidently, he also had been legal counsel to Susan B. Anthony in 1873 when she was arrested for voting... because she was a woman.

George Eastman - A self-portrait on experimental film

In 1880, Eastman rented a loft space in a building on Rochester's State Street and began selling his dry plates to professional photographers. Economic necessity required that he retain his day job at the bank.

The fledgling company struggled in its initial years. On more than one occasion, poor quality plates failed to perform as intended and were quickly replaced with suitable products. While this remedial action was costly to the struggling company, Eastman recognized the long-term value of building a reputation for quality and integrity. He was quoted as saying: "Making good on those plates took our last dollar but what we had left was more important -- reputation."

By 1881, Eastman realized that he needed outside financing to successfully expand his business. He sought out the former boarder in the Eastman home, mentor and entrepreneur Henry A. Strong. Strong and his buggy whip business partners were rewarded handsomely with the profits from one million buggy whips that the company sold each year. While his partners preferred to invest conservatively, Strong liked to take risks on new ideas and concepts. He had nearly squandered a significant portion of his inherited fortune by placing risky bets on residential rental property, local banks and the dry docks infrastructure in the emerging town of Tacoma, Washington. He escaped these investments just prior to suffering large losses. He was immediately attracted to the radical ideas of his former landlord's son who, by now, was convinced that he would change the world by changing the world of photography.

They formed Eastman Dry Plates Company and Eastman resigned his position at the bank. Within two years, the business had grown substantially and new, larger facilities were acquired at 343 State Street. This four story building would become the company's long-time headquarters. Future manufacturing locations were located adjoining the Genesee River perpetuating a pattern of the earlier flour milling industry. The mighty Genesee provided the power to run manufacturing facilities and, in that pre-"green" era, provided an easy disposal route for the assorted chemical effluence produced in the photographic plate manufacturing process.

In 1884, fourteen investors contributed a total of $200,000 and the business was incorporated to form Eastman Dry Plate and Film Company. The name was changed for the last time when it became Eastman Kodak Company in 1901.

Mr. Strong was named the first president of the company in 1884 and remained in that post until his death in 1919. The differences in styles between Eastman and Strong could not have been greater. Perhaps each saw in the other, the perfect compliment. Where one saw a personal shortfall in himself, he perceived the same trait as a resounding strength in the other. Eastman was viewed as analytical, calculating and careful, Strong was considered a bit of a river boat gambler. Strong was the ever popular, loquacious, consummate salesman who liked to heartily embrace acquaintances upon meeting and was known to "pitch" Kodak stock to whoever would listen. In contrast, Eastman tended to avert his eyes in one-on-one conversations with strangers and stare at his shoes. He was particularly ill-at-ease in large groups. In the early years, he awkwardly attended company summer picnics but ceased doing so after he decided, perhaps correctly, that everyone could relax and have a better time if he were not in attendance.

While normally taciturn, Eastman was far more comfortable in small group interactions. He was known as a diligent listener who sought out and valued the opinions of all levels of employees. While cautious, he was also decisive and would freely provide his opinion on a range of topics. He placed great value on the contributions of employees and felt a deep obligation to reward loyalty with pay and benefits never before considered by American industry.

"Shy" was the adjective most often used to describe Eastman. His attempts to mask this shyness frequently resulted in awkward social interactions and his efforts to engage socially sometimes yielded inept jocular exchanges that some found to be uncomfortable, ungraceful or lacking humor. Eastman had a habit, which many found to be annoying, of assigning nicknames to acquaintances that they viewed as unflattering and not welcomed.

As he got older, he eventually developed a cadre of close friends with whom he spent considerable time. Presumably these relationships were warm, sincere and cordial. Among this small group, he was known to be warm and even funny.

Throughout his life, a defining personal characteristic was his intense modesty. His self-esteem was tied solely to the success of Kodak. When it prospered, he felt complete. He did not need personal recognition; if Kodak excelled that was quite sufficient. In his later philanthropic years, he would orchestrate his travel schedule so as to be out of town, preferably out of the country, when press releases were anticipated announcing a major donation.

Through most of his life, Eastman looked a decade younger than his age. He found this troubling in his early years and tried to grow facial hair to affect an older appearance. During his final decades, he found his youthful appearance humorous. On several occasions, visitors who had never met Eastman thought that the youthful figure sitting in the Chairman's office must be George Eastman's young son.

In the last twenty years of the nineteenth century, Kodak was Eastman's life. He bicycled to work carrying his bag lunch. Arriving early, he was often the last one to leave; sometimes as late as 3:00 a.m. Despite his social awkwardness, his hard work, determination and singular sense of purpose to bring photography to the masses was contagious among employees. He "walked the talk" and they reciprocated with hard work, long hours and intense loyalty. While many employees would not have chosen to interact socially with Eastman, he earned their unwavering respect for his dedication to the mission.

Maria Eastman was George's mother. The lifelong bachelor lived with her until her death in 1907. As Kodak prospered and her son became one of the world's wealthiest men, she gradually and reluctantly began to share in the spoils of his success. She had experienced the depletion of her husband's assets since his death at an early age. This caused her to cling to her frugal habits despite her son's growing affluence. She resisted his earliest attempts to move to a more spacious home in a more expensive part of Rochester. She declined his offers to buy her a fashionable fur coat for the Rochester winters; finally agreeing to a cloth coat with fur trim.

As he reflected on the market's early acceptance of his groundbreaking dry plate products, Eastman experienced his epiphany: "The idea gradually dawned on me that what we were doing was not merely making dry plates, but that we were starting out to make photography an everyday affair." Later he simplified that message by stating, what was perhaps one of the business world's earliest mission statements…"to make the camera as convenient as the pencil."

To this end George recognized that the expensive, bulky glass plates had to be replaced with a more compact and affordable imaging medium. Even though market demand for his dry plates was robust, he purposely set out to make these plates obsolete by inventing a superior process. Eastman had investigated a "roll holder" for sensitized photographic paper that had been invented in 1854; the year of his birth. He improved on the original versions and patented his unique roll holder (the Eastman-Walker roll holder) in 1885. So improved was his product that it won the gold medal at the International Inventions Exhibition and was similarly acclaimed at events in France, Italy, London, Moscow and Geneva.

He began experimenting with various flexible film mediums that could be stored in roll form in the camera. He gradually developed a suitable system whereby the natural tendency for the grain in the paper film to manifest itself in the photograph was mitigated.

Eastman's dry, transparent film product was slow in gaining acceptance by professional photographers. While the speed and efficiency of the process held great appeal, they viewed the finished product as of inferior quality to traditional methods. Professionals with a broader business perspective also viewed Eastman's breakthroughs as a threat to their livelihood. The complicated nature of traditional photography combined with the significant expense in equipping oneself to take photographs, limited the number of people who were able to capture images for the public. They correctly viewed Eastman's inventions as allowing amateurs to replace the services heretofore available only from professional photographers. Eastman soon realized that he had to capture the interest of the broader amateur photographer population in order to realize his dreams.

To lure the masses to the joys of photography, Eastman was convinced that he needed to create and sell small hand-held cameras that would accommodate the rolled film he had invented. "Small", at the time, was defined as smaller than the bulky professional cameras that required awkward tripods and multiple bulky cases to contain the requisite plates and development equipment.

There emerged a generic category of cameras called "detective cameras". The first such camera was patented in 1883 by William Schmid. It is considered the first readily available hand-held box camera. The origin of the name "detective cameras" was an attempt to describe a product that was small enough not to be conspicuous when capturing images of cheating husbands and illegal or clandestine activities. Rather than requiring a tripod and large format plates, detective cameras were held in the hand at chest level. Soon after their introduction, clever entrepreneurs disguised the detective cameras as hats, wrapped packages, suitcases and binoculars.

In 1886, Eastman received a patent on his own detective camera. It held 6" X 6" X 10" negative film with 48 exposures in a roll holder. The detective camera used a Bausch and Lomb lens but had no view finder. You pointed, clicked and hoped not to cut off the extremities of your subject. The camera was introduced in 1887 and priced at $25. This initial foray into small cameras was not successful. While Eastman had been intent on introducing one of the first detective cameras, his real focus was on leapfrogging the competition with the first of the original Kodaks.

In 1888, he introduced the Kodak Camera that would forever change photography. In the earliest days of amateur photography, no network of film processors was in place. Producing photographs from exposed plates was mainly a do-it-yourself proposition. Eastman decided to offer the consumer a complete photographic service. The Kodak Camera, loaded with 100 exposure film, could be purchased for $25. After the film was exposed, the camera was returned to Eastman Kodak and for a $10 processing fee, the photographs would be developed, prints produced and the camera reloaded with film. Unfortunately, the price[8] precluded all but the most affluent from becoming customers.

[8] *$35 for camera and processing in 1888 compounded at 4% for 120 years equates to over $2500 in 2010 dollars.

G. EASTMAN.

CAMERA.

No. 388,850.   Patented Sept. 4, 1888.

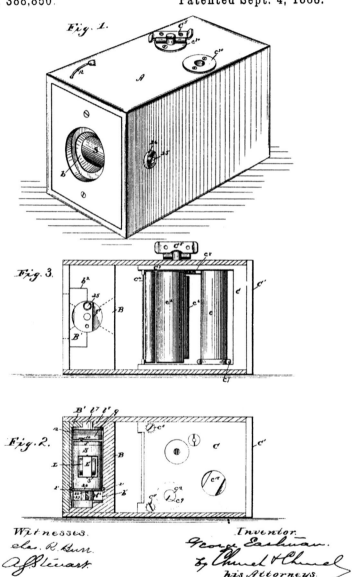

The original Kodak Camera of 1888
"You press the button, we do the rest"
Courtesy of Eastman Kodak Company

Eastman was more than a lab geek. Early on, he recognized the power of advertising to sway the buying habits of the masses. Before he had the luxury of an advertising department, he wrote ad copy himself. To introduce the first Kodak Camera in 1888, he is credited with creating the enduring slogan... "You press the button, we do the rest".

Eastman advertised broadly. The signature yellow color and Kodak logo were always predominant. Over time, frequency-of-observation and consistency created an iconic world brand. Consumer polls overwhelmingly associated the color yellow to Eastman Kodak in much the same way that today green is linked to John Deere and pink to Owens Corning. The Kodak name and the Kodak yellow are among the strongest and most valuable brands and trademarks in the world.

Before there were such trendy leadership tools as mission statements and core values, George Eastman led his company based on four clearly defined principles:

- Drive low cost by mass production
- Offer broad, international distribution
- Advertise extensively to the consumer
- Focus on the customer

Today this may seem simple but... in 1888 it was pioneering business leadership. To reach the masses, he understood that he must drive down the cost of the total picture-taking experience; both of film and camera. Today, nearly everyone feels a need to own at least one camera but, in the late nineteenth century, the populace did not <u>know</u> they "needed" a camera. Advertising was a cost-effective way of creating awareness and a "need" for the product. Eastman recognized that the consumer had to have ready access to the product via a broad distribution network. Finally, the product had to meet the customer's newly perceived needs.

It worked. Within eight years, the company had sold its 100,000[th] Kodak camera. George was not satisfied. Though he had driven cost down and made his cameras far more affordable, the pocket Kodak was still priced at $5 and out of the reach of many potential customers. He established a goal of producing and selling a camera for $1. In 1901, the company introduced the first Brownie camera priced at...$1.

Eastman's goal was to convert his targeted mass amateur photographer audience at the earliest possible age. The Brownie was the precise vehicle to do so. Cheap and simple was the key...load the 15 cent film into the $1 Brownie, aim and shoot; no fiddling with shutter speed or aperture opening. The tradeoff for low cost and simple use was photographs of predictable but average quality. But good enough quality and affordability for the emerging photographer who Eastman hoped would become addicted to the pleasures of permanently capturing a lifetime of memories. And... a lifetime buyer of little yellow boxes.

EASTMAN KODAK CO.'S BROWNIE CAMERAS $1.00

Make pictures 2¼ x 2¼ inches. Load in Daylight with our six exposure film cartridges and are so simple they can be easily

Operated by any School Boy or Girl.

Fitted with fine Meniscus lenses and our improved rotary shutters for snap shots or time exposures. Strongly made, covered with imitation leather, have nickeled fittings and produce the best results.

Forty four page booklet giving full directions for operating the camera, together with chapters on "Snap Shots," "Time Exposures," "Flash Lights," "Developing" and "Printing," free with every instrument.

Brownie Camera for 2¼ x 2¼ pictures, ... $1.00
Transparent-Film Cartridge, 6 exposures, 2¼ x 2¼, ...15
Paper-Film Cartridge, 6 exposures, 2¼ x 2¼. 10
Brownie Developing and Printing Outfit. 75

The Brownie Camera Club.

Every boy and girl under sixteen years of age should join the BROWNIE CAMERA CLUB. Fifty Kodaks, valued at over $500.00, will be given to the members of the club as prizes for the best pictures made with the Brownie Cameras and every member of the club will be given a copy of our Photographic Art Brochure. No initiation fees or dues if you own a Brownie. Ask your dealer or write us for a Brownie Camera Club Constitution.

Send a dollar to your local Kodak dealer for a Brownie Camera. If there is no Kodak dealer in your town, send us a dollar and we will ship the camera promptly.

EASTMAN KODAK CO.
Rochester, N. Y.

Courtesy of Eastman Kodak Company

So who was Kodak? Several alternate theories have circulated over the years as to the derivation of the company name. Some hypothesized that "Kodak" onomatopoetically described the actuating sound made by the shutter in the new cameras. Another woman claimed that Eastman told her that he conceived of the name while staring into a bowl of alphabet soup.

The truth is that George Eastman made up the name while playing anagrams with his mother. His favorite letter since childhood was "K"; perhaps influenced by the fact that it was the initial letter of his mother's maiden name. He decided the new company's moniker should have not one but two K's. It was his company, so he could have as many K's as he desired. He explained his process…"I devised the name myself. The letter 'K' had been a favorite with me -- it seems a strong, incisive sort of letter. It became a question of trying out a great number of combinations of letters that made words starting and ending with 'K' ". Over the years, he further explained his reasoning by stating that he was drawn to the name because it was easy to pronounce and it would sound alike in any language. He said he thought the name was "strong and incisive…firm and unyielding". <u>Pathfinder Magazine</u> quoted him as describing the unique name as "euphonious and snappy". The name Kodak was trademarked on September 4, 1888 and would become one of the world's most recognized and valuable brands.

George Eastman was a true pioneer in creating, funding and introducing innovative employee benefit strategies to earn and reward loyalty. It remains a mystery why most twentieth-century business leaders chose to ignore the sterling relationships that he fostered between Kodak's salaried and hourly employees. He introduced the concept of employee pay incentives based on company performance. In 1912 he directed the company to pay every employee an amount equal to 2% of their total pay over the preceding five years. As the company prospered, he tied this "wage dividend" to changes in the dividend paid to shareholders; if the latter went up, so did the wage dividend.

His gratitude and appreciation for employees was further demonstrated in 1919 when he pioneered one of the country's first employee stock ownership programs where employees could acquire shares in the company at a substantial discount. He made a gift of $10 million of his own stock holdings to initially underwrite the program.

He placed an additional $2 million of his money in an employee "welfare fund" to assist those who were injured on the job or were forced to miss work due to prolonged illness. This was the first version of what would later become "workman's compensation insurance"; now an employee benefit staple. This was followed by the establishment of precedent-setting retirement plans and company paid life insurance. These benefits were provided to Kodak workers forty years prior to them becoming commonplace in American business.

American industrial leaders were not adequately observant of the Kodak model of harmony between labor and management. It took fifty years of labor/management animosity and strife before strategies that George Eastman originally introduced began to resurface and be deployed to usher in a new era of cooperation and enhanced productivity.

Interestingly, Eastman was equally adamant in his lifelong opposition to organized labor. He did not understand their value in an organization where management demonstrated a sustained commitment to treat all employees with respect, dignity and provide fair wages and benefits in exchange for good job performance. He insisted that the company pay superior wages and offer better benefits than companies having union work forces. As a result, Kodak always experienced employee turnover rates far below the averages of American business.

Eastman shared the characteristic vision, tenacity and intense drive of the century's industrialist icons. He was decisive as it related to hiring and firing employees; terminating under performing employees with alacrity. Maybe his feeling towards organized labor was associated with a common perception that their presence hampered the company's ability to promptly terminate employees who failed to meet the requirements of their jobs?

Eastman remembered that he was passed over for a promotion in favor of a non-employee relative of a superior while working at the bank. Recalling the wound of this injustice, he committed to a philosophy of "promoting from within" and opposed the hiring of employee's relatives for fear of fostering an environment of nepotism. He routinely declined the opportunity to hire friends and relatives seeking to use him as a "connection".

Until his final years, George Eastman maintained his remarkably active schedule. However, as the nineteenth century concluded, he diverted his time and attention away from the day-to-day leadership of Kodak. By the late 1890's, Kodak dominated the photography industry. Between 1885 and 1902, they introduced sixty different models of cameras for any budget; ranging from the $1 Brownie to $50 models for the dedicated enthusiast and professional.

Kodak product development labs were busy creating replacement versions of products the day the initial new version of the camera or film was introduced to the market. New, improved renditions were introduced to replace popular selling products before demand had declined. This presaged the automobile industry's concept of planned obsolescence. In this environment, competitors had little hope of capturing market share.

Eastman was the first in the industry to hire a full time laboratory scientist to work exclusively on new product development. The first fruit of this investment was the creation of a commercially acceptable transparent film.

By 1889, Thomas Edison had a successful string of inventions that were changing the world. He had introduced the popular electric incandescent light. Among his 1100 patents were the phonograph, the electric vote recording machine and telephone transmitter. In August, 1922, Edison attended a gala at the Eastman House where the first color movie film was introduced. He had been consumed working on his research on "motioned pictures" and was frustrated by the products offered by competitors that could not withstand the rigors of his projection equipment without tearing. Eastman's transparent film was the first that worked. The motion picture industry was born.

This lock on the photography industry was a result of Eastman's domination of patent rights, aggressive new product development efforts and persistent acquisition of competitors. He insisted on securing patents to every new product or process developed in the Kodak Laboratories. With equal vigor he pursued and purchased the patents held by others that he viewed could either enhance Kodak products or processes or could represent a future competitive threat. Frequently he would buy the entire company in order to secure coveted patents. This market domination would ultimately capture the attention of the U.S. Justice Department.

In retrospect, the public's continued fascination with photography seems obvious. Who would not want to record the images of today to be recalled and appreciated in the future? But at the time, many thought picture-taking was just another fad that would run its course. Some were certain that the growing popularity and availability of bicycles would displace the camera as the latest craze.

Eastman's steadfast devotion to his mother raised eyebrows among biographers. By today's mores, the fact that she was such an integral part of his adult life seems unusual. Not only did they share a home until her death, but by all accounts, they shared an intense emotional bond. Eastman told friends that he wept the entire day that she died. The year was 1907 and he was fifty four years old.

Within the context of the time however, their relationship might not have been so unusual. Other twentieth century iconic Americans had equally strong maternal ties. When Franklin D. Roosevelt was accepted to attend Harvard, his mother promptly moved to Cambridge so as to enable her to keep a watchful eye over her son. Similarly, Douglas MacArthur's doting mother took up residence on the Hudson River near West Point where her son was a cadet prior to embarking on his illustrious military career.

The doting on his mother and the fact that Eastman never married did not escape the notice of the gossip columnists. Some questioned his masculinity and sexual orientation when they observed that he liked flowers and gardening, pursued the arts and music, subscribed to Vogue Magazine and, heaven forbid, enjoyed ...cooking! He supposedly amused and confused the Eastman House kitchen staff when he spent hours recreationally cooking. At the time such activities were seen as mainly of interest to the female gender. By today's standards, where "real men wear pink", and Dennis Rodman cross-dresses, perhaps he would be viewed as simply having a healthy sense of himself and confident enough in his own skin that he could spend his time doing what ever he damn well wanted to do without regard to what others thought. Maybe he was Pleasant Valley's first metrosexual?

He was asked by the press, no doubt tactfully, about his bachelorhood. He responded that during the traditional marrying years, his singular focus was on bringing photography to the masses by building Eastman Kodak Company. He did not have the time to devote to relationships outside of the workplace. The cliché of describing Kodak being "his bride" often surfaced in editorials.

While this explanation was reasonable in the years prior to 1895, after that year, Eastman devoted far fewer hours to Kodak and most of his time pursuing a wide array of personal interests. He focused on building Eastman House, recreational motoring, extended travel both domestically and abroad, sojourns to his North Carolina retreat and the significant chore of giving away his money. If finding a mate were a priority, he had ample time to pursue such an interest during this period of his life. Any active sex life that he may have enjoyed was well hidden from the public.

While no one ever accused Eastman of chronic women-chasing or of even being regularly in their company, the press did follow every clue that might have demonstrated a serious interest in the opposite sex. After all, he was the most eligible of wealthy bachelors in all of Pleasant Valley.

There was an unsubstantiated rumor that Eastman had a brief affair with a married woman. She allegedly divulged the affair to her husband; a lawsuit was filed and Eastman paid $50,000. Some contend that this prompted an overreaction in Eastman leading to intense skepticism in future personal relationships. Could he ever be certain that those who demonstrated interest in him were not simply interested in sharing his fame and fortune?

Eastman's longest relationship with a woman was with Josephine Dickman, the widow of a Kodak executive. They shared an interest in some common charities; both loved music and automobiles. His household staff opined to the press that they thought Josephine may become the first Mrs. Eastman. Another source described Dickman as the "love of his life" and inferred that they would have married if she had been in good health. Dickman's husband left her with substantial wealth in Kodak stock so Eastman's fear of a gold-digger must have been at least partially mitigated.

Other rumors included supposed letters from a Susan Brown that referenced "love that never dies" but the relationship was reportedly brief. Marion Gleason told friends that she "rebuffed" Eastman's numerous sexual advances.

Between 1895 and 1901, Henry Strong returned as President of Eastman Kodak. This allowed Eastman, at age forty one, the luxury of taking three month bicycle excursions through Europe. He pacified his own modest guilt by establishing new Kodak dealers while en route. Imagine the quizzical look on the faces of candidate Kodak dealers upon learning that George Eastman was calling to solicit their business.

By any standard, Eastman's business goals had been far exceeded by midway through the 1890's. Unlike many successful entrepreneurs who cling desperately to the identity that brought them fame, or professional athletes who refuse to retire at "the top of their game", Eastman seemed to have little trouble transitioning to a post-business life. With seemingly equal enthusiasm, he focused his attention on his personal life and his growing influence as a philanthropist. Many thought after the dawn of the new century, he "played" as hard as he had worked in his prior forty six years.

As he eased into a post Kodak mode, an early priority was the design and building of a formidable new home at 900 East Avenue; The Eastman House. This undertaking monopolized his time during the period of 1902 – 1905. When complete, he and his mother moved in to the most spectacular residence in Rochester; viewed as even more opulent than estates occupied by the Sibley's and the Watson's – the founders of Western Union.

The Eastman House captured the attention of the city. Even the wealthiest residents pondered a life surrounded by a household staff of forty. Eight maids, two butlers and a pantry girl were deployed on each of the ground and second floors. On inclement days, Eastman would leave his bicycle at home and have one of the coachmen drive him to his office. This allowed Eastman to enjoy his signature Lucky Strike cigarette en route. Coachmen would take Maria on her daily excursion to Highland Park in the morning and to Seneca Park after her mid-day meal. Howard Gleason moved from New York City at Eastman's request to play the home's organ each morning at 7:30 a.m. during Mr. Eastman's breakfast. He returned Wednesday and Sunday evenings to perform with a string quartet for Eastman and his guests.

The socially bumbling Eastman made even less effort to be civil to those around him as he grew older. He treated the household staff coldly; sometimes even rudely. Those closest to him attempted to excuse his cold demeanor by referencing his incredible ability to focus exclusively on a single person, report, subject or piece of music. They contended that this focus was so intent that his lack of warmth was not conscious; rather he was just focused elsewhere and did not realize you had spoken to or greeted him.

When the Eastman House was nearing completion, Eastman turned his attention to newly discovered and soon-to-be favorite past times: visits to his North Carolina retreat and driving his motor cars. He rented private train cars for his regular trips to Oak Lodge, a former plantation south of the Mason Dixon Line. Six cars would be reserved for the use of Eastman and his guests to travel in comfort from Rochester to North Carolina. The final thirteen miles was more adventuresome as the transportation options were limited to horseback or carriage. So fond was he of Oak Lodge that he typically spent six weeks there each year.

Most of Eastman's southern neighbors either fought in the Civil War or had fathers and uncles who did. Eastman's frame of reference was quite different. He had grown up in liberal Rochester; the gateway to freedom for runaway southern slaves. He had been greatly influenced by "Up from Slavery", the autobiography written by his father's friend Booker T. Washington. The fact that Eastman's father was a conductor on the Underground Railroad when they resided in Waterville further influenced his moral compass.

Eastman reportedly angered his new southern neighbors by hiring former slaves "Aunt Fannie" and "Uncle William" as cook and handyman respectively. He built comfortable quarters for them on the property. The neighbor's animosity grew more intense when they learned that he had hired Fannie and William's son, Henry to be the overall manager of the property. Out of respect for Eastman and his regular guests, Fannie and William named many of their fourteen offspring after them.

Upon learning that the Black children of the area attended a dilapidated one room school that was open just five months of the year, Eastman donated land to the local municipality and agreed to pay one half of the construction costs to erect a modern five room education facility. These actions only affirmed his neighbor's suspicions regarding the Yankee from Rochester; the home of Frederick Douglas and his radical rag, the North Star. Upon hearing that his neighbors suggested that he lacked understanding of the "ways of the South", he rejoined that he had "no sympathy with those who try to exploit the colored man".

Late in his life, Eastman's faith in human nature was shaken when it was determined that Henry Myrick, the African American manager of his Oak Lodge properties had been falsifying payroll records in order to embezzle funds. Henry was fired.

Eastman was fascinated by the newest phenomena of the twentieth century…the horseless carriage. By 1903, he had a stable of six different motor cars and spent much of his time recreationally motoring with the Rochester elite. After considerable arm twisting, he was able to convince Henry Strong to take a spin with him, but not before Henry hurriedly purchased a life insurance policy. Eastman prophetically thought electric powered vehicles held the greatest long-term promise, but felt that they had a few minor technical issues to resolve before they completely displaced vehicles powered by internal combustion engines. He became the popular face of motoring in Rochester and was elected to be the President of the Automobile Club. He declined to serve.

While Eastman spent most of his time after 1895 pursuing personal interests and philanthropy, the time he did spend at Kodak was consumed with two extended lawsuits. While he thought his company either had originated or purchased every significant patent that could impact the company's domination of the photography industry, Kodak lost a significant infringement case brought by Ansco[9] in 1913. When company attorneys predicted that the case appeared to be favoring the opposition, Eastman decided to settle out of court. The negotiated settlement was $5 million. While this sum could have financially ruined Kodak and many companies its size, Eastman decided that this settlement amount dwarfed what could have been a $25 million verdict if the penalty had been decided by the court.

Eastman decided not to jeopardize the value of existing Kodak shares. He kept the news of the settlement confidential until he paid

---

[9] *Ansco was founded in 1842 and produced inexpensive cameras for 150 years under various brand names. A main factory was located in Binghamton, New York. They merged with the German company Agfa. In 1941, the U.S. based facilities of Agfa-Ansco were taken over by the U.S. government and sold as enemy assets. The company re-emerged after WW ll and was renamed GAF in 1967.

the $5 million settlement from his own personal assets. Perhaps his metaphorical "marriage" to Kodak was apt.

A second concurrent lawsuit, brought by the U.S. Department of Justice was potentially more damaging. The Justice Department estimated that, through Kodak's aggressive acquisition of over sixty competitors in the twenty years leading up to 1912, the company now held 75-80% market share in the domestic photography industry. They brought suit accusing the company of monopolistic practices. On August 24, 1915 a decision was handed down that directed Kodak to split the company into at least two competing film producing entities and provide knowledge and assistance to other companies wishing to enter the photographic film business using Kodak technologies. Kodak appealed to the Supreme Court in 1916.

World War 1 substantially delayed all of the activities of the Supreme Court. While the case was in abeyance, the company garnered substantial public support as it became known that Kodak was reaping profits formerly enjoyed by German competitors.

Perhaps tied partially to post-war euphoria, the case was settled in 1921 by the issuance of a dissent decree. Kodak agreed to sell three manufacturing plants and the equipment they contained. This "slap on the wrist" required that they divest themselves of dry plate cameras and plates; the dying sector of the photography industry. Kodak estimated at the time that they would retain 80-90% of their prior business.

George Eastman
Official Portrait

Eastman decided that there was no future in a business model that relied almost exclusively on proprietary patents and buying up competitors. In order to retain industry leadership in the twentieth century, creative product innovation and talented, hard working, loyal employees would be the key to the company's continued leadership. Retained earnings could no longer be used to only acquire competitors. The company began reinvesting earnings to reduce their manufacturing costs through vertical integration. Factories were built to produce raw

materials and chemicals. Kodak purchased forestlands to control wood sources, maintain quality and reduce costs in producing camera bodies.

George Eastman gave up all day-to-day operational duties in 1925 when he was appointed Chairman of the Board. He named William G. Stuber as his successor and President. At the time, he decided he had personally accumulated sufficient wealth and henceforth he would focus his attention on using those assets to benefit society.

Eastman found inspiration for his philanthropy in the "Meditations of Marcus Aurelius". Echoing the values of the local Seneca Nation, Aurelius believed that, while personal possessions may result from one's own accomplishments, we are merely caretakers of physical objects; not permanent owners.

Much of Eastman's accumulated wealth was contained in shares of Kodak stock. He considered the health and prosperity of the company and its employees his personal responsibility not only during his years building the company but also after he ceased active management. He made sure that his vast holdings of Kodak shares were gradually sold and the funds used to support his philanthropic activities. He did so to preclude his massive holdings being dumped on the market upon his death and thereby depressing the share price and negatively effecting the assets of employee shareholders.

Mr. Eastman was a lifelong philanthropist. While still young, he began donating money to the Mechanics Institute of Rochester which would later become Rochester Institute of Technology (RIT). His interest in RIT waned over time as he donated more aggressively to the University of Rochester, MIT and the historically Black colleges of Tuskegee and Hampton.

While Eastman's philanthropy may have focused on education, he was also committed to improving healthcare in Rochester and throughout the world. Through most of the nineteenth century, dentists were mainly itinerant tooth extractors. There was no established protocol for the practice of preventative dentistry. Those whose genes favored good oral health, managed to retain their teeth longer than others. Maria Eastman suffered through many toothaches prior to having all her teeth extracted. George Eastman eventually sported a complete set of dentures after many years of painful tooth decay.

Initially prompted by his camera lens supplier Henry Lomb, Eastman joined a group of local residents in contributing $200 per year to the Rochester Dental Society to fund the establishment of a free clinic. Lomb had originally donated $600 of dental equipment to a clinic at a local public school and subsequently paid the salary of a dentist to attend to children from disadvantaged backgrounds. When

Henry Lomb died, Eastman partnered with William "Billy" Bausch, the son of Henry's partner, in funding a group of clinics that vastly expanded affordable oral healthcare for those with lesser means. They provided a wide range of healthcare procedures including treatment for the adenoids, for assorted birth defects including hair lips and cleft palates as well as tonsillectomies. Eastman's commitment to these clinics ultimately totaled one million dollars.

Eastman understood and appreciated the greater suffering of children residing in parts of the world without modern oral health facilities. Accordingly, subsequent donations funded dental clinics in Paris, London, Stockholm, Brussels and Rome.

Eastman's largess was focused on establishing healthcare in the Genesee Valley on a par with the premiere medical centers of the nation and the world. He did so based on his longtime love affair with his adopted hometown and his desire to assure Kodak employees access to the best available healthcare.

Thirty million dollars is a substantial sum of money even in today's inflated dollars. In 1924 alone, Mr. Eastman made gifts totaling that amount to the University of Rochester, MIT, Hampton and Tuskegee Institute. His contributions to Hampton and Tuskegee, which served mainly African American students, were a reflection of his long-term commitment to helping the so called "negro colleges" level "the playing field of life" for its students. At the time they were made, his gifts to Tuskegee and Hampton were the largest donations ever made to Black colleges. While he normally shunned such publicity, he allowed these contributions to be made public in hopes that such news would inspire others to contribute.

After writing $30 million in checks one day, he reportedly said: "Now I feel better". Over his lifetime, he gave away an estimated $68 million. Upon his death, an additional $25 million was donated to the University of Rochester resulting in total lifetime philanthropic gifts of $93 million.

Assuming a modest five percent annual rate of inflation and the magic of compounding interest, $93 million in 1930 would double five times to the equivalent of $3 billion in the first decade of the 21st century. While perhaps no match for the $33.5 billion endowment of the Bill and Melinda Gates Foundation (significantly augmented by Warren Buffet), this still places Mr. Eastman in the top echelon of the most generous philanthropists of any generation.

When interviewed regarding his generous gifts, he stated: "The progress of the world depends almost entirely upon education. I selected a limited number of recipients because I wanted to cover certain kinds of education, and felt I could get results with those named quicker and more directly than if the money were spread."

While he did not aspire to have his name forever associated with his gifts, he did intend his donations to have impact that survived him. He added "Fortunately the most permanent institutions of man are educational. They usually endure even when governments fail." An interesting statement coming from a "not especially gifted" high school drop-out!

Another endearing Eastman characteristic was his self-effacing, modesty. His $20 million gift to MIT was given anonymously from a "Mr. Smith". The identity of "Mr. Smith" was only made known when the Kodak stock he donated was sold and it was revealed the stock certificates bore Eastman's name. He was once described as "America's most modest and least known millionaire". At the height of his philanthropic efforts, he was thought to be the sixth richest American and the country's wealthiest bachelor.

In 1922 his generosity led to the founding of the Eastman School of Music at the University of Rochester. It remains today one of the premiere arts institutions in the country. The school and theatre that Eastman funded was declared Rochester's "most beautiful building" by a poll of architects in the 1980's. John D. Rockefeller teamed with Mr. Eastman in splitting the costs associated with building the university's School of Medicine; each contributing $5 million.

There was little doubt that Susan B. Anthony had mixed feeling towards George Eastman. While he was the world's most generous donor to Black colleges, he was not a supporter of higher education for women. He never donated to women's colleges. When asked about his reluctance to do so, he stated that "I have always drawn the line on women's colleges...simply because I am more interested in other branches of education". He did donate modest amounts to <u>anti</u> suffrage causes and he publicly opposed married women working outside of the home...definitely not politically correct by today's standards.

Eastman similarly "drew the line" at donating to religious organizations. He did appreciate and was a living example for America as the "land of opportunity". He manifested this patriotism by, on his own volition, refunding to the U.S. Government all $384,000 of Kodak profits earned on government contracts (38% of total profits) during World War l.

Ironically, Mr. Eastman was reluctant to be photographed. As a result, much to his satisfaction, he was seldom recognized as he walked or bicycled through Rochester. His face was not well recognized even around Kodak. On one occasion, a security guard prevented him from entering a new company facility. The guard thought it a weak attempt at humor when the "stranger" identified himself as George Eastman. An intensely private person throughout his life, he was reluctant to grant interviews and refused to support numerous efforts to write his biography.

Chronic back pain in later life drastically impeded his active life style. Modern medicine would subsequently diagnose his ailment as spinal stenosis; a narrowing of the lumbar spinal column that produces pressure on the nerve roots.

On March 14, 1932, George Eastman wrote a note and placed it on his bedside table. It read:

"To my friends
My work is done –
Why Wait?"
GE

Months earlier he had asked his personal physician to outline on his chest exactly the area where his heart was located. George Eastman placed a pistol to that spot and ended his own life. He was seventy-seven years old.

At the time of his death, a New York Times obituary tried to distill his extraordinary life to its quintessence…

> *"Eastman was a stupendous factor in the education of the modern world… of what he got in return for his great gifts to the human race he gave generously for their good; fostering music, endowing learning, supporting science in its researches and teaching, seeking to promote health and lessen human ills, helping the lowliest in their struggle toward the light, making his own city a center of the arts and glorifying his own country in the eyes of the world."*

After Eastman's death, William G. Stuber became Chairman and Frank Lovejoy was appointed President to replace Stuber. In 1945, Perley S. Wilcox replaced Stuber. The spectacular Eastman House became the International Museum of Photography in 1949.

Eastman Kodak prospered through most of the twentieth century. Employment grew from 5000 in 1907, to 20,000 in 1927, 60,000 in 1946, 75,000 in 1962 and 120,000 in 1973. The company invented, commercially developed and successfully introduced a succession of innovative film and camera products throughout this period including color film, 8 mm and 16 mm home movie films and cameras, the Instamatic camera, film cartridges and disc photography.

Color photography was the biggest breakthrough in the first half of the twentieth century. It was also a study in patience. The product-to-be was given the copyrighted name of Kodachrome in 1914. Eastman was so intent on being the first to offer commercially acceptable color film, that uncharacteristically he introduced a product that did not meet his normally rigorous quality standards. The resulting blurred images dulled the interest of the anxious public. It was not until 1935, three years after Eastman's death, that a truly acceptable color film product was introduced and popularized.

In response to a perceived shift in customer demands, Kodak "introduced" the single-use camera in the latter part of the 20th century. Mr. Eastman would have been humored; it was a variation on his original Kodak of 1888 that was sold loaded and then returned to the company for processing. Was this testimony to Eastman's legacy or simply a refection of nimble marketing efforts responding to ever-changing contemporary consumer preferences? Like most market leaders, sometimes Kodak's new product development efforts were exactly on target in anticipating customer needs. Occasionally sales of new products were disappointing but each discovery, innovation and resultant new product was directed towards George Eastman's original mission of… putting cameras in the hands of the masses.

24

Flour City or Flower City

Mount Hope Nurseries was started in Rochester in 1840 by partners George Ellwanger of Germany and Patrick Barry of Ireland. Business was brisk and the enterprise prospered. By 1888, it was thought to be the largest and most complete nursery in the world. In 1892, the owners orchestrated some self-serving philanthropy by donating twenty of their 650 acres of nursery fields to the City of Rochester for development as a public park. The park's paths provided visitors a comprehensive view of the nursery products available for sale at the adjoining Mount Hope Nursery.

The city was caught by surprise and scurried to form a parks department to convert the donated land into the city's first public park. Frederick Law Olmsted, fresh from his work on New York's Central Park, was hired to design the project.

Horticulturist John Dunbar, was aware that some of the area's first settlers had brought lilacs with them to the area. The Common Lilac (Syringa Vulgaris) is a member of the olive family and is just one of twenty species. Because these plants seemed to thrive in the area's climate, he acquired cuttings from original plants to seed the first of twenty varieties that were planted.

Indeed the harsh Pleasant Valley climate was much to the liking of the lilac bush. Within a few years, crowds descended on the park in May and June to view the flowering lilacs at their peak. Three thousand attended Rochester's first Lilac Festival held in 1898. More than a century later, crowds are estimated to exceed one-half million at what is believed to be the world's largest celebration of the lilac bush. The original twenty varieties have grown to five hundred and the number of individual plants to 1200. As a result, some suggested that The Flour City be rechristened The Flower City!

25

What Happened to Big Spring?

As the new century dawned, a growing number of beneficiaries of Rochester's vibrant milling and shipping industries sought country homes, estates or second residences removed from the bustle of the port city. Many chose the reasonable accessibility and small village charm of Pittsford. While the village continued to prosper with strong agricultural production, food processing and storage businesses combined with easy access to the shipping lanes of the country via the Erie Canal, a portion of the increase in population consisted of Rochester's affluent seeking new or second homes. As public transportation improved and became affordable to the working class, the village's population grew still further. The greater job opportunities afforded by the mills and factories of Rochester became accessible to villagers as first rail and then trolley service was extended to Pittsford.

The growing efficiency of larger, powerful, steam driven tugboats allowed the use of larger barges and made Erie Canal tow animals obsolete. The larger barges prompted the doubling in both breadth and depth of the old Erie Canal in 1910-1911 and the gradual elimination of towpaths. In order to minimize transportation downtime during construction, a parallel channel was dug directly south of the original canal with an earth berm separating the two. Narrow gauge railroad tracks were laid in the new dry canal bed to accommodate the movement of steam shovels and the removal of dirt. The parallel trenches ultimately became one wider, deeper canal when the center berm was removed.

The widening affected only the south side of the canal through the Village of Pittsford. Many of the original nineteenth century warehouses and mills located on the northern edge of the canal remain on present day Schoen Place.

An expensive element in expanding the canal's infrastructure was the need to enlarge or replace hundreds of bridges that had been built a century before. The Monroe Avenue, Main Street and State Street bridges all had to be expanded to accommodate the greater width of the new Erie.

Within two years of the opening of the new and expanded canal, there were two significant breaks at nearby Bushnell's Basin. The first (in 1911) was just west of Bushnell's Basin and resulted when the towpath gave way and washed out Marsh Road and the adjoining trolley tracks. Greater disaster was barely averted as a fully loaded commuter trolley had passed the location of the breach just moments before. A year later the culvert that carried the canal over Irondequoit Creek a half mile west of Bushnell's Basin failed, just moments after work crews responsible for repairing it were ordered to evacuate. So as to avoid closing the canal at the height of the fall harvest shipping season, the state hired a contractor to build a wooden aqueduct to temporarily reconnect the canal. This temporary fix worked satisfactorily until a new culvert was installed during the winter of 1915-1916.

Located between the village and Bushnell's Basin on Irondequoit Creek was the old Stone-Richardson-Jaeschke Rye Flour Mill. This mill had been in operation since the 1790's and was near the popular swimming hole on the creek known as Jaeschke's. After the 1960's double murder of a young couple near this location, the prevalent rumor was that the ghost of Jake Jaeschke did not take kindly to trespassers on the old homestead. From that point forward, local teens ventured to this swimming venue only in large numbers in the full light of day.

Pittsford was home to a continuously operating flour mill for 150 years. The Pittsford Milling Company (originally called Vogt's Steam Mill) was built in 1882 and is depicted in the photo below as it appeared in the 1930's. The warehouse was added in 1915 and the tile silo in 1920. At the time, it was producing 400 barrels of flour a day. The operation was acquired by Henry Perrigo in 1921, renamed the Victor Flour Mills and production increased to 1000 barrels per day. After a succession of owners, the facility was purchased by Theodore J. Zornow in 1953. He ran a successful flour mill and red bean business from the facility over the next 43 years; until 1996.

Theodore (Ted) Zornow was Pittsford's last nationally known business leader whose focus was the area's dwindling agricultural base. While the village became a residential haven for the wealthy of Rochester, the asheries, distilleries, fruit drying and pickle processing businesses were slowly closed. During this period, Ted Zornow continued to run successful milling and food distribution businesses. He was president of both T. J. Zornow Inc, which distributed grain and beans, and Pittsford Flour Mills Inc. His leadership had national impact when he served as president of the New York State Bean and Grain Shippers Association and as a director of the National Grain Council.

Like his brother Gerald Zornow, Ted was a gifted athlete at the University of Rochester. He captained the baseball team and was President of the Student Government. He graduated as the depression began in 1929. While an eminently successful business person, he was best known for his life-long interest and contribution to harness racing. He was nationally known as a breeder and owner of some of the best Standardbred race horses in the world. He served as a director and then president of the U.S. Trotters Association and was inducted into the U.S. Harness Racing Association Hall of Fame.

Ted Zornow also owned Pittsford Farms Dairy and Avon Farms. He purchased Pittsford Farms Dairy in 1946. Successful livestock breeding continued with a focus on Standardbred race horses and Guernsey dairy cattle in the last half of the 20th century. Sweet corn and pumpkins were added to satisfy the local population's yearning for locally grown produce. The eco-friendly returnable glass milk bottles from the days of Frank and Estelle Hawley remain today. Mr. Zornow died in 2001 at the age of ninety three.

So what happened to Big Spring? It remains in its original location but simply not discernable to today's observers. The answer to this puzzle lies in the building and subsequent expansion of the Erie Canal. The original "Clinton Ditch" was only four feet deep and approximately twenty feet wide. Its original course was slightly north of its present location. As it passed through the village between 1825 and 1909, there was a noticeable widening along State Street across from the flour mill. This expansion in width was the result of the canal absorbing the pond created by Big Spring. The greater width at this point allowed villagers to erect boat houses on the southern shore; essentially in the waters rising through Big Spring. The foreground of the photo below depicts the location of Big Spring's confluence with the Erie Canal.

When the Erie Canal was substantially deepened and widened, the pond created by Big Spring was irreversibly consumed by the new and "improved" canal. Big Spring was forever lost to the eye but presumably continues to feed the canal.

Pittsford Milling Co. (Big Spring in foreground).
Courtesy of Paul M. Spiegel

The Pittsford Milling site was sold to Schoen Place LLP in 2004 by the family of Ted Zornow. The developers demolished the warehouse and silos due to purported safety hazards inherent in their deteriorated state. Their intention is to restore the remaining structures in keeping with their original appearances (including the Pittsford Milling signage) and to convert the mill and grain elevator into office space; office space that will be reflected in the waters of Big Spring.

Immediately to the west of the flour mill, the Schoen Brothers operated an apple drying business. Today, much of the eastern portion of Schoen Place has been developed into retail shops known as Northfield Common. Many of the buildings were remodeled from former lumber sheds or structures built by the state to support the ongoing maintenance and repair of the Erie Canal. The original mule barn for sheltering Erie Canal dray animals presently houses Mustards Eatery and Bar. Beneath the building are remnants of a tunnel (now sealed) that purportedly was a receiving station on the Underground Railroad.

Train service between Pittsford and Canandaigua began in 1835 and made Mr. Hildeth's stage service to the area obsolete. Service was completed to Auburn by 1840 and, in the next decade, the Rochester and Auburn became part of the New York Central system. Passenger service continued for 124 years until it was discontinued in 1959. The passenger terminal is shown in the foreground of the photo below. The freight office and storage area is to the rear. The two were joined to form the Depot Restaurant in 1963.

Rochester & Auburn/New York Central Railroad.
Courtesy of Paul M. Spiegel

Steady job growth in the enterprises associated with the storage, processing and shipping of the areas agricultural output combined with the continued influx of Rochester's affluent, resulted in a growing need for housing in and around Pittsford. Farms located close to the village were the first targets of local developers who added the requisite streets, sewers and water to accommodate the demand for housing.

The village center added an array of retail and service establishments to support the expanding population. Retailers opened markets and dry goods stores. Early service providers included a fine tavern, hotel and blacksmith. By adding water, sewer, power and telephone infrastructure as well as space for government offices, the village became a fully functioning, independent entity.

The Four Corners' Parker Building was the first home of Burdett's Grocery (Burdett, Wilbur and Burdett) prior to their acquisition of the Zeitler and Burg General Store at 21 South Main. The photo below was taken around 1926 at the time that Burdett's occupied the northern half of the building. By this date, the Central Pharmacy building had been built in the gap between the Parker Building and Pittsford Town Hall.

Burdett's in the Parker Building location.
Courtesy of Paul M. Spiegel

The building that would eventually house Burdett's (21 South Main Street) was originally a store owned by Charles Armstong. The second floor of the building was called Armstong Hall and served as a community center that was the regular venue for dances, plays and even opera performances. It also housed the village's government offices prior to 1890 when the current town hall was built.

Mr. J. B. Bacon purchased the store from Armstrong in 1886 and Armstrong Hall became Bacon Hall. The store became Phillips and Agate in 1905 when he sold to Will Agate and Morris Phillips. Agate and Phillips ultimately sold their store to Zeitler and Burg and they, in turn, sold to Burdett's in 1937.

From its opening, Burdett's was a veritable institution and community mainstay during the fifty-five years it provided old fashioned neighborly service in satisfying the grocery needs of villagers. In the 1950's the store was run and actively managed by James W. Burdett and his two sons, James G. Burdett and Richard Burdett. If a patron had a question, special request or guidance in selecting the best cut of meat or freshest vegetables, chances were good that Jim Sr. or one of his sons were available to provide expert guidance.

Burdett's of the mid twentieth century is shown in the photo below. It is evident the always dependable Department of Public Works crews had been dutifully clearing the streets of the normal seasonal snowfall. It is hard to explain the presence of shadows in the picture as that would suggest sunshine on a winter day in the Genesee Valley.

Burdett's in the 1960's.
Courtesy of Paul M. Spiegel

Most local families had charging privileges at Burdett's. At a time when credit cards were mainly issued by and used exclusively at gas stations, the simple request to "put it on my account" added not just convenience, but a genuine neighborly touch to the shopping experience. This also made it convenient for the children of customers to pick up the occasional quart of milk or box of cereal on their way home from school.

It is not as well known that in the 1930's, Pittsford was home to a thriving shipbuilding enterprise. Remains of a long-abandoned section of the Erie Canal remained intact above the Long Meadow subdivision well into the mid twentieth century. With the expansion and deepening of the Erie Canal in 1910, some original routes were modified and slightly altered leaving abandoned sections such as this. The Odenbach Company obtained the rights to build ships in the bed of the abandoned section of the canal located just south of French Road and a short walk northwest behind homes on Westbrook Road in Long Meadow.

The ships were only partially completed at this site because the canal could not accommodate the height or displacement of a fully completed tanker. From the French Road location, they were sailed back to the main canal and ultimately to the Atlantic coast where the ship's superstructure was added.

The community of Long Meadow was developed in the early years of the twentieth century. It was one of the first "planned unit developments" in the country. It remains a desirable residential community characterized by its large lots, spacious lawns, serpentine streets and meandering creek-side setting. The existence of a shipbuilding facility at its perimeter remains a curious juxtaposition.

In the early twentieth century, the Post Office occupied the southern section of the Parker Building and The Federal Telephone office was upstairs. Federal Telephone later became Home Telephone and subsequently was acquired by Rochester Telephone. In 1945, the Parker building was purchased by Lawrence Bridge. After acting exclusively as a landlord to a succession of furniture stores, grocery stores and a Ben Franklin variety store, he remodeled the complete structure to form a single retail enterprise. At the larger site, he opened The Pittsford Department Store. At that time it was mostly soft goods, mainly clothing; none of which could be charitably described as "leading edge" fashion. Regardless, every family with children had due cause to patronize The Pittsford Department Store to purchase Pittsford Central School's official gym clothing as mandated by Coach Charlie Miller and his staff.

The Pittsford Department Store operated as such until 1966 when the store was sold to William H. Reinhard and W. Buel Hendee. They added greeting cards to augment their product offering beyond clothing. It looks much the same today as it did in 1966.

Pittsford's first high school was built in 1894 on Lincoln Avenue. The building was destroyed by fire in 1916. In just a year, the replacement building, costing the local taxpayers $25,000, was completed. The building has continued to serve the community; as the district's administrative offices and in recent years as the Paul M. Spiegel Community Center. (Mr. Spiegel is the author of the Pittsford Scrapbook Series and generously furnished many photographs for this book)

Town Hall and Pittsford Department Store
(Parker Building) in 1966.
Courtesy of Paul M. Spiegel.

A new high school was erected in the early 1950's on the former Lomb family farm where Sutherland Street meets West Jefferson Road. The new facility was necessary to ease overcrowding at the Lincoln Avenue School. It greeted its first students in 1952. Classes were held for grades five through twelve at the new Pittsford Central School while younger students continued to attend the Lincoln Avenue School.

A substantial addition was made to the high school in 1960 but continued population growth led to the decision to build a second school to serve the community. In 1972 Pittsford Mendon High School opened to serve families in the southern part of the district. With two world-class high schools in the district, Pittsford "Central" no longer correctly described the original high school. At the time that Pittsford Mendon High School opened, the name of the original Pittsford Central School was changed to Pittsford Sutherland High School.

During the nineteenth century, two of the three original buildings anchoring the Four Corners burned to the ground. The third, Spiegel's Wagon Shop, would meet the same fate in the early twentieth century. The original Phoenix Hotel opened in 1807 and was destroyed by fire in 1814. That same year, the structure that survives to this day, was built. The first Wiltsie and Crump building was built in 1816 and had a decent life-span of fifty years before it was devastated by fire in 1866. Add to the above, the demise of the old Birdsall Hotel (the site later to be occupied by Stephanys) in 1906 and the 1916 fire that destroyed the Pittsford High School and the need for a well-trained, volunteer fire department became clear to all.

The Pittsford Volunteer Fire Department has been a vital element in the fabric of the community for over a century. The first public water system in Pittsford became operational in 1899 and provided the impetus to form the first Volunteer Fire Department that same year. Perhaps as a result of the fires at Wiltsie and Crump and the Phoenix Hotel, the first fire station was erected on Monroe Avenue adjoining Wiltsie and Crump in 1908. That original structure was replaced after WW ll. Fifty years later, in the last decade of the 20th century, the current modern facility was erected on essentially the same site.

The tower in the first fire station held the original "alarm", a well-used rim from a railroad train car wheel that was struck vigorously to beckon the volunteers. The tower height was helpful in broadcasting the alarm and as a drying rack for the cotton fire hose. In the second decade of the century, the miracle of electronics allowed a modern alarm to be activated by the local telephone operator.

26

Pittsford Inn to Fortune 100

John Wegman's parents owned a grocery store in Rochester. By 1916, he grew tired of the modest earnings afforded by selling fruits and vegetables from his pushcart. He opened his own business, Rochester Fruit and Vegetable Company, from the front of the family's home. In 1917, his brother Walter joined him and in 1921 they purchased Seal Grocery Company. John's pioneering spirit was evident from the beginning as he quickly expanded to offer meats, dairy products and baked goods. In 1930, John and Walter opened their "showplace" store on Clinton Avenue featuring a cafeteria and seating for 300 people. If not a "first", surely this expansion into serving prepared food in a grocery store setting was a bold move contrary to centuries of tradition.

Their penchant for innovation continued when the brothers introduced the heretofore unheard of concept of self-service. That unique strategy was credited with revolutionizing the grocery business. Over the years, they added vaporized water spray to the fruits and vegetable sections of their stores and refrigerated cases with display windows; both new concepts to the industry.

John Wegman made the first of several attempts to broaden his business portfolio when he purchased The Pittsford Inn in 1933. He expanded and remodeled the dining area in a Bavarian theme. The restaurant called Old Heidelberg served thirty-five cent lunches and fifty-cent dinners and offered "the best German and American food". It was not a successful financial venture. Perhaps Wegman should have been more cognizant of the ominous actions of Nazi Germany and the effect that would have on American's appetite for German cuisine? Or maybe this venture was simply a valuable lesson that would further sharpen his keen business acumen and force him to take a more worldly view in the future?

Walter Wegman's son Robert (John's nephew) gradually took the helm at the grocery business in the 1930's and 1940's and led the company to national prominence in the latter half of the twentieth century. He continued the pioneering initiatives of his father and uncle. Wegman's was the first grocery store in the country to use UPC laser scans. Initial trials were in the East Rochester store.

Robert Wegman's legacy will be his pioneering (but now common) concept of one-stop shopping. Under his leadership, Wegman's was the first to place video centers, photo labs, child-care facilities, bakeries and full-service restaurants under the same roof with their full-line of grocery products.

Wegman's continued its leadership in the food service industry growing to become the sixty-sixth largest privately held company in America in 2006. By 2005, they were the seventieth largest retailer in the US. Today there are seventy five stores in the states of NY, PA, NJ, VA and MD generating $5.15 billion in annual revenues. More than one half of the stores are located in Upstate New York.

In 2002, Wegman's opened their first full-service restaurant at their Pittsford store. This store is often Wegman's "test store" and, as a result, has been home to many industry innovations. The upscale dining experience offered in their Tasting Restaurant, where patrons may interact with chefs preparing their meals, was initiated at the Pittsford store. The newer "superstores" are 120,000 square feet in size and include retail restaurants serving Italian and Chinese cuisine as well as the obligatory selection of pizza. They were among the first retailers to offer ATM's on-site and child-care for shoppers.

After John Wegman's diversification play with the Pittsford Inn in the 1930's, Wegman's mainly focused on what they did best; running innovative and successful grocery retailing operations. Robert made another attempt to diversify in the 1980's when he purchased the Chase-Pitkin Home and Garden chain whose original principals were Pittsford residents. During the 50's and 60's, there was a small Chase-Pitkin retail store on South Main Street in Pittsford's village.

This bold but misguided move was predicated on the assumption that Wegman's proven expertise at running highly successful grocery operations was transferable to other retailing categories. While they stayed within their retailing roots, effectively competing with Home Depot and Loews required a disproportionate amount of top management attention and diluted their efforts to retain their leadership position in their core supermarket business. Both efforts to diversify were unsuccessful but, there were positive lessons learned as a result of these failures. Most importantly, neither venture required an investment of the magnitude that, if lost, would threaten the solvency of the core enterprise. Secondly, having tried and failed in their attempts to diversify, John and his key leaders gained a renewed appreciation of how very different the various retail segments are and the equally specialized expertise required to excel in each. After these aborted attempts to diversify and vertically integrate, his company focused all future efforts exclusively on retaining their reputation as a world leader in grocery retailing.

In late 2005, Wegman's announced their intention to close all Chase-Pitkin stores. All units were shuttered in 2006.

In addition to being on the leading edge of innovative approaches to marketing grocery products, the Wegman's followed George Eastman's lead in creating and introducing progressive approaches to hiring, training, motivating and retaining employees. The company was one of the first to offer on-site day care for employee's children. As a result of such leading-edge programs, turnover is comparatively low among Wegman's employees. Wegman's has been on the Fortune list of "100 Best Places to Work" each year since its inception, capturing the top spot in 2005, second place in 2006 and third in 2009. Upon learning that his company earned the top spot, in 2005, Mr. Wegman proudly stated: "This is the culmination of my life's work".

Wegman's has been a perennial winner of various awards for outstanding customer service. Ethisphere Magazine named the retailer one of the most ethical companies in 2007. Consistent with that recognition and their continuing efforts to place the health and safety of their employees and the community ahead of short-term profits, Wegman's took the bold step of announcing that they would cease selling tobacco products in early 2008.

Food Network named Wegman's the nation's Best Grocery Store. It was ranked as the number one grocery chain by Consumers Report in 2009.

With innovation and risk-taking comes some controversy and Wegman's has not been immune. They tangled with New York State regarding item-pricing and their attempts to eliminate coupons, with environmentalist over their advocacy of plastic rather than paper bags and with animal rights advocates regarding the treatment of hens at their mega egg production facility. They have weathered each of these minor storms with grace.

Robert Wegman was Chairman of the Board until his death at age 87 in 2006. His son Danny, of Canandaigua and Rochester, remains as CEO and Danny's daughter Colleen serves as President. She lives in Brighton. Daughter Nicole, a resident of Pittsford, serves as VP of Restaurant Operations.

If the Old Heidelberg concept had proved successful, perhaps there would be fifty Pittsford Inn's containing Old Heidelberg restaurants located throughout New York, Pennsylvania, New Jersey, Virginia and Maryland where there are now Wegman's Markets.

27

Pittsford's Pickles, Mustard and Piccalilli

With the exception of some limestone quarrying, ship-building and gun powder manufacturing that occurred in the 19th century, most of Pittsford's economy was driven by agriculture and its supporting trades. Warehouses, lumber mills, malt houses, storage silos and fruit drying facilities sprang up around the transportation arteries at the train depot and Erie Canal docks.

During the first half of the twentieth century, Pittsford could have been considered the "Condiment Capital" of the world. This was due to the substantial contributions of local pioneering food entrepreneurs L.C. Forman and the French brothers.

One of Pittsford's earliest "captains of industry" was L. C. Forman. Some contend that L. C. Forman Pickles put Pittsford on the map. This is not a source of shame as our country was named in honor of an Italian explorer and pickle merchant. Amerigo Vespucci, was a purveyor of pickles who traveled with Columbus in his search for the new world. He wisely insisted on ample stores of vitamin C rich pickled cucumbers to thwart the ravages of scurvy while at sea. Perhaps in recognition of his contribution to the health of his crew, Columbus recognized Amerigo by naming the newly discovered continent after him. Ergo.... America!

Until 1912, Mr. Forman's substantial pickle processing and bottling plant was in a barn located on East Avenue. Like nearly every significant original structure in the village, it experienced a devastating fire and was a total loss.

The cucumber harvest of the summer of 1912 could not wait for the usual extended construction schedule in erecting a new processing plant so L. C. Forman executed an early version of fast-track construction technology. He had his new facility ready for the earliest cucumbers harvested that same year. The new facility dominated the greater part of Grove Street and was the largest pickle factory in the state. The replacement building is shown in the photo below. Forman's capable staff is seen sorting some of the day's production in the second photo.

L.C. Foreman Pickle Factory.
Courtesy of Paul M. Spiegel

L.C. Forman Pickle Factory Staff
Courtesy of Paul M. Spiegel

According to one account at the time, among the 25 workers who worked in the new plant on Grove Street, were a number of German Prisoners-of-War who had been transported from the brigs in Wayne County after World War ll.

The signature product of L. C. Forman and Sons was Forman's Piccalilli. Some proud residents are of the opinion that Forman invented Piccalilli and that it was proprietary to the company. In fact, there are recipes dating to the 18th century that describe the ingredients as "a pickle" of finely chopped vegetables combined with hot spices, mustard, vinegar, salt and sugar. The addition of turmeric contributed the bright yellow color. Virtually any kind of vegetables can be used but often green tomatoes, cauliflower and onions are included. It is thought to be of English origin as it is often served as a condiment in their pubs offering the popular "Ploughman's Lunch". In contemporary America, it was a popular addition to hotdogs and hamburgers; at least in Upstate New York. At the time that its sales peaked, Piccalilli reportedly represented seventy five percent of the Forman Company's production.

Another well known condiment purveyor was the R. T. French Mustard Company. The company got its start in nearby Fairport, New York when the French brothers (Robert and George) purchased a flour mill there in 1883. By 1904, they had expanded into processing and selling a broad array of spices. In that year, they introduced French's Cream Salad Mustard at the World's Fair in St. Louis. The legend is that its introduction coincided with the first unveiling of the hot dog at the same event. Both were hits; presumably in combination. The ice cream cone, peanut butter and iced tea also debuted at this fair.

Fires must have been commonplace in this part of the century, as yet another conflagration destroyed French's Fairport facility in 1912. This prompted the French brothers' move to Rochester's Mustard Street. While there is no official record of the company being headquartered in the village, for decades, R. T. French Mustard Company proudly proclaimed on every jar of their ubiquitous yellow mustard that Pittsford, New York was their home. They did have a large warehouse and distribution center off East Avenue for many years through the mid 20th century. Known as innovators, the company introduced power machinery to their process in 1920 which lowered their costs and facilitated them becoming one of the largest food purveyors in the country.

While mustard seed has been used in various flavorings for thousands of years, the yellow mustard that we identify as "American" has been a condiment mainstay for only the last century. It was the milder, smooth, cream style mustard "seasoned for American taste" that the French brothers created and introduced. While diversified in flour and other spices, it was French's Mustard that allowed the company to survive the great depression and ultimately prosper.

In 1926, French's was purchased by the UK food conglomerate Reckitt Benckiser but its original name was retained. In 1960 R. T. French Mustard Company (subsidiary of Reckitt Benckiser) purchased the L.C. Forman and Sons Pickle Company. R. T. French departed Rochester in 1987 and consolidated its operations in Springfield, Missouri.

Every great condiment needs a special hot dog on which to stake its claim to fame. "White Hots" are exclusively a Genesee Valley creation. Introduced by the Zweigle's Company, they were styled after the German sausage called a weisswurst. Nowhere else on earth when you order a hot dog, does the vendor bark back "red or white buddy"? They remain the unique food product of a proud upstate customer base. While perfectly palatable, culinary diva Alice Waters of Berkeley's Chez Pannise (St. Alice in the "foodie" world) is not likely to popularize the white hot to a broader audience anytime soon.

How interesting and good is the cuisine of the Genesee Valley? For "interesting" we have the white hot. For "good"...not very is the honest answer. As testament to that observation, one only has to consider the area's "signature" dish – the "Garbage Plate".

Characterized as an example of American "extreme cuisine", Garbage Plates were originated at Nick Tahou Hots; a Rochester landmark since 1918. While variations of the Garbage Plate are popular at a host of late-night diners throughout Genesee Valley, only Nick Tahou Hots can legally call their creation a "Garbage Plate" Consistent with the long local tradition of legally protecting inventions, Nick applied for and was granted the trademark rights to the Garbage Plate. Competitors have resorted to variations on the theme such as "dumpster plate" or "trash plate".

Nick Tahou originally called his creation "Hots and Potatoes". For over fifty years, the dish has been a popular choice among local college students who brought their ravenous appetites to Nick's after the 2:00 a.m. bar closings. In their compromised state of sobriety, it was the rare patron who could remember the true name of this gargantuan heap of starches, protein and hot spices. Late one evening, a young patron simply requested "one of those plates with all the garbage on it". The name was born.

Garbage it is. The classic Garbage Plate begins with a generous layer of home fried potatoes on one side and macaroni salad on the other half...yep macaroni salad. Nick's original creation then received a heap of Zweigle's red hots or white hots, onions, French's cream style mustard and a giant ladle of Nick's proprietary Greek hot sauce.

The latter contained ground beef, onions, red peppers, paprika, chili powder and assorted other spices.

Over time, hungry diners were offered choices on key elements of the recipe; both in the starchy base layer and toppings. In recent years, two quarter pound cheeseburgers have displaced the red hots/white hots as the preferred protein layer. Some restaurants offer French fries or baked beans in the initial layer and choices ranging from chicken tenders, fried ham, fried haddock, Italian sausage, grilled cheese or eggs as toppings. Onions, French's Mustard and Greek hot sauce remain mandatory elements.

While Pleasant Valley's contribution to the culinary world was mainly in creating or popularizing new condiments, the area has an equally long history of being a challenging environment to find high quality, interesting and innovative restaurant dining. For a good part of the 1950's and 60's, many thought that the only "decent" adult meal in or around Pittsford was offered at The Maplewood Inn. John Clifford (father of Thirsty's proprietor Gerry Clifford) was the longtime owner/operator. The building was originally the home of Mrs. C. Alverson where she welcomed the public for "home cooked meals". In summer months, the grounds of her home were a popular spot for picnics. Her son Charles, branched out and erected a small building adjoining The Maplewood Inn and called it Charlie's Chicken Hut. Both The Maplewood and Charlie's prospered but Charlie's burned down in the 1930's.

28

"Hanging Around is an Old Custom"

Paul Spiegel's remarkable collection of books titled Pittsford Scrapbook provide a pictorial chronology of generation upon generation of young and old "townies" passing time in the village. He declares that "hanging around is an old custom" in Pittsford. Though the most popular spots to "hang" changed over the decades, the culture of "hangin with the homies" surely was prevalent throughout the last century. While evident in his fine collection of photos, Mr. Spiegel does not mention that this propensity to "pass time in the village" was largely a providence of the male gender.

The taverns at the Phoenix Hotel, The New Exchange/Hotel Stephany and the Fire Station provided adult male residents with warm, dry locations to casually congregate and socialize at all times of the year. But, after a long bitter winter, even the adult male populace was anxious to fraternize in the fresh air and occasional sunshine.

Prior to the (most unfortunate) creation of the shopping mall, it was a longtime tradition for the youth of the community to congregate in the village center. During late spring, summer and early fall, the choice of al fresco congregating venues was transitory but almost always on the west side of South Main Street. Because it was typical to congregate for the better part of an afternoon or evening, those locations allowing the participants to be seated, became the preferred spots to meet. It was the good fortune of the locals, that nearly every store on Main Street was constructed with a concrete or wooden stoop at its entrance. Concrete was fine in the summer months and even provided some cooling effect on hot August nights. A wooden stoop offered greater resilience and was clearly a better insulator from the chilly weather in the spring and fall months.

These store stoops provided a welcoming location for the male youth of the area to sit and pass the time in the company of friends. Some stores even had two or three steps leading to the entrance which could be occupied bleacher-style by a small pack of acquaintances.

"Pack" is perhaps the operative word as there existed a clear pecking order of who could legitimately claim preferred seating. Generally higher was better. The alpha male, chose his seat independent of whether it was presently occupied. Generally he chose to sit at the top of the stoop thereby affording him better views, shade and the option of ducking out of sight.

While an integral part of the community's social fabric, this tradition was not without conflict. Merchants considered it a mixed blessing at best. Surely, it was good for the overall vitality of the community that the village center appeared vibrant; an active retail center presumably begets additional customers. Largely offsetting this benefit, was the near constant battle waged between the merchants and local youth when the latter's presence became a deterrent to customers wishing to access the merchant's place of business.

There were two main elements that caused conflict. The first occurred when the shear number of townies congregating in a particular location resulted in the obstruction of the merchant's entrance. This prompted merchants to regularly monitor their entrances to assure easy customer access. This, in turn, resulted in occasional hostile exchanges between merchants and stoop-dwellers.

Secondly, young men hanging out in the village seldom restricted their remarks exclusively to one another. What began as harmless banter, sometimes grew to a competition to outdo one another with what they considered "clever" comments directed towards passing villagers. Those "passing by" were normally the regular customers of local merchants who had a choice of shopping venues; too many "clever remarks" and they chose to take their business elsewhere.

As has been the norm throughout history, young women strolling the village were sure to attract the attention of men of all ages. The young male generation often felt compelled to verbalize their approval of the well-turned calf or callipygian.

October through May weather presented greater challenges for local youth wishing to congregate in the village. The coldest winter months precluded idle sitting and chatting.

Fresh fallen snow prompted a resurgence of interest in youthful rowdiness. The typical cycle of escalation began with a harmless contest to see who could strike, with a snowball, the highest point on the church steeple across from Hicks and McCarthy's. As a winner was declared or boredom displaced interest, random teams would form and snowball "fights" would commence. Parked cars, alleyways, parking lots and recessed store entrances emerged as bases of operation for opposing forces. Once this competition played itself out, the targets became cars passing on Main Street. Popular teens were as treasured a target as those deemed not so popular. School teachers were prime targets as long as the spineless perpetrators were well hidden. During the fifties and sixties the ultimate high priority target was the village's favorite law enforcement official, Monroe County Sheriff Officer Bill Jarvis.

Officer Jarvis was simply a classic. He was affectionately known as "Jelly Belly"... except to his face. He was a product of a different time; known as much for his willingness to give a tipsy villager a late night ride home in his cruiser[10]* as for his spirited pursuits of Pittsford teens who bombarded his black '57 Chevy patrol car with snowballs.

"Spotters" typically watched for Officer Jarvis commencing his predictable late afternoon beat through the village; down Lincoln to Main, left on Main and slowly cruise the commercial center of the village. The testosterone-laden perpetrators would wait in the alley between Burdett's and Pierce's for the signal that "Jelly Belly" would soon be passing. As Officer Jarvis drove by the entryway, a barrage of snowballs would erupt from the alleyway; thump, thump, thump into the side of his patrol car. The alleyway was one-way leading onto Main Street so Officer Jarvis had few options other than to activate his overhead flashing emergency lights, hope that he could get through the Four Corners signal and screech into Burdett's parking lot from Monroe Avenue in an attempt to catch the guilty. By this time, the offenders would typically be ensconced in a rear booth at Hicks' or hidden in the loft of John Patterson's barn on Washington Street. The few who were caught were given a stern "talking to" and released to the custody of their admiring friends.

Clearly the need for a warm, friendly establishment that welcomed the youth of the village to congregate was substantial. Several local merchants satisfied this demand.

Ike Hicks and John McCarthy were brothers-in-law. They worked together as clerks at the Phillips and Agate General Store (latter to become Burdett's) in the first decade of the twentieth century.

In 1913 they pooled their savings and acquired Frank Bryant's Ice Cream Shop located just two doors south of Phillip's and Agate. The store would become a village institution. In the spirit of George Eastman, they squashed the remaining competition, by immediately

---

[10] New York State had an anomalous set of rules regarding drunk driving at the time. They resembled current boating regulations in many states. It was illegal to drive while drunk but NOT illegal to drink while driving. So...as long as you did not meet the minimum threshold of blood alcohol level to be declared drunk, it was quite permissible to enjoy a cold beer while behind the wheel. This led to the common practice of describing travel distances in terms of the number of "travelers" that would typically be consumed en route; Canandaigua was one traveler away while Buffalo was three.

acquiring Les Whiting's Ice Cream store located on the east side of Main Street. An ice cream monopoly was thus formed.

Opening day was April 1, 1913. The photo below shows Ike Hicks (left) and John McCarthy looking relaxed and confident.

Ike Hicks and John McCarthy.
Courtesy of Paul M. Spiegel

Perhaps this was the mid-afternoon lull between the lunch and after-school crowds. The store fixtures are either remarkably similar or identical to those still in use at mid-century and beyond. John McCarthy is standing behind what would become the penny candy section in the 1950's and 1960's. Fifty years later his son, Larry McCarthy, would not-so-patiently deposit the chosen selection of young patrons into small paper bags as they pointed in the direction of their desired sweet.

"Babe" Hicks, Norm Hicks and Larry McCarthy (left to right) are shown in the photo below minding the store in the 1960's. At the time, patrons could nurse a ten-cent cherry Coke for hours at Hicks' and enjoy the company of multiple generations of village characters. For its first fifty years, the proprietors resisted customers' suggestions to add anything requiring cooking. A wide range of deli sandwiches were available; American cheese on Wonder Bread was the thrifty option at twenty cents, the ever-popular egg and olive or tuna salad were available for an additional nickel. Not until the late sixties were a grill and deep fryer added to satisfy the local demand for burgers and fries.

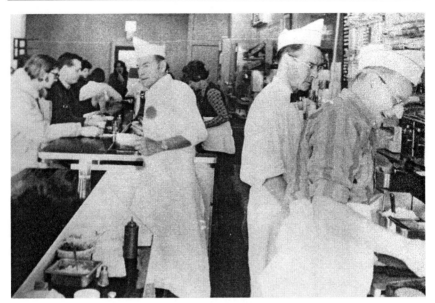

"Babe" Hicks, Norm Hicks and Larry McCarthy
Courtesy of Paul M. Spiegel

Around mid-century "Pete the Greek", hoping to capture some of the Hicks and McCarthy overflow, opened a "Hicks' Light" a few doors south on Main Street. For several decades, he catered to the contrarians not wanting to follow the crowd to Hicks' or those who simply preferred more personal space and less of the constant aural din that accompanied the hordes of high school students patronizing Hicks'.

The photo below captures Hicks' storefront to the left and, equally importantly, Pierce Rylott's paint and electrical supply store to the right. This must have been the mid afternoon of a weekday, as there are no "townies" ensconced on Pierce's Steps.

Upon careful observation, the Hicks and McCarthy store appears as if it could have been a house of worship in an earlier life. In fact, the building's first incarnation was as the Christ Church Episcopal in 1848. Over its first seventy five years, the back room was reportedly used as the Village horse barn.

Hicks & McCarthy's and Pierce Rylott's store (to right)
Courtesy of Paul M. Spiegel

Pierce Rylott's stoop was THE premiere location to congregate for many years. It had it all…three full steps, each with adequate breadth to accommodate three or four butts, it was relatively soft (wooden construction) and it offered an ideal view of the parade of patrons passing to and from Hicks and McCarthy's.

Mr. Rylott offered an odd product mix. His sign describes the business as Pittsford Electric but the larger advertising image was for Dupont Paints? Customers were rare; perhaps one or two patrons would darken his door on a busy Saturday. Even Pierce entered through the rear entrance so there was seldom reason to move from his steps.

Adding to the appeal was the excitement created by the proprietor. By most measures Pierce Rylott was a patient man. His steps were rarely empty. Perhaps he eventually got bored waiting for customers or maybe he assigned the lack thereof to the youth obstructing the entrance to his establishment, but when he decided to clear his entrance his actions were vitriolic. Rather than deterring the use of his steps, his ranting seemed to add to the excitement, embolden the locals and even heighten the desirability of the venue.

The photo below shows perhaps one of the earliest contingents of village boys, "hanging on the steps" of Phillips and Agate's Store in the first decade of the last century before it became Burdett's. Either: a) this group had little need for "personal space" or, b) the preferred squatting territory was just to the left of the store's entrance or, more likely c) Messrs. Agate or Phillips had recently barked one of their repeated demands not to block the way for customers entering the store.

Phillips and Agate's Store (subsequently Burdett's)
Courtesy of Paul M. Spiegel

The undated photo below shows perhaps one of the first images of a foursome of local businessmen "hanging around" in front of the cigar store which later became Hicks and McCarthy's on a "warm Sunday morning". The Inscription declares that "Hanging around...is an old custom". The photo was taken sometime before 1913; the year of Hicks and McCarthy's opening.

Local Businessmen "Hanging Out" in the Village
Courtesy of Paul M. Spiegel

At some point in the 30's or 40's the preferred place to congregate moved north to the Four Corners. Surely there was a benefit of seeing both the east-west as well as the north-south traffic flow from this vantage point. The photo below was taken in 1942 and shows Eddie Nobles (second from right) hanging with his buddies at the Four Corners at the entrance to the Pittsford Department Store. This group was no doubt convinced that they were looking "cooler than the other side of the pillow". Subsequent generations of Nobles' spent their time similarly in the village.

Eddie Nobles & friends "hanging out" in the village in 1942
Courtesy of Paul M. Spiegel

The caption on this Paul Spiegel photo describes the "men of the Village" gathering to "discuss politics, or to sit quietly, chew or smoke". I suspect the "younger men" did not sit so quietly; Ed Nobles is clearly conjuring up some pithy comment for the photographer. Given the long tradition of "hanging around" in the village and the physical discomfort portrayed on the faces in many of the accompanying photographs, it is a mystery why the village's Chamber of Commerce never advocated for placing clusters of benches on Main Street to accommodate and nurture this fine tradition. It would have mitigated much of the hostility between merchants and youth who were interrupting the free flow of customers.

Alpha Males "hanging around" the village
Courtesy of Paul M. Spiegel

The building erected directly to the south of Hicks and McCarthy's was initially the residence of the Lockwood family. Early in the century, Royal Newcomb acquired the property and operated his undertaking business from the front portion of the building. From the barns in the rear, he operated a livery stable. Around 1920, Royal could see that business was "dying" so he converted the facility to the Newcomb Oil Company which sold household heating oil to villagers.

In the early years of the twentieth century, a great trolley system served the state of New York. The Rochester and Eastern trolley service began service to Pittsford in 1904. The trolley station shown in the photo below functioned as such until 1930 after which it laid dormant until Al Stephany opened the Trolley Grill in the abandoned station.

Rochester & Eastern Trolley Station; then Trolley Grill McConnel's and Wahl's
Courtesy of Paul M. Spiegel

Al ran the eatery for just three years and in 1936, moved his restaurant business up the street to the ground floor of the Exchange Hotel; later to become Hotel Stephany. Replacing Stephany in the old trolley station were Scott McConnell and his sons, Lloyd, Red and Frank who moved their milk and ice business from Washington Road. Their natural expansion into ice cream was a major hit with the local populace. Warm summer evenings would find lines of patrons extending out the door and winding through the parking lot. McConnell's Dairy prospered in that location until 1966 when the business was sold to Bill Wahl.

The photo below depicts a thriving McConnell's in the middle of the century. It joined Hicks and McCarthy's and The Pittsford Inn as village "institutions" and hospitable places to congregate.

McConnell's Dairy in the late 1950's
Courtesy of Paul M. Spiegel

Henry Hifiker owned the old Birdsall Hotel that burned to the ground in the late 1890's. He immediately rebuilt on the same site and christened the new facility the New Exchange Hotel and Livery. Passengers traveling on either the Rochester and Eastern Trolley or the New York Central found his location adjoining the train depot to be ideal. They could easily haul luggage to the New Exchange and access horses or horse-drawn vehicles from the adjoining livery stable.

Al Stephany eventually purchased the New Exchange from Henry Hifiker. He succumbed to his yearning for immortality and renamed the hotel and popular meeting place to bear his own name. The photo below depicts Hotel Stephany in the 1940's.

Hotel Stephany in the 1940's
Courtesy of Paul M. Spiegel

29

"Dry Writing" to Xerography

"We were spending money we didn't have for a product nobody wanted"
John H. Dessauer, The Haloid Company

Chester Carlson sounds like the name of a lab-rat inventor. Born in Seattle in 1906, he and his family moved to Southern California soon after his birth. At age twelve, he declared to his cousin that "Someday I'm going to make a great invention". His father was incapacitated by arthritis so his mother cleaned homes to support the family. She died when Chester was seventeen.

Not unlike George Eastman, young Carlson sought night and weekend work when he became the primary breadwinner of his family as a teen. He attended the local community college for two years before completing his physics degree at the prestigious California Institute of Technology (Cal Tech).

Carlson was laid off from his $35 per week job at Bell Telephone Labs in NYC and found work as an assistant to a patent attorney. Inspired by the concept of protecting one's inventions, he earned his law degree at night and began practicing as a patent attorney. Research remained his passion however and he spent all of his free time in quest of discovery. Like George Eastman, Chester Carlson spent his days performing paid work; nights and weekends conducting experiments in the kitchen of his apartment.

Chester perceived a problem for which he was intent on finding a solution. Each day he observed clerical employees grow bored and frustrated when asked to make multiple hand copies of the firm's patent documents. In his view, there was a great need for a method to efficiently duplicate exact copies of office documents at a reasonable price. The contemporary options were either: a) expensive - using conventional photographic technology or, b) messy - using carbon paper or, c) laborious - retyping documents and then proofreading for accuracy. He began studying reports on European experiments that used a chemical reaction and dry process to create exact duplicate copies.

Carlson was quoted as saying:

> *"Work outside of school hours was a necessity at an early age, and with such time as I had I turned toward interests of my own devising, making things, experimenting, and planning for the future. I had read of [Thomas Alva] Edison and other successful inventors, and the idea of making an invention appealed to me as one of the few available means to accomplish a change in one's economic status, while at the same time bringing to focus my interest in technical things and making it possible to make a contribution to society as well."*

Carlson's original research consisted of laboriously searching the New York Public Library for information regarding photoconductivity. This concept in which light is used to increase the ability of certain substances to conduct electricity seemed to provide a possible solution to the problem he perceived. He studied the premise that when both light and shadow are cast upon certain materials that have been electrically charged, the dark (shadowed) parts will attract any magnetic powder that may be introduced at the time. Conversely, the lighted area will reject the magnetic powder. He postulated that if a method could be developed by which the powder attracted to the dark images could be fused to the page, a duplicate copy would result. It took great tenacity to see his theory become a commercially viable business venture; fifteen years of continuous research to be exact.

He was granted his first patent on "electrophotography" in 1938. The beauty of his technology was that it did not require any liquids or expensive light sensitive papers. Rather, electrophotography used only a fine powder, heat and an electrostatic process.

Chester Carlson with first prototype of
electrophotographic machine.
Photo courtesy of Xerox Historic Archives.

Once he obtained his patents, the real work began in trying to convince others that he had the solution to a problem they did not acknowledge existed. Mr. Carlson spent the years 1939 – 1944 attempting to sell his idea. He was turned down by more than twenty companies that did not see the commercial viability of his technology. These included General Electric, IBM, Eastman Kodak, Remington Rand and RCA. He found it particularly disheartening when the National Inventors Council characterized his invention as "impractical".

The most substantive negotiations to emerge occurred in 1940 with IBM. Discussions took place over a period of eighteen months and Carlson grew optimistic that, at last, someone would recognize the value of his pioneering work in electrophotography and provide the funding and infrastructure to bring his invention to market. Growing frustrated, Carlson proposed to give IBM an exclusive license to his patents in exchange for the greater of $10,000 per year or a 5% royalty fee. The offer remained dormant for several years before IBM ultimately decided the concept had little commercial viability. They declined.

Finally, in 1944, Battelle Memorial Institute of Columbus, Ohio, a nonprofit organization, expressed interested in his technology. They agreed to a royalty sharing agreement in exchange for conducting further research and development.

Also in 1945, John H. Dessauer, head of research at Rochester's The Haloid Company was perched on the toilet perusing a copy of the "Kodak Monthly Abstract Bulletin" when his attention was drawn to an abstract involving electrophotography. The article discussed a broader study on electrophotography that had appeared eight months earlier in the esoteric trade journal "Radio Electronic Engineering News". It described the pioneering work of Carlson and his joint venture with Battelle Memorial Institute.

Dessauer brought this article to the attention of his boss, Joseph C. Wilson. He knew that Wilson was keenly interested in new technologies that might help reinvigorate his company after World War ll.

By all accounts, Joseph C. Wilson's early childhood was far less taxing than either George Eastman's or Chester Carlson's. He was named after his grandfather who had founded the M. H. Kuhn Company in 1903; renamed the Haloid Company in 1906. "Haloid" was a reference to the group of chemicals known as halogens. The salts of halogens were a critical component in the emulsions used in the photographic process. The company invested heavily in research and developed a sensitized photography paper deemed to be the best in the industry. This product, which was marketed as Haloid Record, was a resounding financial success and the "cash cow" needed to keep the company solvent through the Great Depression.

The first Joseph C. Wilson was more interested in politics and had little time for his business once he was appointed Rochester's mayor. Duties at the Haloid Company soon fell to his son, Joseph R. Wilson.

The second Joseph C. Wilson was born in Rochester in 1909 and attended the University of Rochester and Harvard Business School before joining the family business in 1936. Joseph worked closely with his father in adapting the company's product line to support the country's efforts during World War ll. Sales more than tripled to $6.9 million by 1946. Young Joseph was convinced however, that he had to reinvent the Haloid Company in order to survive and prosper in a post-war economy.

At the time, Haloid's primary competitor and raw material supplier was the mighty Kodak. While Haloid Record possessed unique characteristics that were highly desirable in certain high-end photographic processes, the company held less than 10% of the photographic paper market and was dependent on Kodak for most of its raw paper stock. Mr. Wilson was concerned that Haloid was vulnerable on both fronts. If Haloid were to irritate Kodak, could they depend on them as a long-term supplier? Secondly, with Kodak's vast financial resources, they could invest substantial funds in research and development and potentially create improved specialty papers that could make Haloid's most profitable lines obsolete.

In his seminal 1960 essay titled Marketing Myopia, Dr. Theodore Levitt of the Harvard Business School warned business leaders against a narrow or restrictive definition of the marketplace in which they competed. As an example, he suggested that oil companies should not limit their business to oil but rather define their business as the energy market. Some feel that his essay represented the birth of modern marketing. Others built on his classic work to suggest that true leaders should constantly be researching and seeking the next technology that will make their own business obsolete. They encouraged business leaders to lead by embracing the new technology, re-inventing their own company and capitalizing on their established strategic strengths – IE brand loyalty, distribution effectiveness, research et al. In other words, purposely make your own technology obsolete before someone else does.

Mr. Wilson was intent on leading the company in a direction that could utilize its existing strengths while capitalizing on new or emerging technologies. Encouraged by his director of research, John H. Dessauer, Mr. Wilson vigorously pursued knowledge regarding the innovative new process called "electrophotography". It appealed to him because the technology fell within their "imaging" industry, but what he found particularly exciting was that the process was based on physics not chemistry. Kodak had floor upon floor of chemists but few if any physicists. He speculated that they, his local supplier and nemesis, would be reluctant to abandon their core chemistry-based processes.

This led to a series of meetings with Battelle. Joe Wilson was intent on capturing the exclusive rights to manufacture Chester Carlson's invention and prove its commercial viability. He was not certain who else might be simultaneously negotiating for these licensing agreements. His strategy was to convince Battelle that Haloid should be their partner of choice because only they were truly committed to the success of the invention and were "small enough" to provide the necessary focus. While perhaps not mentioning competing suitors by name, the subtle message for Batelle to digest and consider was…would electrophotography simply get lost in the multidisciplinary labs of a corporate giant? Worse yet, would this technology be buried forever as a means of avoiding a future competitive threat?

Joe Wilson's enthusiasm, drive and commitment was apparent. In 1947, Battelle agreed to license the Haloid Company to develop and market machines designed to perform electrophotography. In 1948

Battelle and Haloid introduced "xerography" to the public. In 1949 the Model A xerography machine was offered for sale. Wilson was convinced that this technology would revolutionize the office place. He had to be very convinced because his small, privately held company did not have the resources to ultimately fund decades of additional research and development.

While Haloid was granted the exclusive rights for office copying, the contract with Battelle required them to aggressively seek well-capitalized partners to research and develop ancillary or specialized applications of this technology. Consistent with this commitment, they initiated discussion with GE regarding licensing the technology as it related to the X-ray process, RCA pertaining to imaging of facsimile recordings and IBM as it related to the imaging of tabulating machine output.

The discussions with IBM were the second of a series of serious negotiations centered upon "Big Blue" playing a far more substantial role in the commercialization of electrophotography. (Recall Chester Carlson had discussions with them in the early 1940's) Haloid's core strengths were in the sale and production of a specialized coated photographic paper. IBM had a proven record of efficiently manufacturing and selling high quality office machines. IBM's customers were the target audience for office copiers. Their world- class manufacturing expertise was in leading-edge office equipment; exactly what Haloid was intending to manufacture but lacked a single plant or manufacturing line to do so. By most definitions, IBM represented the perfect partner. Haloid had the technology but IBM had the customers, sales force, service technicians and specialized manufacturing plants.

Wilson proposed that IBM manufacture, sell and service machines that would bear the IBM logo. Haloid would receive a generous royalty on each unit and retain the right to manufacture and sell their own machines under the Haloid name.

Fortunately for future Xerox shareholders, IBM demanded exclusive rights to manufacture and sell machines. Under their plan, only IBM would manufacture and sell office copier machines. They proposed that Haloid do what they did best; profitably supply paper and supplies to the buyers of IBM branded machines. Wilson recognized that at some time in the future, the copy paper supply business would become a cut-throat, low margin commodity business; just what Haloid was trying to escape. He declined and discussions ceased in 1954. IBM walked away a second time.

Battelle scientists felt that the electrophotography technology was so unique and compelling that it deserved a name that more clearly differentiated it from conventional forms of photography. They sought the guidance of a professor of classical languages at Ohio State University. He translated the English words "dry" and "writing" to the Greek "xero" and "graphy" or xerography.

After considerable discussion, it was decided not to copyright the word "xerography" that describes the electrophotographic process. The rationale was that by not inhibiting the use of the word, its broad acceptance would be hastened.

During the five years beginning in 1953, Haloid spent $23 million in their research laboratory on xerography. In the same period, the company spent an additional sixty million dollars on manufacturing plants, equipment and inventory of machines on lease to customers. Head researcher John Dessauer stated at the time, "We were spending money we didn't have for a product nobody wanted". And...it was money Haloid didn't have! Over this period Wilson spent each year an amount equal to two times the average annual Haloid earnings on developing xerography technologies. He did so by both debt and equity financing. Wilson was so committed to this unproven technology that he personally mortgaged his personal wealth to invest in the company. That is commitment!

IBM initiated a third series of talks in 1957. As an agreement appeared more likely, IBM commissioned the consulting firm of Arthur D. Little to confirm their assessment of the business potential for xerography. The study took nearly a year to complete and recommended that IBM not consummate the deal. The consultants concluded that the limited market opportunity for office copiers did not warrant their client's further expenditure of time and money. IBM walked a third time.

It became clear that the tired moniker of the Haloid Company no longer matched the completely new charter of the enterprise. The total focus on a revolutionary technology needed to be reflected in an equally fresh brand name and image.

Brand discussions centered first on Xero with some thought given to the name Xerex. Wilson liked the book-ended letter X's as they had the same hard consonant bite and repetitive pattern as highly regarded neighbor Kodak. He decided the name was too similar to the then popular automotive antifreeze, Zerex. Instead he opted for Xerox and changed the company name to Haloid Xerox in 1958.

On September 20 of that same year, Ursula Burns entered this world. She grew up in "the projects" of Manhattan's lower east side with an ethnically diverse mix of playmates. In a New York Times interview in 2003, she described her early years spent with "lots of Jewish immigrants, fewer Hispanics and African Americans, but the common denominator and great equalizer was poverty."

What did distinguish this Black child from her peers was a hard-working single mother that had high expectations for her children. When income from her home-based day-care center, was inadequate to pay for private Catholic school tuition, she started a second career ironing clothes for neighbors.

The Xerox 914 Copier was introduced in 1960 and remains one of the most successful product introductions ever. In its prime, it cost Xerox an estimated $2000 to produce a single 914 and each unit generated $4500 in annual revenues. When viewed over its entire product life cycle, many feel that it was the most profitable machine ever produced and sold in this country.

Joseph C. Wilson with 914 being assembled at
Orchard Street Facility.
Photo courtesy of Xerox Historical Archives.

The 914 designation was a reference to the maximum size copy that could be accommodated on the machine ... 9" by 14". The 914 drastically changed the way the world communicated in the written form; no more carbon papers or mimeograph machines. Perhaps this was the earliest chapter in the information age; where individuals were provided their very own exact copy of information that may have been transferred in earlier years verbally or by the archaic method of a "distribution list". With the latter, recipients were requested to read a document and pass it to succeeding persons on the attached list. The 914 added speed, efficiency and accuracy to the transmission of information. It could duplicate typed, hand-written, printed or drawn information. As anyone who occasionally stayed late in the office and had a sense of humor can attest, it could even attempt to capture three dimensional objects like the human face or buttocks...all in a dry process on ordinary paper.

The 914 was so successful that, the company name was changed to Xerox Corporation in 1961. Xerox became the world-wide darling of entrepreneurial success stories. The one-ton machine was so well engineered that Xerox had little competition for nearly twenty years.

In 1963 IBM initiated a fourth series of negotiations. Nine years of perfect hindsight prompted them to take a quite different tactical approach. They suggested that it would be prudent for Xerox to voluntarily license IBM to make their brand of copiers for surely the U.S. Justice Department would soon be investigating Xerox's monopoly in the office copier business and be initiating anti-trust actions. Xerox's legal staff did not blink; neither did Wilson. They respectfully declined IBM's generous offer. Years later, IBM head Thomas J. Watson described the biggest error in his illustrious business career as failing to acquire Haloid.

As it turned out, the company eventually did face growing pressure from the Federal Trade Commission. Perhaps Xerox benefited from careful review of Kodak's prior experience with the U.S. Department of Justice. Rather than enter a costly legal battle, the company tacitly ignored competitors as they boldly infringed on their xerography patents. Eventually those competitors began to take market share.

While Joe Wilson clearly demonstrated a bias for action, he was far from capricious. Rather, he was considered brilliant, driven and analytical. When he was not comfortable that Haloid or Xerox had the expertise in a particular discipline within its employee ranks, he was quick to retain expensive, well-respected independent consultants to provide unbiased analysis and make recommendations. More importantly, he had the uncanny wisdom to know when to take the advice of consultants and when to ignore it. An early study commissioned by Haloid described the potential for the 914 as "extremely limited" and that such technology would be used only for limited specialized purposes.

Likewise he summarily rejected the recommendations of a McKinsey Company compensation strategy study that urged him to assign incentive compensation and stock options exclusively based on an individual's performance and their specific contribution to the company's success. While consistent with contemporary business management principles of many highly regarded firms, this strategy was categorically at odds with Wilson's commitment to share the bounty of the company's success with all employees; white collar, blue collar or no collar at all.

Joseph C. Wilson
Photo courtesy of Xerox Historical Archives

Many chief executives seek and obtain independent, specialized advice from members of their board of directors rather than hiring costly prestigious consulting firms. Often times board members are selected for the specialized knowledge a candidate director might bring to boardroom discussions. Wilson did not subscribe to this approach. Instead he usually selected non-controversial board members from within the community or the ranks of Xerox senior executives with backgrounds similar to his own. This would prove to be a costly error when it came time to implement a top-level management succession plan and subsequently provide oversight to new senior executives.

While he recognized that he was given unusual leadership opportunities at a young age because of his father and grandfather's legacies at Haloid, he earned the respect, admiration and loyalty of the vast majority of employees because of his hard work, dedication, incredible listening skills and exuberance for the mission of the company. He earned the loyalty of both internal and external constituents by his self-effacing charm, willingness to applaud the accomplishments of others and uncompromising integrity.

Wilson had an internal compass that allowed him to see the "right" course as it related to fair dealing with all manner and levels of employees, suppliers and customers decades before it became fashionable to do so. He dealt honestly and forthrightly with organized labor when tradition held that the prudent course was to maintain an adversarial relationship.

In making the tumultuous transition from being a fabricator of specialty-coated papers to manufacturing precision office equipment, Wilson partnered with Rochester Institute of Technology (RIT) to develop and fund a training program for all employees having at least ten years tenure. This allowed for re-training of his existing loyal factory workers for completely different jobs. He proposed that the employees on the shop floor should benefit from the success of the corporation just as the sales, marketing and executives did. In exchange he obtained their understanding that they needed to be prepared to share in the belt-tightening when times got tough.

His sense of fair play extended to suppliers as well. One day Wilson learned that a normally diligent and dependable vendor had incurred a $135,000 loss on a parts contract with the company. Wilson directed that the supplier be paid a supplemental amount to offset the loss.

The company broke new ground in the world of advertising. Under Wilson's leadership, Xerox embarked on what, at the time, was a risky strategy of "blind sponsorship" of hopefully enriching but potentially controversial television programming. By definition, Xerox had no right to edit or selectively opt out of programs. This was before the days of public radio and TV and their well-earned reputation for quality content. Xerox agreed to sponsor several series of provocative, uninterrupted ninety minute television "specials" and only receive a modest "this program has been brought to you by Xerox Corporation" banner ad at the beginning and conclusion of each program. This style of sponsorship and the documentary format which Xerox helped pioneer has gone on to become a successful new genre of television.

The first documentary was a series on the United Nations. Others included more testy subjects such as our country's handling of the Cuban Missile Crisis. Another was titled "Of Black America". After the latter was aired, the company received a copier contract cancellation… from the Ku Klux Klan. Surely Joe Wilson viewed this as a badge of honor.

Joe Wilson was not a prototypical leader. In fact, he had some unusual proclivities. The vast majority of his decisions were thoughtful, insightful and prudent but, like all mortals, his judgment was imperfect. He managed to recruit a stellar and committed core of dedicated executives that shared his vision as their own. Once he chose a course of action, he tended not to vacillate or second-guess that decision. This also applied to his selection of his closest circle of key executives. On rare occasions, these leadership choices were mistakes. A couple of his most senior executives became addicted to their own self-importance and significantly strayed from Wilson's vision. This jeopardized the continued prosperity of one of the world's most successful enterprises. Wilson could be blinded by his intense sense of loyalty and fail to act to correct these errant executives.

Unlike many CEO's, Wilson did not have the need to be the center of attention. He recruited and hired smart, dedicated leaders, delegated effectively and was quick to applaud success. While not one to personally seek the spotlight, he never passed up an opportunity to share his vision of xerography's amazing future with whomever would listen. He sought compromise in negotiations and, while no fool, he understood the long-term benefit in agreements that both parties found rewarding.

While an unusual trait for such a likable, successful leader, Joe Wilson was a naturally shy person. It was a characteristic he recognized, acknowledged and worked to neutralize. This was not evident in his public persona however as his relentless drive and enthusiasm for the company's mission easily masked this tendency. It is an interesting coincidence that this trait was shared with the world's other pioneering imaging leader - George Eastman.

Wilson did not feel compelled to always lead discussions. He thought that he gained as much from listening carefully to erudite people as sharing his own thoughts. Nobody listened as intently and thoughtfully as Joe Wilson. When engaged in conversation with him, you had his full attention; you felt as though there was nobody else in the universe.

Some found it frustrating that he insisted on having important information submitted to him in writing. To promote this concept, he had company notepads emblazoned with "Don't say it, write it". Subordinates sometimes viewed this as an impediment to prompt decision-making.

Heartfelt compassion for "the individual" was both Wilson's defining strength and Achilles heal. Wilson was a pioneer in recognizing both the business and social necessity of hiring and training a "diverse" workforce. In the early 1950's, he observed that there were only two functional areas in the company that included women employees; the factory floor and the secretarial pool. He described the situation as "disgraceful". Xerox soon began hiring women for management and executive roles. Anne Mulcahey was named President and CEO of Xerox in 2001.

Wilson had a reputation for being unable or unwilling to terminate underperforming employees. This was perhaps tied to his tendency to avoid confrontational situations as well as his intense loyalty to those who were committed to his vision for the company. His style was to compromise and seek solutions that partially appeased both parties. Rather than insisting on the summary dismissals of employees who repeatedly failed to meet their standards of performance, he would direct the redeployment of such persons into areas where their skills more closely matched the assignment. On occasion he suggested that perhaps it was equally the company's fault for placing the individual in a position where they were not trained or otherwise capable of succeeding. Following Wilson's lead, this informal practice was applied throughout the organization without regard to pay scale or collar color. This style is in clear contradiction with conventional leadership protocols that suggest that managers are doing a disservice to the underperforming subordinate, the colleagues that are dependent on his or her work and the company by not promptly terminating their employment.

Wilson was not interested in repetitive activities that he perceived to yield little added value. Among such activities was the routine exercise of briefing the board of directors on issues they were certain to rubber stamp with their approval. Accordingly, he appointed board members that had ultimate faith in him and were not interested in hearing a rehash of the company's many successes. Some were former executives with the company that were effective or perhaps even stellar contributors at Haloid (a small specialty photographic paper company) but did not have the talent or interest in adjusting to the demands of leading a sophisticated company marketing and manufacturing precision office equipment. Wilson was reluctant to fire his friends so some of them found a comfortable "home" on the board of directors.

Because he knew they would support his initiatives as CEO, Wilson rarely felt compelled to fully advise, let alone seek particular guidance from his board. He felt that his most important constituents were the key operational executives charged with implementing his vision. He was a master at effectively convincing them to take on his vision as their own. When he wanted an independent opinion, he hired a consulting firm. Accordingly, despite the remarkable success of Xerox, its board of directors was perhaps equally unremarkable.

When new CEO's assume the reins from visionary legends, they often struggle. By nature, such leaders usually possess a sturdy self-esteem and desire to quickly establish their own significant mark on the enterprise. Some are not aware that a portion of their prior success can be attributed to the normal checks and balances of working under the tutelage of their predecessor. Others are so consumed in making the company "their own" that they abandon their normally prudent judgment.

Joe Wilson carefully selected Peter McColough to succeed him. Consistent with his established style, Wilson left him alone to run the business as he saw fit. By most accounts, McColough stumbled through a series of dreadful decisions. The biggest blunder was the acquisition of Scientific Data Systems. He was so consumed with broadening the Xerox product mix that he traded $1.5 billion in Xerox shares for a company whose revenues were just $100 million and earnings were $10 million. Contemporary prices for acquiring successful, profitable companies are in the range of 5 to 10 times annual earnings (before interest and taxes). Peter McColough paid 150 times earnings; this for a company whose business was providing esoteric scientific computer calculations to a very small segment of the business community.

Soon after the acquisition, the full effect of the 1970 recession impacted the overall tempo of business spending. Profits promptly disappeared at the newly named Xerox Data Systems Division and losses mounted to $500 million over the next few years. By the time the decision was reversed, Xerox had pounded $2 billion dollars down the "rat-hole" called Scientific Data Systems. All this because McColough was convinced Xerox had to enter the computer industry in response to IBM entering the copier business.

Often times newly appointed CEO's attempt to visibly stamp their identity on the company by redesigning the logo, altering the company name or building a new headquarters campus. McColough was clearly the new operational leader of Xerox and Joe Wilson's role as Chairman was more titular than functional. This was, after all, how Wilson had designed and nurtured the board to function.

Despite Joe's clear willingness to allow McColough full authority to run Xerox (reference the Scientific Data Systems fiasco), McColough felt threatened by the proximity of his former boss to the vast cadre of key lieutenants that Wilson had trained and developed to hold critical leadership roles in the company. McColough, not so rationally, concluded that Wilson would be viewed as the true Xerox leader as long as he remained in Rochester. But... Joe Wilson was clearly a Pleasant Valley boy and not going anywhere. In order to make Xerox his company, McColough moved the headquarters to Stamford, Connecticut. Whatever small gain was realized in lower state taxes and in having key executives closer to the banking center of NYC, was more than offset by the inherent inefficiencies of the daily flights between the Stamford headquarters and the Rochester operations by dozens of those same executives.

When Xerox most needed an experienced, judicious and involved board of directors to challenge senior management and provide oversight and guidance, such talent either did not exist or refused to act. A responsible, talented board could not have rationalized the investment in Scientific Data Systems or agreed to move the headquarters from Rochester. Wilson's involvement, or lack thereof, in these significant strategic blunders is enigmatic. Clearly he felt obliged to allow his hand-picked successor considerable latitude in running the business. But the scope and magnitude of his costly strategic errors, leads one to question whether Mr. Wilson, the Chairman of the Board, was emotionally absent?

30

It Takes a Village!

The volunteer fire departments of this nation have filled a great civil duty. These institutions efficiently marshaled local teams of trained fire-fighting men and women without the financial burden necessary to retain a full-time paid staff of firefighters on call 24/7 - 365. The exceptional value of the volunteer system was particularly evident when significant distances separated villages from neighboring communities and horse-drawn fire fighting equipment was slow and cumbersome traversing the winter snows and unpaved roads. Perhaps more than just filling a vital community need, the department evolved quickly into an important social entity that thrives to this day. Even if there was a more fiscally prudent option to satisfy this need, it is doubtful that the intensely loyal volunteer members would allow the institution to be displaced without a protracted fight.

A special bond was formed when a group of a small town's young men gathered to train and develop the requisite skills to protect the life and property of their neighbors. Not much has changed between 1899 and 2010. Pittsford's volunteer firefighters still fraternize over talk of fires, friends or the state of the nation. Through the Second World War, one could always find a game of cards being played upstairs; particularly in the winter months. Many of the young men described in earlier chapters who treasured the social interactions of "hanging around" in the village "graduated" to become volunteer firefighters after finishing school, starting a career and a family. Pleasant, sunny weather always drew a group of volunteers to relax and chat in front of the fire hall... just as their fathers and grandfathers did and their sons and grandsons are likely to do. The current Chief of the Pittsford Volunteer Fire Department is Jared Lusk. His great-grandfather, grandfather and father were all Pittsford Volunteer Firefighters before him. He is an eighth generation villager descended from John Lusk; the first white settler in Pleasant Valley.

Throughout its existence, the core members of the Pittsford Volunteer Fire Department have been local merchants, tradesmen or farmers. This made sense given that fires don't respect the fact that many Pittsford residents commute to jobs in Rochester and are not able to hear and respond to the beckoning wail of the village siren.

The adage "It takes a Village" comes to mind when observing the beehive of activity prompted by the wail of the Pittsford Village Fire Station siren. Bryce Chase of Bryce and Don's Atlantic Station was often the first in the door. His business was directly across the street. "Dutch" Earl would dash from his barber shop on South Main Street asking his customer to wipe off their own shaving cream or come back in a few hours to allow him to finish their "trim". By the time "Dutch" departed, he would be joined by the Burdett brothers leaving their meat or vegetable departments in the capable hands of employees. Sole proprietors with no employees would hurriedly place the "Closed" sign on their door and adjust the hands on the "back at....O'clock" sign to reflect their anticipated two or three hour absence.

Some local farmers, who were volunteer fireman, were well within the audible range of the siren but too far to walk or run to the station. Partially hidden within the grillwork of their cars and trucks were small fire department medallions and flashing red lights. It is unclear what special sanction allowed them to exceed the posted speed limit but it was generally understood that you pulled over and made way for the local heroes. There was a sense that some of the volunteers experienced an awakening of a childhood dream to be a career firefighter as they made the mad dash from home or farm to the fire station with horn honking and red lights flashing.

To many volunteers, this activity represented far more than a casual pastime. A large number had fire/police band radios at their places of work (garage, store or barn) and in their homes. These would be permanently tuned to the frequency reserved for firefighters. Ostensibly Bryce Chase <u>slept</u> with this burping cacophony on his bedside table. Being elected Fire Chief was equivalent in many admiring eyes to becoming the mayor.

Rabid volunteer Fritz Milliman sometimes got the roles confused. He was jokingly called "The Mayor" because of his take-charge attitude. He regularly chased speeders through the village with his fire department mini lights flashing. It is not generally known what transpired when the offenders pulled over.

Reliable reports indicate more than one enthusiastically committed firefighter family, when considering a move to a different home, informed realtors that "proximity to the fire station" was their highest priority. One lucky family delayed their move until the home directly adjoining the Fire Station became available for sale. Whether the demand for such properties caused them to carry a price premium is not known.

Alfred "Dutch" Earl was himself an institution within the village; having cut the hair of successive generations of Pittsfordites. "Dutch" is seen facing the camera in the photo below in the early years of his shop. Two fellow barbers are busy at work.

Dutch Earl's Barber Shop – Dutch in center foreground
Courtesy of Paul M. Spiegel

He moved his shop's location around over the years. In the 1920's he was located on the east side of Main Street but from mid-century forward, was mainly located on the west side of the street. He was the quintessential small town barber with quick wit, the latest joke and a good array of frayed "skin magazines". Few married men intent on maintaining domestic tranquility subscribed to Playboy at home but would fight over the most recent tattered copy at "Dutch's". The availability of these publications no doubt hastened the average time between visiting Dutch. Some patrons had near equal loyalty to Dutch's colleague Jim Vitalone. Patrons tended to be a "regular" of either Dutch or Jim's. For some time there was a competitor of Dutch's shop located next to Tallo's Town Tavern but he was rarely busy. During this period, only women made hair appointments. Men stopped by and asked "how many in front of me Dutch?" and decided to wait or return later depending on the response.

Dutch was a bit of a risk-taker. When the youth of the community showed an interest in Mohawk haircuts, he offered to provide the early-adapters with complimentary cuts. Most of these pioneers, after exposing their parents to their newest act of self-expression, returned to have the remaining center strip shorn to the height of the adjoining stubble. Some concerned parents reportedly "had words" with Dutch regarding their displeasure with his decision to offer incentives (free haircuts) for rebellious acts. They suggested that he require written permission from parents or guardians. Within the context of 21st century tattoos and lip/tongue/nipple/genitalia piercing, Mohawk haircuts seem innocuous. Perhaps local youth were simply paying tribute to the Mohawk Nation; brothers/sisters of the local Seneca and fellow members of the Iroquois Confederacy.

While the social, retail and commercial focus of the area has always been the village center, Pittsford's roots are in its farms. While income-producing crops have dominated, some local rural properties have a long history as recreational venues. Griffith Farms Stables was located on Marsh Road for many decades of the early and mid twentieth century and offered horse boarding, rentals and riding lessons. In the 1930's and 1940's the stable hosted Sunday Matinee Races which drew substantial crowds. Also on Marsh Road, Roger Young's stables offered similar services for a more upscale client base willing to pay his higher prices.

Transportation has played a key role in the evolution of Pittsford. The pony express mail delivery was followed by the stage lines and the building of the Erie Canal. Then railroad and trolley service was followed by bus service. The only thing missing was an airport.

Not far from Griffith's Farm Stables was Pittsford's own airport. Roy Harmon's Airport was located on Marsh Road in the 1950's. Before long, developers took over the property and created another charm-less subdivision. At one point, the airport was called Brizee Field; perhaps having to do with the fact that it was located across the street from the Brizee house.

The village's sick and injured did not have a local clinic staffed with a broad array of attending physician "specialists" and laboratories. Rather villagers sought the aid of one of the two local family physicians. Dr. Foster J. Hamilton worked from his home on Rand Place and Dr. Lloyd Allan from his on South Main Street. There was no gatekeeper nurse to take your vitals and prescreen your symptoms. A visit to Dr. Allen's South Main Street home was akin to visiting your grandfather in his comfortable living room.

Dr. Allen had sad eyes. He was a quintessential gentleman and compassionate healer. It is not unusual for grieving parents to bury their sorrow and focus on their work. In retrospect, one can consider the probable thoughts of Dr. Allen as he tended the fortunate who were merely sick; wishing only to have his son return from World War ll to ease his own pain.

31

The "Wake-Up Call"

Rochester's healthy business climate fostered population growth in The Genesee Valley through the middle of the twentieth century. In 1950, the population of Rochester peaked at 332,488. Despite many remarkable success stories in the area of imaging technology by Bausch and Lomb, Eastman Kodak and Xerox, as well as leading positions in the garment industry, the city's employers could not offset the reduced need for workers as the agricultural, food processing and transportation sectors transitioned to more efficient, less labor-intensive business models.

In the last half of the twentieth century, the fundamental process used by businesses to determine plant, office and facility locations was drastically altered. Throughout the Industrial Revolution, traditional "smokestack" industries were located in close proximity to cheap energy, abundant raw materials and low cost transportation. As the country transitioned to a broader economic base, energy became uniformly less costly and the trucking industry became amazingly efficient; neutralizing the former advantages of port cities. As a result, business owners had far greater latitude in locating their new factories, warehouses, research centers and administrative offices. When business owners and managers selected new facility locations, they increasingly focused on choosing sites that would attract qualified employees. Year-round recreational opportunities, affordable housing and a favorable climate became paramount in importance. The Genesee Valley did not fare well in competition with the Sunbelt.

Rochester's boomtown years were based on a plentiful supply of cheap energy, close proximity to fertile grain-growing agricultural areas and a barge transportation system that could efficiently move commodity agricultural products to a broad market. As energy became affordable across all of America and railroads and trucking became more efficient and practical than barge transportation, Rochester lost its strategic advantages. Concurrently, technological advances in farming and food processing, reduced the number employees required to effectively run agricultural businesses.

Job growth ceased, unemployment increased and some portion of the population migrated to the available job opportunities located elsewhere. In the fifty years since its population peaked, Rochester lost 113,000 souls; more than one-third of its population. Census numbers for 2000, reflected just 219,773 inhabitants of the city.

At the same time, the demographics of Rochester were undergoing a significant change. Rochester's African American population quadrupled in the fourteen years leading up to 1964. Many of these new arrivals were southern plantation workers who had lost their work as a result of mechanized farm equipment; most notably the automated cotton-picker. These southerners had become accustomed to joining the agricultural workforce as soon as they were big and tall enough to physically perform the work. There was no perceived need for formal education beyond grammar school for vocations focused exclusively on manual labor. Accordingly, when the northern migration began, Rochester's newest residents did not meet the minimum requirements for employment at Kodak, Bausch and Lomb or Xerox. The hope and promise of a better life was clearly not available to most new arrivals in the African American community. An editorial in the Rochester Democrat and Chronicle stated frankly that: "Most (Black) people got into Kodak in those days behind a broom".

The city's Black community was disproportionately affected when the pink slips were distributed. And, while the area's major employers were perfectly willing to accept applications from all who applied, such efforts were almost always unsuccessful when the applicant did not meet the initial educational screen; a high school diploma.

Abject racism was less overt. The Ku Klux Klan had some presence in Pittsford although little is written about their activities. There is record of a significant gathering of the hooded ones at the Pittsford Cemetery presumably to honor one of their departed comrades. This racist expression seems enigmatic given the community's strong support of abolition and its leadership on the Underground Railroad; prompting more questions than answers. Could these participants all be residents of adjoining towns and villages? How cautious must the "conductors" have been if in fact there were significant numbers of the Klan within the community? As small and seemingly close knit as the Village seemed, was a resident's liberal sympathies generally known and, if so, was there a noticeable rift between groups? How could you "hang out" at the Four Corners or the Fire Station and not discuss the burning social-cultural issue of the century and in the process identify with one side or the other?

America's "wake up call" happened in Rochester in the summer of 1964. The adopted home of Frederick Douglass and the northern most embarkation point on the Underground Railroad was the site of the first major urban riot of the Civil Rights Movement. Watts burned the following summer.

Per the <u>Rochester Democrat and Chronicle</u> of July 18, 2004:

"Forty years ago this week, Rochester festered with racial tension that exploded in the first major riot of the Civil Rights era. It began at a street dance on a hot July 24th in the Joseph Avenue area and ended three days later with the arrival of the National Guard –The first time they'd ever been called to duty in a Northern city."

"...whether the volatile event was merely a spontaneous, violent response to a hot night, too much beer and a destructive attitude or a more deeply etched social rebellion, triggered by severely limited job opportunities, poor housing and institutional racism"

"...According to most interview subjects, the problems were found not with the neighbors but with Rochester industry, insensitive police (and their cruelly employed dogs), housing restrictions and a general aura of community smugness."

"Dr. Walter Cooper, a scientist and retired New York State Regent, applied to 69 different homes outside the proscribed black neighborhoods 'only to be denied for all of them'"

From the University of Rochester "Rochester Race Riot Papers, 1964 –1966":

"Violence and looting in Rochester spanned a period of approximately sixty hours, resulting in four deaths, at least 350 injuries, over 800 arrests, and property damage totaling more than a million dollars. Dubbed 'Smugtown" in the 1950's because of the comfort and complacency borne of the economic prosperity and amicable labor-management relations fostered by the Eastman Kodak Company and other large, successful, high-tech corporations, the riots represented a profound blow to Rochester's positive self-image. As the flames of discontent were replaced by the glare of the media spotlight, black and white Rochester residents were forced to reflect – from different perspectives and with different conclusions – on the causes and meanings of this devastating event"

"The 'riot' was precipitated by the arrest of an allegedly drunk and disorderly African-American at a Joseph Avenue street dance. But even in its immediate aftermath, many looked to underlying social and environmental conditions to explain the events that followed. These conditions were analogous to those that existed in many Northern cities. They included a large and rapid influx of African-Americans from the

South, the de-facto segregation of black arrivals in specific areas of the residential urban core, a failure to extend economic opportunities from white to black residents, the physical decay of black neighborhoods due to poverty and inadequate services, the routine exploitation of African-American tenants by white landlords, the neglect of an overwhelmingly white police force, inequities in educational instruction and facilities, and the inability of African-Americans to redress grievances through legitimate political channels. Rochester's was one of a trio of 'riots' in the summer of 1964. Together, they inaugurated the 'long hot summers' of racial strife that marked the mid and late sixties."

The violence of the 1964 Rochester Race Riots came to the front door of Xerox's corporate headquarters. This had significant impact on Joseph Wilson and prompted his commitment to be part of the solution to a systemic social problem. Wilson quickly determined that the high school diploma requirement was the initial barrier that had to be addressed. Rather than simply lowering hiring standards, he demanded his Human Resources Department develop solutions that would help satisfy Xerox's continuing need for capable and dependable employees and make a contribution to solving the unemployment epidemic in the African American community.

"Operation Step Up" welcomed its first student/workers to the newly built Xerox classrooms in 1965. In exchange for waiving the high school diploma requirement, newly hired employees agreed to attend classes for a half day studying to earn their high school diploma and work in the Xerox factory the remaining half day.

While the riot's embers were still warm, Wilson sought out Reverend Franklin Florence, the most respected of Rochester's African American clergy. He traveled alone to Florence's second-story office in Rochester's ghetto at 9:00 p.m. one night. He introduced himself and declared that the two leaders could and should help each other. There were plenty of able constituents of Reverend Florence who needed and sought work that paid a fair wage and Xerox was always in need of qualified people.

When Operation Step Up was ready for its first class to matriculate, Franklin Florence personally selected the students. He sent only the best. On the rare occasion when a student worker did not perform to their expectations, Reverend Florence promptly replaced that underperforming student with a more deserving and committed one. In 1966, six classes, averaging nearly two dozen students each, graduated from the visionary program to become loyal, productive employees.

Under Wilson's leadership, the company forged additional new ground in 1968. Xerox joined with the Department of Labor to co-sponsor a program with Reverend Florence called FIGHT (Freedom, Integration, God, Honor, Today). It was the first time that a U.S. Government agency had partnered with a private entity to enable the creation of African American owned businesses. Enterprises created through assistance from FIGHT successfully supplied parts to Xerox plants and other Rochester area firms.

32

Imaging Re-invented for the 21ˢᵗ Century

Chester Carlson originally postulated that he could "change his economic status", utilize his technical skills and make a contribution to society by becoming a successful inventor. He was proven correct on all counts. Xerography revolutionized office processes and he was rewarded handsomely for his accomplishments; mainly in shares of Xerox stock. Over the remainder of his life, these shares were valued at over $150 million. He donated two thirds of his estate to charities prior to his death in 1968. The main beneficiaries were a variety of organizations aligned with the peace and civil rights movements. He was reportedly a follower of the Indian guru Ramakrishna and donated money to support their cause. There are no reports of Mr. Carlson wandering American airports during that period with shaved head, incense and peach colored robe preaching the Krishna gospel however. Mr. Carlson lived in Pittsford with his wife Doris.

Joe Wilson led Xerox as CEO and Chairman until 1968. In May of that year, he appointed Peter McColough as CEO. Wilson continued to serve as Chairman until his death in 1971. During his tenure, sales increased from $7 million in 1956 to $3 billion. Employment increased from 735 to 25,000 in the same period. Xerox common stock performed accordingly. In the late 1960's it was not uncommon to read about little old blue-haired ladies that had purchased 100 shares in the old Haloid Company and become millionaires. That was when millionaires were a rarity and newsworthy.

What was Wilson doing while McColough was running (or not running) Xerox? He was back focusing on his strength as a visionary. He was following Dr. Levitt's mantra to make yourself obsolete; do not wait for others to run you out of business. Wilson focused his efforts on shaping the long-term fate of the company he created. What could and should replace xerography as the Xerox core business? He found renewed inspiration to find or create a technology with which the company could duplicate its magical success with xerography.

By the early 1970's it had become clear that the photocopier business was saturated with competitors. All were seeking to reduce manufacturing costs and ultimately drive down selling price. Wilson correctly viewed Xerox as an innovator and technology company; not one focused exclusively on low cost manufacturing of commodity business machines.

A year before his death in 1971, Mr. Wilson orchestrated the creation of Xerox Palo Alto Research Center (Xerox PARC) to expand the company's leadership into new technologies and businesses. This strategic decision was demonstrative of his unique talent as a gifted visionary. He could see the day that either the company lost its competitive advantage or advancements in imaging technology made xerography obsolete.

While Wilson preceded Dr. Levitt's tenure at Harvard Business School by nearly twenty five years, he probably subscribed to the Harvard Business Review and read with great interest the <u>Marketing Myopia</u> essay published in 1960. Wilson had studied and admired 3M's research efforts in what they called their "skunkworks". Their scientists were given the freedom to break beyond established boundaries and explore new technologies that might change the world. It is easy to imagine the mission at Xerox PARC as being to redefine the office of the coming century and chart the path for Xerox to continue to revolutionize that environment.

While Steve Jobs and Steve Wozniak are often credited with "inventing" the Personal Computer, they, rather like Henry Ford or Joseph Wilson, had the insight to see a great invention and figure out how to bring it to the masses at an affordable price. While not without controversy[11], many who will ultimately write the history of the personal computer believe that Xerox PARC researchers were the first to create the mouse and graphical user interface (GUI) that ultimately made computers "user friendly". They also were the first to introduce Ethernet networking technology.

Had George Eastman been around, he might have challenged researchers to "make the computer as convenient as the pencil". These user-friendly elements defined Xerox PARC's development of the first personal computer, called Alto, in 1973. While ultimately these

---

[11] The definitive history of the PC has not been written, in part because of the difficulty, perhaps impossibility of identifying single persons to credit as the exclusive "first" to develop the key technologies (mouse, graphical user interface, Ethernet networking) that allowed the PC to become a reality. The challenge is exacerbated because multiple individuals, teams and laboratories were working on these elements simultaneously. As engineers moved from one lab to another and shared research ideas, it became increasingly difficult to assign a technological breakthrough to an individual.

breakthroughs were the essence of what would become the personal computer industry, Xerox researchers could not fully envision the significance of their accomplishments. Because they lacked confidence regarding its commercial viability, the Alto was never offered for sale.

Instead, they redirected their R & D efforts to a workstation for the business community. Xerox Star was introduced with a selling price of $16,000 per unit in 1981. It was the first computer available to the business world that offered Ethernet networking, print servers, window-based graphic user interface and email; all common elements of the most successful of today's personal computers. In the clarity of hindsight, the Xerox Star contained the correct combination of innovative elements to kick-start the information age.

The vision was right on target. The technology was spot on. Xerox was <u>very</u> close to capitalizing on their revolutionary research and earning the leadership position at the very dawn of the information age. But... they did not execute!

So what was missing? It is easy today to suggest that Xerox simply screwed up. Why didn't they evolve to be the present day Dell, Apple or Hewlett Packard? Was it timing? Were they too early? If Joe Wilson had been alive, would he have had the vision to lead Xerox in the next giant step of the information revolution?

In the 1970's there were not personal computers in every home, on every office desk and nearly every airline seat-back tray. The economic challenge was not simply a single $16,000 investment but rather $16,000 times the number of employees intended for the network. Al Gore had not yet "invented the Internet". Office managers could not look across the hall or at a competitor and see a more efficient, cost effective way of communicating. There was no precedence.

Perhaps one can draw an analogy with the visionary pricing strategy deployed to sell the $20,000 Xerox 914. The ground-breaking tactic was not to sell the machine at all but, rather to sell copies produced from the machine for five cents each. It was the rare office manager who would risk investing $20,000 in an unproven piece of office equipment from a company who had never before sold office equipment. But who could resist the temptation to make copies on-sight for a nickel a piece? With no Joe Wilson to challenge conventional thinking, the Alta sat idle until its key elements became the bounty of Silicon Valley pirates.

Steve Jobs and some colleagues from the fledgling Apple Computer toured Xerox PARC in 1979. The significance of the mouse and graphical user interface in simplifying the world of computing for the common man and woman was evident to them. Within four years, Apple offered the Apple Lisa for sale to the public. It was a commercial flop. Perhaps the $10,000 price tag was a significant deterrent to achieving mass appeal? Apple clearly needed to take a page from either the George Eastman or Henry Ford schools of business leadership of six decades prior. Mr. Eastman recognized that to reach the masses, he had to reinvent the $5 pocket Kodak. His answer was the $1 Brownie which brought photography to the common people. Likewise, Henry Ford focused on taking cost out of the Ford automobile so as to make it affordable to the average wage earner. Steve Jobs' challenge was to similarly reengineer the personal computer. We are left to speculate; would Joe Wilson have envisioned that the manufacturing cost of the Alta-like personal computer would drop by seventy five percent ($12,000 to $3,000) in just four years?

The personal computer industry was born of such efforts. Jobs and Wozniak realized that the mouse and graphical user interface were the keys to user friendliness. They introduced the Apple Macintosh in 1984 and thereby became the first to make this technology available and affordable to average consumers.

As the commercial success of the Macintosh became apparent, Xerox filed suit against Apple Computer over their use of graphical user interface. By then, the three year statute of limitations had expired and the case was thrown out of court. Steve Jobs stated at the time that had Xerox fully appreciated and pursued the long-term possibilities contained in the Alta personal computer, they could have become the dominant high-tech company in the world; surpassing the combined size of IBM, Microsoft and Xerox.

Joe Wilson's accomplishments as a twentieth century business icon were remarkable. Under his leadership, Xerox achieved unparalleled growth in sales and earnings, significantly altered the very nature of office work which, in turn, led to advances in productivity that favorably affected the world's standard of living.

During the decade he was re-inventing Haloid, Wilson was known to take long weekend walks with key lieutenants around Mendon Ponds; seven miles south of Pittsford. As decisions were made and strategies agreed to, these items were scratched off his typed agenda.

The water from Mendon Ponds has been feeding Irondequoit Creek for thousands of years. The creek, in turn, has provided the power and nourishment to Pleasant Valley; power to turn the Stone's grist mill and nourishment for the fertile farmlands of the area surrounding Big Spring. Not unlike the impact of Joe Wilson making strategic decisions as he hiked around the ponds; decisions that would empower and nourish Xerox.

Wilson was a longtime trustee of the University of Rochester and served as Chairman of the Board for several years. He generously donated \$23+ million to the University during his lifetime. Before his death, he established an irrevocable trust that bequeathed his estate to the University of Rochester upon the death of his wife.

Joe Wilson died in 1971 at Governor Rockefeller's NYC home where he was a dinner guest. Fortunately he did not live to see the price of Xerox shares plummet, learn of the corporate fines for accounting principles that were deemed fraudulent or the deterioration of the firm's reputation that resulted in their corporate bonds being designated as "junk". Nor did he meet Ursula Burns.

At the time of Wilson's death, Ursula Burns was a thirteen year old African-American math whiz living nearby in "the projects" of Manhattan's lower east side and attending local Catholic schools. She excelled academically and ultimately earned an engineering degree from Brooklyn's Polytechnic Institute and a Masters in Mechanical Engineering from Columbia. She joined Xerox as a summer intern in the summer of 1980.

The development of the world's first laser printer in 1977 was a welcome boost to the eroded morale of dedicated Xerox employees. It ultimately became a multi-billion dollar business for the company. In the last thirty years, the company successfully redefined its mission as "document management and service". While remaining proud of their xerography roots, they added a corporate signature to their core promotional message to more broadly define their business focus. They began calling themselves "The Document Company". Consistent with this redefined mission, they have been successful in leading the industry in developing innovative high speed laser printers, word processors, fax machines, printing and publishing systems, "book factories", scanners, digital photocopiers and work flow software. Concurrently they have offered their customers full "document services" of user support, materials supply, maintenance and the creation of on-line web services in support of processing, archiving and transmitting documents.

The Xerox mission statement reads: "Our strategic intent is to help people find better ways to do great work -- by constantly leading in document technologies, products and services that improve our customers' work processes and business results". As long as documents continue to represent a significant communication medium, Dr. Levitt would be satisfied.

Mr. Wilson's legacy has continued in the 21st century. Ursula Burns rose from summer intern (in 1980) to become the company's first African-American president in 2002. On July 1, 2009 Ms. Burns succeeded the retiring Anne Mulcahy as CEO and thus became the first African-American woman to head a Fortune 500 or S&P 100 company.

The tandem of Mulcahy and Burns became the first woman-to-woman CEO transition team in Fortune 500 history.

Ursula Burns worked hard and delivered exceptional results through her three decade career at Xerox. Joe Wilson's vision and courage in creating an environment for all employees to be recognized for their achievements paved the way for her success. Of the nearly four thousand executives at Xerox, fully one third are women and nearly a quarter are members of a minority group. These results are a direct product of Joe Wilson's mandate that all company leaders be evaluated on their success in hiring, mentoring and developing members of underrepresented groups. In describing contemporary Xerox, Professor David A Thomas of the Harvard Business School, stated: "You have a culture where having women and people of color as candidates for powerful jobs has been going on for two decades."

The Bausch and Lomb rubber eye glass frames were never the commercial success that young Mr. Bausch had anticipated. Fortunately, the company prospered for decades based on its focus on high-end optics and precision manufacturing.

Late in the twentieth century, Bausch and Lomb introduced the country's first optical quality glass. This was followed by their crafting of the satellite mounted lenses that photographed the moon's surface for the first time. The company was an early leader in the development of the contact lens industry.

By definition, the free enterprise system attracts additional competitors to industries perceived to be profitable. Bausch and Lomb was not immune to that reality. As machine tools were developed and refined to perform the precision crafting of optical products, the historical strategic advantages of the company dissipated. As the patents on their proprietary products and processes expired, competition entered the market with lower priced products and drove down profits. For a time, the company's research and development staff could not invent and commercialize proprietary products fast enough to offset the pace that traditional products were becoming low profit commodities.

In the later half of the century, the company's 14,000 employees have focused on a broad range of "eye health products"; from contact lenses to equipment and instruments to perform eye surgery. They became and remain the world's largest supplier of eye care products. A significant milestone was the introduction of the first "soft" contact lens; a market in which they remain dominant.

Today, Bausch and Lomb's Mission Statement reads:

"Bausch & Lomb is the eye health company dedicated to perfecting vision and enhancing life®. At Bausch & Lomb, our history of innovation continues today as we invent new materials, engineer new technologies, and create pioneering ways to help people see better"

They have clearly re-invented themselves several times over the century and are now considered a leading "healthcare company" rather than an imaging company.

George Eastman's original focus on broad, captivating advertising was rekindled in mid century. Beginning in 1950, the company initiated the Kodak Colorama display in the main terminal of New York's Grand Central Station. The mammoth (18 feet by 60 feet) transparency was seen by nearly one half million commuters each day until it was discontinued after the station restoration in 1989. Several Pittsford residents have been the subject of these mega photos. Pittsford's Shaw family was shown one summer enjoying a family barbeque with Rochester's own Tobin First Prize White Hots.

Kodak continued to prosper in the third quartile of the twentieth century with sales reaching $1 billion in 1962 and $10 billion in 1981. During this period, the Justice Department took issue with Kodak's effort to limit the photo processing of their color film exclusively to company laboratories. A settlement was reached, again, via a consent decree that required Kodak to allow others to use Kodak technology to process Kodak color film.

There was a transition in senior leadership in 1962 when Dr. Albert K. Chapman was appointed Chairman after fellow Pittsford resident Thomas J. Hargrave died. Pittsford resident Dr. Louis K. Eilers was promoted to President in 1967 and became Chairman of the Board in 1970. Succeeding Dr. Eilers as President at that time was Gerald B. Zornow. In 1972, Mr. Zornow became Chairman and Walter A. Fallon succeeded him as President. Mr. Fallon commuted from his home in nearby Victor.

Gerald Zornow was a Pittsford lad and three sports star at the University of Rochester. He pitched for the Rochester Red Wings in 1937 after signing a contract with the Saint Louis Cardinals. In 1975, he was appointed by President Gerald Ford to serve as Chairman of his newly formed President's Commission on Olympic Sports. He was the recipient of the Theodore Roosevelt Award from the NCAA, awarded the Gold Medal by the College Football Hall of Fame and the Amos Alonzo Award by the American Football Coaches Association.

Continuing the pattern, Mr. Fallon became Chairman in 1977 and was succeeded in the presidency by Colby H. Chandler. When Mr. Chandler was elected Chairman and CEO, he was succeeded as president by Kay R. Whitmore in 1983. Mr. Whitmore resided in Pittsford. Mr. George M. C. Fisher led the company in the late 1990's and, it appears, that he too was a Pittsford resident. Daniel Carp succeeded Mr. Fisher for the first five years of the 21st century before Antonio M. Perez assumed that role in 2005. Mr. Perez makes his home in Pittsford.

The company's growth trajectory came to an end in the last twenty-five years. Sales declined to $7.6 billion in 2009 and the company incurred a loss of $232 million.

Two major factors contributed to the end of this impressive century-long-run of business leadership and increasing sales and profits. Fuji Film challenged Kodak's near-monopoly on the consumer film market by introducing a film product that most viewed as at least equal in quality and performance to Kodak film. Some viewed the Fuji film superior in certain color ranges. Fuji took a page from George Eastman's marketing strategy by investing heavily in consumer advertising. This coupled with a significantly lower price provided sufficient motivation to convince many amateur photographers to try a roll. In the main, they liked the results.

With little advantage perceived in Kodak film by the non-professional picture-taking community, Kodak had little choice but to reduce their price to match Fuji's. This resulted in a loss in profit margins and market share for Kodak.

Far greater impact was wrought by the second major revolution in imaging technology; digital photography. The ultimate irony is that Eastman Kodak engineer Steven Sasson invented the first digital camera. His eight pound jury-rigged prototype utilized cannibalized parts from: a Motorola analog-to-digital converter, a charge coupled device (CCD) from Fairchild Semiconductor and the lens from a Kodak movie-camera. The first image took 23 seconds to capture and was recorded on a digital cassette tape. While it was clear that the clumsy prototype needed significant refinement before it would become "as convenient as the pencil", the modest Sasson declared that his creation "was a little bit revolutionary".

Indeed it would be. Today, the digital camera is the world's most popular electronic gift. More than 50% of homes have at least one such camera.

The first digital camera is depicted below. Not exactly a "detective camera".

The First Digital Camera
Courtesy of Eastman Kodak Company

Not unlike the wide latitude given by Joe Wilson to Xerox PARC researchers, Sasson was casually asked by his supervisor Gareth Lloyd if a camera could be built using only solid-state imagers. After demonstrating viability of the concept in 1975 via his bulky prototype, Sasson tinkered with his invention for three years before he and Lloyd were granted the first patent on an "Electronic Still Camera". In the clarity of hindsight, it is fair to characterize Garth Lloyd's challenge as a courageous step consistent with Theodore Levitt's doctrine of making your own company's technologies obsolete...before someone else does.

Mr. Eastman's initial business partner and family friend, Mr. Strong made his fortune in the family buggy whip business. He clearly was a man who paid attention to the market place and, no doubt observed the impact that Henry Ford was likely to have on the market for buggy whips.

Perhaps Kodak leaders revisited the principles on which George Eastman had established the company one hundred years earlier. Recall Mr. Eastman's fourth tenet ... "focus on the customer" and his tag line of "You press the button, we do the rest". Would a modern- day Mr. Eastman have recognized that digital photography clearly focused on the customer by making it easier for both amateur and professional photographers to "make the camera as convenient as the pencil"?

Since obtaining Sasson's patent, Kodak has been at the forefront in investing in digital imaging research. While not generally known or appreciated by casual observers of the electronic consumer goods industry, Kodak continued to lead the industry in the design and development of digital photography technology over the last quarter century. They invented a number of solid-state image sensors that advanced the industry in the years following Sasson's original prototype. In the mid-eighties, they greatly enhanced the commercial viability of digital photography by creating the first mega-pixel sensor that allowed high fidelity prints up to a 5X7 size; a breakthrough at the time. This was followed by a succession of new products for storing, transmitting, recording and printing digital images. In the early nineties, the company commercialized the CD storage system for digital photos and created the first professional camera based on the format. While not the first to market an amateur digital camera with home computer interface capabilities, they followed Apple's pioneering product with the Kodak DC40 one year later in 1995.

Kodak was effective at leading the introduction of digital photography to the amateur photographer through their team efforts with Kinko's and Microsoft. These collaborations yielded digital image-making software and the photo printing kiosks that advanced digital photography one step closer to being "as easy as the pencil".

Consistent with George Eastman's mandate of the 1890's to obtain tight patent protection on all proprietary product development achievements, Kodak attorneys have been busy over the last thirty-five years securing in excess of 1000 patents on digital imaging. Most manufacturers of digital cameras depend on the technologies protected under these patents to design and build their imaging products.

It is reasonable to assume that Mr. Eastman would have used patent protection on this pioneering technology to allow Kodak to once again monopolize the photography industry. Kodak executives chose instead to move cautiously; perhaps hoping to simply deter others from pursuing digital imaging by virtue of tight company patents. Surely, these executives shared many sleepless nights imagining the potential obsolescence of Kodak's enormous investment in people, plants and equipment dedicated to film technology.

Recognizing the unmistakable momentum of the second imaging revolution, Kodak began licensing their technology to others in 2000. This did not eliminate the temptation of some eager high-tech competitors from testing the legal strength of Kodak's digital patents. The result was a series of protracted legal battles and patent infringement lawsuits.

Under CEO Antonio Perez, aggressively pursuing legal action against those who infringed on protected technology has become a core income-producing strategy. In the 2009-2010 period alone, Kodak revenue from patent infringement suits totaled nearly $1 billion from just two defendants; Samsung Electronics and LG Electronics. Perez set minimum income goals from lawsuit settlements and licensing patented digital technologies of $250 million per year for the years 2008 through 2012.

The boardroom discussions in the last decade must have been spirited and controversial. In that period digital photography threatened the core film technology that the company had invented, perfected, commercialized, brought to the masses and dominated for a century. The choice to lead the digital revolution and perhaps hasten the obsolescence of your core technology and worldwide manufacturing base is clearly not as easy as Theodore Levitt might suggest.

Second guessing Kodak's strategy is easy when you do not have a personal stake in the fate of hundreds of millions of dollars of equipment and the livelihood of thousands of loyal employees. But, it is reasonable to suggest that if Kodak was convinced that digital photography represented the future and they were committed to quickly emerging as the market share leader in this medium, that stealing a page out of the Apple playbook would have been prudent. The technology and performance details of the IPhone were purposely kept confidential until the well-orchestrated public unveiling. The product was in stock, distribution channels were established and a partnership with a cellular service provider was in place. The competition could not begin developing alternate products until the IPhone was already in the hands of eager consumers. That head-start has been key to Apple's continued dominance in the sector.

If Kodak were allowed a re-do, perhaps they would have refined and miniaturized the digital camera product, developed storage systems, reached agreement with Walgreens and CVS to have printing kiosks ready to roll out and introduced the entire digital photography platform in a single world-wide introduction? Perhaps they would have decided not to license patented digital technology to others and, rather, to fight to protect against patent infringement.

Perhaps easier said than done? In recent years, Eastman Kodak has been intent on recapturing its former market dominance in the imaging industry. It has not been easy. Recent decades have been marked by a series of layoffs and downsizings in order to retain profitability. Concurrently senior leaders have redirected the company's efforts to compete aggressively in a market now dominated by digital photography.

Recent results have been promising. In 2009, 77% of sales revenues were from digital sources and only 23% from traditional businesses. While photographic film products remain profitable, this is a result of focusing on the higher margin segments and allowing competitors to harvest market share on the lower profit product lines.

33

Pittsford "Another Fort Lauderdale!"

"There is nothing which has yet been contrived by man by which so much happiness is produced as by a good tavern or inn"

Samuel Johnson, 1776

In <u>A Brief History of Pubs,</u> pubs are described as being "very much part of the social fabric...a place to meet friends and neighbors, a focal point for various community activities and a source of local information and contacts." In <u>A Brief History of a Typically English Pastime</u> the local tavern is further defined as "an important social gathering place... the place to meet your friends and neighbors for a good old chinwag (chat). It was somewhere you could drown your sorrows over a pint of ale, enjoy a sing-song with your mates, play games, warm your frozen toes in front of a crackling log fire, woo a lover or perhaps escape a nagging spouse and noisy children. In short, a community just wasn't a community without its 'local'."

Hundreds of years later, the local taverns of Pleasant Valley served much the same purpose. As Paul Spiegel aptly states in his <u>Pittsford Scrapbook</u> series, "hanging around is an old custom" in the village. The taverns of Pittsford have long served as a warm and friendly venue to satisfy this tradition.

Surely the "chin-wagging" remains a staple. The few, older customers who arrive soon after the 7:00 a.m. opening do their share of sorrow drowning. There is not much singing although most local taverns offer music; occasionally from live bands but more often from a juke box.

The card game euchre was often the "game playing" of choice with occasional ventures into pinball. Thankfully video games had not been invented. Darts, popular in British Pubs, was a rarity.

Maybe it's the weather? The winters in Pleasant Valley are long, gray and bone-chilling. Pleasant Valley taverns perhaps serve the same function as the British Pubs...its been a hard day at work, dinner sated the appetite, you feel a need for some "space" from your family and a breath of fresh air but it's too cold and miserable to partake in outdoor activities. A short stroll to the corner pub is the answer.

Or...maybe it's the summer weather? Even those that subscribe to the opinion that beer is an acquired taste, agree that a cold beer does taste especially refreshing in a hot and humid environment. For three summer months every year, hot and humid describes Pleasant Valley. You sweat just being; no movement required. Your clothes stick to you and to the car seat. Think of Hawaii, Mexico or Miami and you think of beers on the waterfront patio. Likewise, think of a Pittsford, New York summer and you think of beers in a tavern.

Like all taverns, the overall experience of the Pittsford Inn (aka The PI) was a product of the physical space, the "mood" as inspired by the owner/barkeeper and the assembled congregation. No Pittsford tavern was neat, clean and modern like the one in "Cheers". Even the PI was modest at best in terms of decor; looking much like the working class bar that it was. Bill Lisi, the proprietor, was rarely around but was inclined to hire tough, no-nonsense bartenders who gave the patrons wide boundaries in behavior before ultimately demanding adherence to the well established rules of the house. Only a fool would risk banishment from the PI for disruptive behavior.

The same charge privileges afforded customers at Burdett's Market were available to regulars at the Pittsford Inn and contributed to its overall neighborly ambiance. While many pubs allow customer to run a nightly tab and settle up at the end of the evening, longtime patrons at the PI could "put it on my tab" and clear their credit balance every week or two; usually on payday.

The Pittsford Inn was really two taverns in one. Five days a week, it was a typical hometown tavern with a steady, multi-generational and eclectic clientele. On Friday and Saturday nights in the summer, it morphed into one of the most popular gathering spots in the county. A key element in this draw was the Black band known as Wilmer and the Dukes. The result was described below in the article comparing everyone's favorite staid, charming New England-like village to Fort Lauderdale.

While a three story building, only the first floor was used as the Pittsford Inn. Little is known regarding the use of the upper two floors during this era. One floor contained the ballroom with the spring-supported floor. Larry the barkeep purportedly had an apartment upstairs and from time to time, a busboy/dishwasher would receive a room as partial compensation for his employment. The action was in the ground floor pub.

So…what's wrong with Fort Lauderdale? "Spring break" has meant a bacchanalia in Florida for generations of college students attending schools in cold climates. In the early 1960's, the popular movie <u>Where the Boys Are</u> caused the southeast coastal city of Fort Lauderdale to become the epicenter of this nonstop drunken revelry. Each March, local papers described the antics of the droves of college students who descended on this otherwise peaceful retirement community. Headlines declared the newest variation of drinking game or provided the running count of the number of students arrested for drunk and disorderly behavior. Each year local officials declared a firm intention to "clamp down" on the rowdies as the week wore on and pool "dives" from balconies and roofs became fatalities. "Fort Lauderdale" became synonymous with the raucous, out-of-control party scene.

Brighton-Pittsford Post

"The Comets, a four piece rock 'n' roll band, wearily filed out of the Pittsford Inn early yesterday and with them went about 300 college youngsters who, some village residents claim, turn Pittsford into a Fort Lauderdale.

Carefully watching the exodus were at least five sheriff's deputies, assigned to the South Main restaurant because citizens and a merchant's association charged recent "rowdyism" in the village stemmed from beer drinking youths having a last fling before returning to school.

In a closed meeting Thursday, the board of directors of the Pittsford Businessmen's Association drafted a resolution asking the sheriff's office and the district attorney's office for "strenuous action" to halt alleged vandalism, littering with beer cans, excessive noise and "immoral" activities.....

Outside, the deputies concerned themselves with stopping persons leaving with beer bottles and checking ages. Throughout the evening there was no indication of violence.

During most of the session two Pittsford Inn employees stood outside the main entrance and asked the more youthful-looking patrons for proof of age. At a dining room door two more sentries prevented youngsters from leaving with glasses and bottles.....

Several neighborhood residents stood outside the inn during the early part of the evening. Asked why, they said they were merely 'interested' or 'amused'.

The inn's proprietor, William Lisi, 18 East Park Road, Pittsford, served principally as liaison between waiters and door checkers and the deputies outside. Officers were not stationed inside the building.

Lisi, who has charged that others besides patrons of the inn have been responsible for much of the village's trouble, denied that beer cans littering stems from his restaurant. He said the inn doesn't sell beer in cans."

The "sentry" (Mike Keating, aka The Senator) charged with checking proof of age of the "more youthful-looking" patrons was, in fact a tad youthful himself. Senator began working at the Inn checking proof of age when he was sixteen. He tried to be discrete in his admission strategies but it was generally assumed that as long as you were a friend of The Senator's and "in your eighteenth year", that was close enough. He was wise enough to understand that if he allowed all of his under-age acquaintances to be admitted, knowledge of such a wide spread caper would become generally known and foil the system.

The band that prompted the overflow crowds at the PI was not The Comets but rather "Wilmer and The Dukes". Lead singer Wilmer was a tall, lean African-American with far more talent than any live band appearing in the area. The band played mostly their rendition of current Top 50 hits but always played an inspired interpretation of Blue Skies...."Nothin but blue sky's from now on". Wilmer played primarily in the greater Rochester area and the Pittsford Inn was a regular venue during the summer.

The PI had two doors; both on Main Street. The main entrance to the tavern was located on the south end of the building and was open all week during business hours. The other was unlocked and operational only when Wilmer and The Dukes were playing and was located at the north end of the building off of the "dining room". The latter became the dance floor on such occasions.

Over the summer, <u>The Brighton-Pittsford Post</u> published an extended editorial battle between those demanding that the Pittsford Inn be permanently shuttered to drive out the undesirable elements and those who found the activities amusing and innocuous. As is so often the case, the more rabid contributors were trying to return the village to the image of a Norman Rockwell painting.

It's not quite like remembering where you were when JFK was shot, but loyal patrons of the Pittsford Inn do recall that fateful Saturday in the summer of 1963. When asked by a customer if anyone had been injured in the previous night's fire at the Pittsford Inn, a gas station attendant reportedly responded "no, thankfully nobody was hurt...the fire occurred two hours after closing". Then he corrected himself and said: "oh except the nigger who lived upstairs". When asked how badly the resident busboy was injured, he replied... "Oh he's dead."

By 1963 we had not come very far since Red Jacket's speech of 1822, or Frederick Baily's beating at the hands of Edward Covey in 1835. Nor had we come very far since the zealous pursuit of escaped southern slaves seeking their freedom via one of Pittsford's busy Underground Railroad stations one hundred years earlier. In the simple, pithy words of Rodney King after the Los Angeles Race Riots that claimed 52 deaths and 3000 wounded..."Can't we all just get along?" Apparently not in 1963. It should not have been a surprise that twelve months later, in July of 1964, the first "race riots" of the modern civil rights movement erupted in nearby Rochester.

The early morning fire that ruined major parts of the PI kitchen in August of 1963 prompted the demise of this historical local drinking establishment. It was more than a place to have your first legal drink at age 18 (the legal minimum age at the time) but a true social institution; a place where "hanging around was an old custom". If they moved with a great sense of purpose, high school seniors with "early birthdays", could dash to the PI for a VERY quick burger and beer at lunch and be back listening to a history lecture for the first afternoon class period. But, for most local youth, the summer immediately following high school graduation represented their first legal welcome to the Pittsford Inn.

The "PI" never re-emerged as a drinking establishment. The property was purchased by Andrew Wolfe, Owner and Publisher of the venerable <u>Brighton-Pittsford Post</u> and reconfigured as an office building to house the newspaper's offices. If it had been "restored" consistent with its proud history, it would have returned as a hotel, eatery and saloon. Imagine the structure's frustration at being dressed as an office building while its heart and soul are that of a raucous public house. Surely its walls have not been witness to nearly as many poignant memories in the last forty-five years as in its initial one hundred and sixty.

Conspiracy theorists are inclined to assign responsibility for the decline and fall of the Pittsford Inn to Andrew Wolfe. <u>The Brighton-Pittsford Post</u> was hardly unbiased in its coverage of the Pittsford Inn's contribution to the village's transition to a raucous, bawdy Northern version of spring break in "Fort Lauderdale". Others contend Wolfe's prompt purchase of the building and reincarnation as the Phoenix Building was simply coincidental.

34

Medals From the President

"Our dad, he was a gentle man
When we all worked at the store
The only time I ever saw him mad
Was when he talked about the war
We lost a boy at Belleau Wood[12], and
I guess he never really understood
What the medals from the President were for"

Lyrics from <u>Oldest Living Son</u> by John Stewart
(The singer/songwriter; not Daily Show host)

The boundaries of Pleasant Valley, Big Spring and Pittsford, New York evolved from a long series of geopolitical events. Over the centuries, the native sons of the area have been called upon to defend and protect their homeland. This "homeland" was originally the boundaries of the Seneca Nation.

Seneca braves were responsible for not only guarding the lands of the Seneca Nation in the Genesee River Valley but protecting the entire Iroquois Confederacy that occupied most of what is now central and western New York State. They were inculcated from early childhood to embrace their role as hunter, fisherman and, most importantly, proud and capable warrior. Fighting to defend native lands was not a matter of choice; brave warrior was the only acceptable identity for male members of the Seneca Nation.

Indigenous people from adjoining territories coveted the area's abundance of natural resources and were occasionally willing to use force to gain control and expand the boundaries of the land they controlled. After repeated attempts by these invaders failed, the French swept in from what is now Canada to try their hand at displacing the Seneca. They too were repelled.

---

[12] WW 1 Battle of Belleau Wood, near Chateau-Thierry, France

Only when they were overrun by vastly greater numbers and superior weaponry in the Sullivan Campaign were the mighty Seneca defeated. Generals Sullivan and Clinton laid waste to fifty Iroquois villages at the direction of (then) General George Washington. Much of this devastation was wrought on the Seneca settlements in the Genesee Valley; no doubt including the villages of Anjagen at or near Pittsford and the capital of Ganonagan located near present day Victor, New York. The resulting loss of life, property and livestock was the death knell of the Iroquois Confederacy.

After the Seneca were forced to relocate to reservations, newly arrived pioneers from New England continued the tradition of regularly sending their young men off to war. Local volunteer militias were mustered to deter the British Fleet from landing and establishing a Lake Ontario beachhead at Charlotte in the War of 1812. As the young nation struggled to ultimately define and defend itself, soldiers from Big Spring willingly enlisted to protect the broader boundaries of an emerging nation. The same sense of duty compelled the youth of subsequent generations to take up arms in the Civil War and the great World Wars of the twentieth century.

Nations choose to go to war. Individual soldiers/warriors participated because of long-nurtured cultural mores, a sense of duty and a powerful instinct to protect their homeland and people. Despite these intense internal forces, the individual decision to volunteer to fight a war can not always be an easy one. Yet history is replete with examples of young men eager to fight for their homeland.

Among the young men who gathered to fraternize in the village center in the first decades of the 20th century were Henry Miller and Homer Rayson. Paul Spiegel described the village's contribution to the war's efforts in his <u>Pittsford Scrapbook, Volume Two</u>, as ... "hundreds of its young men went into uniform". Some of these young soldiers are shown in his moving photographs. The inscriptions reveal many of the well known surnames associated with the earliest history of the village; among them: Schoen, Bacon, Stone, Spiegel and Zornow. Pittsford lost two men in World War l; Homer Rayson and Henry L. Miller. Pittsford's American Legion Post 899 is named Rayson-Miller Post in their honor.

The hoards massed to enlist after Pearl Harbor was attacked. This was to be the "war to end all wars". Eight of Pittsford's boys did not return. Among the dead was Bruce Rylott, son of Pierce and Laura Rylott of South Street in the Village. He was killed in Guam while operating an amphibious tank. His brother Pierce was an infantry soldier in the same assault.

Another casualty was University of Rochester pre-med student Alexander "Sandy" Allen who was killed when the bomber he was navigating was shot down over Italy. He was the son of Dr. Lloyd Allen and his wife Hazel Allen.

These were brave men. Like Seneca warriors, they had an incredible support network that applauded and encouraged their innate patriotism. The returning heroes were greeted by proud parents, parades and swooning females.

The Genesee Valley also sent its young men to fight in what would become America's first broadly unpopular war. The Vietnamese called it the American War. The American's called it the Vietnam War. Republicans called it the Kennedy-Johnson War. Regardless of what you called it, the Vietnam War was a very different "conflict". It was the singular defining event of the 1960's. The threat and likelihood of being drafted to "serve" hung ominously over the heads of draft-eligible males; conscripted to fight, kill or be killed in the jungles of Southeast Asia for the vaguely defined purpose of ceasing the spread of communism throughout the region. Few volunteered.

Many were tormented by self-doubt. Why did they not have the same conviction of their patriotic fathers, uncles and grandfathers who had been eager to take up arms in defense of their homeland? Were they cowards?

An inscription on a cigarette lighter carried by an American GI in Vietnam captured the feelings of many of the nation's young people at the time. It read...

The Unwilling
Led by the unqualified
Doing the unnecessary
For the ungrateful

Maybe Cassius Clay (aka Muhammad Ali) said it best..."I ain't got no quarrel with those Viet Cong". He had few allies at the time.

Blind patriotism died with the Vietnam War. No parades or swooning females greeted returning Vietnam veterans. To many, the main emotion was relief; relief that they had survived their thirteen months of "duty" and could now get on with their lives. Most vets did not return home with great pride in saving Southeast Asia from the Communists; the "domino theory" was as bogus as the weapons of mass destruction in Iraq. For some, perhaps many, it was thirteen months of crossing days off a calendar, keeping their head down and hoping that the guy who "had their back" hadn't succumbed to the temptation to dull his senses by smoking the ubiquitous weed.

On January 2, 1969 Mel Morgan died in Vietnam. He was in the Pittsford Central School Class of 1964. He was one of four Pittsford boys/men who died in Vietnam.

In April 2005, the united Vietnamese people celebrated the 30th anniversary of the end of the "American War". One of the American visitors to that country three decades after the last military helicopter lifted the remaining Americans and American sympathizers from the roof of the U.S. Embassy in Saigon was interviewed by Public Radio International. He stated that "while our troops failed to defeat communist forces in the country, at every turn it is clear that good old fashioned Capitalism is evident throughout the country".

In the concluding few pages of Michael Archer's book <u>A Patch of Ground, Khe Sanh Remembered</u> he reflects on his discouraging conclusions upon returning home.

> *"My experiences in South Vietnam, as much as I disliked thinking about it, had convinced me that both time and history were on the side of the enemy. However optimistic the daily Pentagon news briefing may have sounded, it was not going to change the outcome of things. Five hundred years before the first westerners arrived in Southeast Asia, the Vietnamese General Tran Hung Dao defeated the vastly superior Mongol invasion force of Kublai Khan by employing a strategy of not defending prestige positions. The General later wrote: 'When the enemy is away from home for a long time and produces no victories, and families learn of their dead, then the enemy population becomes dissatisfied... Time is always in our favor. Our climate, our mountains and jungles, discourage the enemy...' It sometimes seemed to me that the only way to avoid defeat in Vietnam was to fight on forever."*

On the BIG decisions (like making war), perhaps having a former General as President holds substantial merit. General Eisenhower admonished "Don't ever fight a ground war in Southeast Asia". He clearly read his military history. It appears that the military strategy of the Vietnamese had not changed in FIVE HUNDRED YEARS! Nobody listened to him.

General Westmoreland, commander of U.S. forces in Vietnam, died in 2005. Not long before, he declared "We won the Vietnam War!" which was, indeed, news to nearly everyone. He suggested that Americans should look at Vietnam today and take pride that we stopped the "domino" of communism in the region and that free enterprise and capitalism was flourishing.

In the final analysis General Tran Hung Dao, General Eisenhower and enlisted man Michael Archer were right. Time, climate and terrain were in favor of the enemy; we should never have fought a ground war in Southeast Asia when the only way to avoid defeat was to fight forever.

What about those who failed to return from Vietnam? Their friends could only weigh their grief against a hollow sense of the "contribution" made by their war heroes in defeating tyranny. A "defeat" that would prove to be temporary. What do we say to Mel Morgan's family, friends and mother?

A mother's grief is universal. The vague notion of defending liberty, or stopping the advancing armies of General Sullivan or Nazi fanatics or preventing the "domino effect" in Southeast Asia does not mitigate the pain of a mother who will never again hold her son in her arms.

The village sent thirty one soldiers to fight in the Civil War. Nineteen returned to their farms after the war. Twelve were lost.

Since then Pittsford's fallen sons include:

WW 1	**WW ll**
Homer Rayson	Bruce Rylott
Henry Miller	Edgar Rowland
Korean War	Lloyd Thornell
Robert Baumer	Robert Patchen
Vietnam	Nicolas Commisso
John Gresens	William Briggs
Michael Lawton	Ferdinand Ballieul
Melvin Morgan	Alexander "Sandy" Allen
Elton Perrine	**Operation Iraqi Freedom**
	Kevin Mowl

The Raysons, Millers, Rylotts, Allens, Mowls and Morgans can only imagine how their brave sons might have affected the shaping of the community, the Genesee Valley and the world had they returned home safely. What do we say to the friends and family of Pittsford's Kevin S. Mowl who succumbed on February 25, 2008 from wounds sustained in August of 2007 when his vehicle was struck by a makeshift bomb while patrolling in Iraq?

The first grieving mothers of Big Spring were here long before the Raysons, Millers, Morgans et al. In terms of the shear magnitude of bloodshed, the 1779 Sullivan Campaign's impact on the mothers of Big Spring/Pittsford was without equal. Hundreds of local Seneca mothers lost sons as a result of General Washington's mandate calling for "total destruction and devastation" throughout the lands of the

Seneca. Pleasant Valley's second highest body count was ninety-two years earlier. Eighty-five Seneca warriors were lost to French General DeNonville's army before he was forced to retreat.

These comparative statistics mean nothing to the twenty-eight mothers of the Pittsford war heroes killed in action since the beginning of the Civil War. They mourn their own flesh and blood.

Many of the survivors "never really understood what the medals from the President were for".

35

The Iroquois Today

Red Jacket's memory lives on. Perhaps Buffalo, New York needed a local hero to immortalize and they found such in the Seneca Chief. The Buffalo Historical Society displays a painting of the peerless orator and visionary wearing the silver medal awarded to him by President George Washington. The original medal is also on display in their museum. Few visiting school children fathom the magnitude of Red Jacket's pride as the President placed it around his neck.

His memory is also retained in the Red Jacket Dormitory complex at the University of Buffalo, the clipper ship Red Jacket (which holds the speed record between New York and Liverpool, England) and Ontario County's Red Jacket School District. Perhaps he is Buffalo's real "native" son? Or...perhaps he who "keeps them awake" continues to disturb the dreams of contemporary Seneca who ponder the multitude of "what ifs".

Despite his final wishes that no white man would bury his remains, the Buffalo Historical Society announced in 1984 their plan to exhume Red Jacket from his chosen final resting spot on the Buffalo Creek Reservation and rebury him at Buffalo's Forest Lawn Cemetery. He who "Keeps them Awake" (Segoyewatha) now lies there with other Seneca Chiefs under a statue of his likeness.

In 1989, one Director of the Buffalo Historical Society was quoted as stating:

> "Why attempt to civilize the Indians, or ameliorate their supposed condition? Only teach them with the strong hand of power to fear our superior race and let them alone in their rapid decay, until like the bison of the western prairies they are obliterated from the earth, as one of the ancient, traditional races of men".

Yes, that declaration was made in 1989. Perhaps this "director" had a preference for white history.

Decisions made two hundred and thirty years ago continue to dictate the fate of the surviving members of the Iroquois Confederacy. Estimates of the contemporary population of Iroquois vary dramatically. The high end of the range is 40,000 to 60,000 living in the U.S. and a similar number residing in Canada. The most dependable census declared a total 29,000 living members.

Those who chose to ally with the British at the outbreak of the Revolutionary War, were offered refuge in British Canada. Accordingly, members of the Mohawk and Cayuga tribes continue to reside in Ontario and Quebec. As of the 2001 census, the Six Nations of the Grand River, near Brantford, Ontario contained 21,474 inhabitants and was the largest reservation in Canada. While the initial migration included mainly Brant's Mohawks, they were soon followed by members of each of the six member tribes of the Iroquois Confederacy plus a band of Delaware. The Seneca Nation is represented by both the Konadaha and Niharondasa tribes. The governing body of the Six Nations continues to preside in the tribal council of chiefs but a titular elected council exists simultaneously to satisfy the requirements of the government of Canada.

The Oneida migrated to Green Bay, Wisconsin. The Onondaga and Tuscarora remain mostly in western New York State.

About one-third of the surviving Iroquois are Seneca. These 10,000 members live mostly in western New York near Buffalo on the Allegheny, Cattaraugus, Tonawanda and Oil Springs Reservations. Some descendants joined Joseph Brant's Mohawks at the Six Nations Reservation near Brantford, Ontario. A relatively small number of Seneca-Cayuga continue to live near Miami, Oklahoma.

Integration into contemporary American and Canadian societies has been a significant challenge for members of the Iroquois Nation. A small number have succeeded in adopting western cultural mores and been fully absorbed by the prevailing socio-economic system. Some Mohawk men carved a niche for themselves as courageous, highly-skilled steel workers on high-rise construction projects. These brave souls walked narrow steel beams, thousands of feet above the ground, without safety harnesses, on landmark structures including the Empire State Building, the World Trade Center, R.C.A. Building, Chrysler Building, Waldorf-Astoria Hotel and the Golden Gate Bridge. When the bridge and high-rise building construction was at its peak, hundreds of Mohawk steelworkers migrated from one construction site to the next and lived in close-knit communities in close proximity to the construction sites. At one time nearly eight hundred Mohawk steelworkers lived in an enclave in Brooklyn called North Gowanus.

But there are few examples of large-scale traditional measures of success. For many and perhaps most, this once proud, independent, self-sufficient society has not succeeded in its attempts of acculturation with the "new" North Americans.

For at least five hundred years, children of the Iroquois Confederacy were inculcated with the virtues of independence, responsibility and community service. But prejudice, racism and bigotry deterred many from venturing beyond the boundaries of their reservations. Those who were the most proud and independent resisted integration with the greatest vigor and endured the greatest indignities; indignities of dependence, public assistance programs and the most debilitating... unemployment.

So confined on reservations, with little commerce or industry and a corresponding paucity of employment opportunities, reservation life offered little opportunity to sustain ones self-esteem. The resultant high unemployment rates, alcoholism, mental illness, prevalent petty crime and destitution are not a surprise.

Prejudice, racism and bigotry were not the sole providence of the Anglo Saxon settlers. Red Jacket's speech in 1822 offered a glimpse of where the Black man fared on his scale of respect...

"And I say that it is a fact, that whenever you find a tribe of Indians that have been 'christionized' and have changed their custom or habit, which the Great good Spirit gave them, you will see that they are a poor, worthless, lying, ragged, miserable and degraded set of beings; and instead of becoming white men, as they expected to have become by changing their customs and habits, they have formed connections with the blacks, and have become black men in their actions and conduct. I say, therefore, that the Great Spirit will not suffer his Red Children to change their religion or custom. But when they attempt to do it punishes them by turning them into Black Men".

Much of the economic success enjoyed by the Iroquois Confederacy in the last century has been a result of the Confederacy's status as an independent nation within the United States. Some of these opportunities are a result of the precedence established by Cornplanter when he successfully protested the tax bill levied on his Cornplanter Tract. This established the basis for a tax-free Indian Nation. Early Seneca entrepreneurs recognized an opportunity and established commercial ventures focusing on the sale of highly taxed consumer goods; mainly gasoline and cigarettes. Without the burden of heavy federal and state taxes, the Iroquois could reduce their selling price well below that charged by tax paying retailers and still reap a handsome profit.

Ironically, the most substantial economic opportunity afforded the Iroquois Confederacy in the last fifty years occurred as a result of individual state's pressing need for additional tax revenues to help offset the huge financial burden of publicly funding the Indian reservation system. These budget shortfalls occurred at the same time that the states were attempting to balance the conflicting needs of their voters as it related to gambling. A significant number of constituents strongly desired access to local gambling while their equally vocal opposition preferred to keep gambling solely in Nevada and New Jersey.

Many states reached, what they considered, a perfect compromise by allowing gambling but only on Indian lands. This satisfied the desires of gamblers and those intent on reducing the cost of public assistance programs. They appeased both constituencies while confining gambling activity to a well-defined geographical area within the reservations. At the same time, they provided a lucrative commercial venture for the hosting tribes who were eager to recapture a sense of dignity in its members by providing jobs. It began with dingy school cafeterias doubling as Bingo Halls in the mid-twentieth century. Within fifty years, gambling activities expanded to include a vast string of profitable casinos that challenged the gaudiest of establishments in Las Vegas or Atlantic City; offering big name entertainment heretofore available only in large metropolitan areas. The Seneca Nation built three casinos on their hunting grounds; the largest consisting of the renovation of the Convention Center at Niagara Falls, New York in 2002.

Red Jacket would be chagrined to learn that Christianity continues its hold on the Iroquois. Contemporary Iroquois are split between followers of various Christian denominations and those that cling to the teachings of Handsome Lake's Longhouse Religion. It is estimated that 20,000 of the surviving 29,000 Iroquois remain in the reservation system today. Twenty five percent of those people are "Handsome Lakers" – IE follow Gaiwiio; the teachings of Handsome Lake or "the good word" of the prophet. Even among his followers, there is not a parochial insistence on strict adherence exclusively to the Gaiwiio. Some spiritual souls keep very busy practicing their faith by participating in all the Handsome Lake rituals but also attend Christian services and celebrate traditional Christian holidays. The center of the Handsome Lake religion is the Seneca reservation at Tonawanda, New York.

Is it singularly quixotic to imagine a sovereign Seneca Nation occupying western New York State in the 21st century? Such a nation could legally exist. If just one or two of the aforementioned series of seminal events had taken a slightly different turn, the Iroquois Confederacy easily could have allied themselves with the Colonists in the Revolutionary War. If that had occurred, presumably President George ("I cannot tell a lie") Washington would have felt compelled to honor and respect the considerable sacrifice of the indigenous people and unequivocally declare in the Treaty of Canandaigua that the lands of the Seneca would never become part of the new United States. It is reasonable to speculate that he would have not been inclined to add the final caveat stating that the Seneca could always decide on their own volition to sell their lands to the white man. The greater challenge perhaps would have been dropped in the laps of Washington's long line of successors who would have been challenged to honor that commitment while faced with the groundswell of momentum for manifest destiny.

Few successful models exist of native people effectively isolating themselves from the encroaching Anglo-Saxon masses and retaining major elements of their traditional lifestyle, culture and independence. American Indians of the Southwest serve as hunting and fishing guides on ancestral lands. They proudly lead visitors on tours of the fascinating ruins of their forefathers but it is clearly a stretch to describe these activities as living-off-the-land.

A significant number of the 22,000 Yup'ik people of Alaska continue to live independently on the rich indigenous resources of the lands first settled by their ancestors 10,000 years ago. Like their forefathers who crossed the land bridge from Asia, they are dependent for their sustenance almost exclusively on harvesting seals, walrus and fish from their homeland and its adjoining seas. Wild berries picked by Yup'ik women in the short summers provide modest variety to their protein-rich diet.

If the Yup'ik people represent the best (perhaps only) example of indigenous people managing to avoid acculturation and retain their independence, it is important to consider what factors might have facilitated that condition. Perhaps they simply have a greater reserve of fortitude to stave off the perceived corrupting influences of modern society? More likely, they clung to a piece of ground that had few alternate commercial uses, a hostile climate and, accordingly, was not coveted by the white man.

Could a Seneca nation state have continued to exist in western New York? The size of the region is comparable to many smaller nations. Geographically the boundary of the Seneca Nation outlined in the Treaty of Canandaigua is about the same size as Israel. Border security would have been less challenging than the U.S. border with Canada and Mexico. Natural geological features clearly define three of its four sides. The Genesee River on the East, Lake Ontario on the North and the Niagara River and Lake Erie delineate most of the western border. Only the southern border with Pennsylvania is less well-defined.

Would there have been the resources to feed, cloth and house a growing population? Available natural resources would not have been a deterrent. The Seneca managed to prosper on this land for at least five hundred prior years. Barring pestilence or natural disaster, the rich fish and wildlife resources would have continued to thrive and provide ample sustenance. The white man has continued to harvest bountiful crops from the legendary fertile soil. Surely the Seneca's "three sisters" of corn, beans and squash could have continued to sustain the native population. Only if...?

The bones of Cornplanter and Handsome Lake lay silently overlooking the waters of Kinzua Lake; the reservoir that covers the former Cornplanter Tract. They are spared the audible assault of man-made sounds emanating from the Seneca Casinos. The "ka-ching" of the slot machines, the high decibel din of crowd noise and the ear-splitting bell that announces "another $100 winner" represents the remaining tenuous thread of self-sufficiency, dependable employment and dignity for the once proud "Keepers of the Western Door".

36

Century Farms

For three-quarters of the two hundred years that the white man dominated Pleasant Valley, the bounty of the area's farms was the economic lifeblood of the area. Those not working directly on farms, were involved in the wholesaling, transportation or processing of agricultural output. Those charged with earning the family paycheck either owned a farm, worked on a farm, transported grain to Pittsford Milling Company or apples to Schoen Brothers Apple Drying or pickles to L. C. Forman's or ash to the ashery or beans to Ted Zornow's or flour to the Erie Canal barges. Or... they may have worked at Forman's Pickle Factory or R.T. French Mustard processing and bottling piccalilli or "cream style" mustard.

Before Pittsford attracted the Rochester affluent in their flight to the suburbs, the village's commercial enterprises were likewise dependent on local agricultural income. Spiegel's Blacksmith & Wagon Shop, Wiltsie and Crump's General Store and the tavern at the Phoenix Hotel needed farm dollars circulating through their cash registers in order to survive and prosper.

While no longer the dominant driver of the local economy, area farms continue to be an integral ingredient in the unique mix of urban village/suburban/family farm that makes up the "charm" regularly ascribed to the Pittsford area. Many of these farms have been passed from father to child to grandchild to great grandchild; some for seven or eight generations.

When recently minted MBA's are awarded six figure salaries and "signing bonuses" it is understandable why many young people considered alternate careers over becoming the seventh generation of Hopkins, Lusk or Knickerbocker to run the family farm. Despite the familial push and genetic pull to perpetuate the family farm legacy, succeeding generations have had to weigh the long hours and exhausting physical labor against the uncertain monetary rewards that were often times adversely affected by uncontrollable weather, erratic consumer taste and the vagaries of farm commodity prices.

An additional complicating factor came into play in recent decades. The long-standing desirability of a Pittsford address resulted in strong demand for the area's residential property. As land close to the village became scarce, prices steadily rose and provided local farmers the sometimes irresistible temptation to attain financial security by succumbing to the constant solicitations by "developers" wishing to purchase their farms and build homes.

There were similarities between the area's original white settlers and the twentieth century "white flight" to the suburbs. Both were an adventuresome lot seeking a better life with more space between neighbors. Both pushed the native people from their homelands; be they Seneca or farm families. The earlier settlers bushwhacked their way here behind a team of oxen from New England; the latter escaped to the expansive lawns of the suburbs in their station wagons and then SUV's. The resounding difference was that the latter version of carpet-baggers paid handsomely for the properties and encouraged the former owners to remain on a small portion of their homesteads to live peacefully among the newcomers.

Pleasant Valley (Monroe County) remains a stalwart among other "aggie" counties in New York State. Of the 62 counties in the state, the value of crops produced in Monroe County ranks fifth. The area was ranked fourth in the category of "vegetables, melons, potatoes and sweet potatoes". Total farm revenue in the county in 2002 was $54 million. While agriculture was an integral part of the defining heritage of the area, this sector's economic impact was dwarfed by other industries. Kodak's annual $10 billion in revenues was nearly 200 times the $54 million in combined total sales of all farms in the county.

Early this century the U.S. Department of Agriculture reported that there were 631 farms in Monroe County. On average, these farms were 169 acres in size and generated about $54,000 in annual revenues. Thirty percent of farm operators in the county describe farming as their secondary profession. Many others find second careers during the long winters; some run dependable snow removal businesses. Plowing snow has been described as the "perfect fit" with the seasonal nature of Upstate New York farming. When the snow drifts are too high to see over, there is not much farming going on and driveways are clogged.

Eighty five percent of the county's farm revenues come from crops and nearly a quarter of those crops are categorized as "nursery, greenhouse, floriculture and sod"; recall Pleasant Valley's days known as "The Flower City". The remaining fifteen percent of sales are in livestock and poultry and the milk, cheese and eggs that they produce.

An accurate description of Pleasant Valley's business of agriculture needs to address both land use and revenue dollars as they yield two distinctly different portraits. Dollars are what pay the mortgage, farm wages and operating expenses so are of paramount importance to farm families. The casual observer biking or driving through the abundant, bucolic acreage that surrounds much of the village will draw a far different conclusion as to the relative importance of various agricultural products.

Sixty percent of the total dollar value of all crops grown in the county is in the category fruits, nuts, berries, vegetables, melons, potatoes and sweet potatoes; twenty percent are in nursery and greenhouse products and the remaining twenty percent are grains and beans. Grains consist mainly of feed corn and wheat. Beans are mostly kidney and soybeans.

Revenue dollars per acre vary dramatically by crop. While fruits and vegetables generate sixty percent of the sales dollars, only twenty percent of the farmland in the county is allotted to growing this produce. The lower dollar yielding crops of wheat, feed corn and soybeans take up fully seventy percent of the available agricultural land. The remaining ten percent is dedicated to pasture and production of hay.

The New York State Agricultural Society recognizes farms that have remained in the same family for 100 years by designating them as "Century Farms". Six such farms have been recognized in Monroe County; three of these are in Pittsford and two of these continue to be farmed by descendants of the original owners. The three Pittsford "Century Farms" are owned by the Lusk, Hopkins and Knickerbocker pioneer families.

The Lusk Farm

The oldest is The Lusk Farm. It was started by Stephen Lusk in 1806. Stephen was the son of John Lusk, the first white settler in Pleasant Valley. The farm was located at the south edge of the village where Mendon Center Road and South Main Street intersect. Number One Mendon Center Road operated continuously as a farm under succeeding generations of Lusks until 1992 when it was sold to settle the estate of Harry Lusk; the sixth generation of Lusk to farm the land.

The Lusk Farm was 140 acres and, for its last fifty years, was exclusively dedicated to a dairy operation. Twenty acres were allotted to pasture; the remaining land was used to grow hay and feed corn to support the herd. The last Lusk to run the farm was Harry A. (Hal) Lusk;

the seventh generation to do so. Towards the end of the last century, Hal's son Jeremy worked beside his father; the eighth generation to milk Lusk family cows.

The Town of Pittsford clearly recognized the significance of the possibility that the Lusk Family Farm might be "developed" into residential housing. In an attempt to retain the unique village/suburban/ family farm mix of the town that defines its "charm", they created a program that allowed the town to purchase future development rights and place the farm in an agricultural conservation easement. This would assure that the farm would be used only for agriculture in perpetuity. In exchange for assigning these rights, it was proposed that the Lusks would receive monetary remuneration <u>and</u> retain the right to continue to operate the family farm. Under the proposed agreement, the original owners would also retain the option of selling the farm to a third party as long as they and all subsequent buyers understood and agreed that the farm could henceforth only be used for farming; not housing.

Hal and Jeremy Lusk were in favor of the town's proposal to permanently preserve the farm but one lone heir to the estate stubbornly disagreed. As a result of the impasse, the farm was sold to developers and now has a herd of predictably boring three bedroom/two bath ranch style homes plying its gentle slopes.

After selling the farm, Hal Lusk bought land near Canandaigua where he grew hay until 2007. The hay was deemed of such high quality that it was hauled to New York's Central Park to nourish the city's carriage horses.

Hal can still be seen occasionally manning a tractor on area farms. In the winter he plows snow for sixty neighbors. When it's not snowing in the winter, he has the time to reflect on the struggles of his great-great- great- great- great- great-great grandfather John Lusk as he and his son Stephen bushwhacked their way from Berkshire County, Massachusetts in 1789. Their only neighbors in this western frontier were members of the local Seneca Nation who were quite accustomed to waiting until spring for the snow to melt.

The Hopkins Farm

War hero and highly respected Town Supervisor Caleb Hopkins' farm is the second oldest Century Farm in Pittsford. Colonel Hopkins was fresh from commanding the 52nd Regiment of Northfield in the War of 1812 when he purchased the land at 3151 Clover Street from Phelps and Gorham in 1812.

George Washington inherited ten slaves and five hundred acres when he was eleven years old. At the time of his death, his will stipulated that all of his 316 slaves would be set free upon the death of his wife Martha. Washington also provided for the care and education of some of his younger slaves as well as financial support for elderly slaves who had been loyal to him.

Thomas Jefferson inherited slaves from both his father and father-in-law. During his lifetime, typically two hundred slaves were working on his estates. He was less magnanimous than Washington, freeing just two slaves in his lifetime and five upon his death.

Both Washington and Jefferson were purported to have fathered children of slaves. Jefferson's relationship with Sally Hemmings is well documented. All seven of the slaves he freed were from the Hemmings family. There is strong oral history to support that West Ford was fathered by Washington but no DNA analysis to prove paternity.

Caleb Hopkins also owned slaves. He bought thirteen-year old Titus Lord in Canandaigua in 1813 presumably to help on his new Clover Street farm. Consistent with the liberal leanings of Pleasant Valley, Hopkins sent Titus Lord to integrate the local school. In 1815, he purchased a second ten-year old slave boy to work on the farm.

In 1814, Caleb was asked to re-name the village. The original District of Northfield had been incorporated in 1796, the name changed to Boyle in 1808 and changed again to Smallwood in 1813. At the time, the village was to be divided once again and was in need of a moniker with staying power. Caleb suggested the name of his original home in Vermont, a village called Pittsford.

At the time Caleb Hopkins established his Clover Street farm, conventional wisdom held that it was prudent to designate twenty percent of one's farmland to remain as woodlot to allow for a perpetual supply of firewood, timbers and framing lumber for homes, barns, outbuildings and fencing material. After designating the recommended acreage to woodlot, Caleb discovered a separate twenty five acre stand of particularly noble virgin timber in another section of his new farm. He decided to preserve this small forest as well. Caleb's wish was passed to subsequent generations and today, nearly two centuries later, the twenty-five acres of old growth forest remains as an element of his legacy. It now contains what are believed to be the oldest living trees in western New York State. Two hundred year old giant maples cast long shadows over adjoining fields of wheat, corn, soybeans and oats.

The Hopkins farm is one of two remaining Century Farms that are run by descendents of the original families. The patriarch of the farm is John Hopkins (Pittsford Central School Class of 1942). In addition to keeping the farm solvent through sixty years, John's legacy will be his foresight and generosity in assuring that the farm will be forever dedicated to agriculture and never be plundered by housing developers. In May of 1999, John Hopkins sold the rights for further development to the Town of Pittsford and the property was placed in a permanent agricultural conservation easement. Cookie cutter tract homes will never replace the Caleb Hopkins maples or fields of corn, grain and beans.

According to the American Farmland Trust, our country loses an acre of farmland every minute. The Hopkins Farm will never be part of that statistic.

The Hopkins Farm is now run by Mark Greene. Mark is the nephew of John Hopkins and the sixth generation of Hopkins farmers. John Hopkins, Mark, his wife Lynn, their children and grandchildren continue to reside on and farm the property. If the latter perpetuate Caleb's legacy, as they are likely to do, they will be the eighth generation to farm the land.

Not unlike the Haloid Company, Kodak, Bausch and Lomb or Wegman's, the farm community of Pittsford has had to regularly re-invent itself in order to survive and prosper. Unusually heavy rains or extended periods of drought are the challenges that every farmer must learn to meet. In order to thrive however, succeeding generations have had to adapt their mix of farm products and services to the constantly changing competitive landscape and the vagaries of the market place.

The Hopkins Farm is a study in market adaptation. While continuing to produce high quality wheat, corn, oats and soybeans, they have diversified by adding fresh fruits and vegetables. They have vertically integrated to operate a farm stand on their property selling fresh sweet corn, vegetables and sunflowers to the local community. They also grow and sell unique seed crops; an additional specialized niche.

In order to add further diversity to their business, the Hopkins Farm is one of a few farms that partner with Cornell University in agricultural research. Cornell researchers develop new hybrid grains bioengineered to increase yields or perform under varying climatic conditions. They supply these experimental seed varieties to the Hopkins Farm and monitor planting, growing and harvesting practices to assure against adulteration of the test samples.

The Knickerbocker Farm

From the time of its opening in 1825 until the commercialization of the internal combustion engine a century later, barges on the Erie Canal depended on mule power to traverse its length. Entrepreneurs were awarded concessions to provide teams of fresh mules at designated points. Mule barns sprang up along the canal's length. Exhausted animals were exchanged for rested mules and after a few days of rest, the teams were harnessed to a barge heading back in the direction of the mule's home barn.

During the early years of the canal, George Knickerbocker managed the mule barn concession in Newark (Wayne County). In addition to the barges that carried the areas agricultural bounty to market, horses and mules housed in canal mule barns powered the packet[13] boats that plied the canal from one end of the state to the other. In 1830, Knickerbocker moved to Pittsford, where, it is generally understood that he continued his livery business in some form. While there is a reasonable likelihood that he was the proprietor of the Pittsford mule barn that provided dray animals to pull barge traffic, there is not agreement among his local descendants on this point.

The mule concession in Pittsford was located near Big Spring on what is now Schoen Place. The original building morphed into Schoen Place Prime Rib and Grill and, more recently, into Mustard's Eatery and Bar. Beneath this building are the telltale remains of a tunnel (now sealed) that purportedly was a receiving station on the Underground Railroad. If Knickerbocker (or an alternate concessionaire), was not a "conductor", they at least collaborated with those assisting runaway slaves on their "last 100 miles to freedom".

While there is not a record of him owning a favored mule named "Sal", Knickerbocker perhaps grew tired of losing his best animals to adjacent concessionaires and, after nearly a decade of providing dray animals, decided to alter his career path. He had long admired a farm not far from the mule barn and, in 1839, sold his business and purchased the property. Later, the road bordering his farm was named Knickerbocker Road and George's farm was assigned the address of 173. A century and a half later, it became the third "Century Farm" in Pittsford.

Knickerbocker decided to do what he knew best; care for equines. He established a business to cater to the wealthiest end of the socio-economic spectrum; the affluent of Rochester. The Sibleys (of department store fame and co-founders of Western Union) and others hired Knickerbocker to board and care for teams of carriage horses.

Teams would be assigned in-town duty for a couple of weeks where they fulfilled their responsibilities of pulling assorted wheeled vehicles that transported family members to their schools, places of employment or social commitments.

---

[13] "Packet Boats" were named originally for the mail "packets" they carried. Because these regularly scheduled boats cut travel time across the state in half, passengers soon became the primary "cargo" during the early years of the Erie Canal.

As the teams grew tired and needed respite and rejuvenation, they were exchanged for a fresh team that had been recuperating under the watchful eye of George Knickerbocker at his Pittsford farm. Boarding fees were $1.50 per week per horse.

Most farms at the time grew food for the family's consumption and generated additional revenues by specializing in one of more crops, dairy or farm animals for resale. George's "cash cow" was the care and feeding of Rochester's finest carriage horses.

Henry Ford made dray animals all but obsolete early in the twentieth century and subsequent generations of Knickerbockers were forced to adapt their farm product offering accordingly. When demand softened for boarding carriage horses, the farm transitioned to a dairy operation with supporting feed corn and hay production. Over the years, significant acreage was planted in potatoes.

Succeeding generations of Knickerbockers have had to monitor consumer tastes, competitor's actions, barriers to entry, human resource needs and prices against the potential economic return in evaluating potential changes in what they produced on their farm. Like most such business decisions, it almost always ended up a question of investment dollars required and hiring quality people. More often than not, "quality people" was translated to "do we have enough children to harvest this new crop or tend these additional animals?"

Brothers Larry and David Knickerbocker are the sixth generation to farm the land. Their children, who contribute considerable farm labor, represent the seventh generation. Larry always "just knew" he'd take over the farm from his grandfather and father. He didn't really think about it; George Knickerbocker and the four intermediary descendent sons collectively tugged at his soul. They too "just knew" they would farm this land... as did he.

Today most Knickerbocker fields are planted in grain corn, oats, wheat and dry beans; mainly red kidney and cranberry beans. Constantly seeking to eke additional revenues from the soil, early twenty-first century crop trials have included peas and sweet corn.

It is perhaps disheartening to work many months of sixteen hour days in the busy season only to see middlemen, wholesalers and retailers earn multiples of the farm's profits. So, the Knickerbockers, like many farm families, have been drawn to the potential added profits of eliminating the wholesaler and retailer. Larry and David added a farm stand to sell their fresh picked sweet corn to the local community.

Until the late 1960's, the family raised significant portions of their own food on the farm. Cattle, hogs and chickens were raised on the property and met the butcher's knife in the family kitchen. The last of thirty head of dairy cattle were sold in 1971 when it became clear that they could not effectively compete with larger, highly mechanized farm operations. In fact, they concluded that to compete with larger farms that had efficiencies of scale, required them to farm far more than the 113 acres contained on the original farm.

The brothers benefited in several ways when they sold development rights to the Town of Pittsford. First they achieved peace of mind... though the agricultural conservation easement program did not exist when their father and grandfather were living, the Knickerbocker brothers are certain that the succession of family patriarchs would have eagerly embraced the principle of keeping the family farm forever a farm. It simply felt like the right thing to do.

Secondly, it had become increasingly difficult for small farmers to compete with the lower cost structure afforded competitors who cultivate five hundred, a thousand or more acres. The funds received from selling the development rights allowed them to expand their operation by purchasing an additional 206 acres of farmland. Consistent with their commitment to retaining the agricultural heritage of Pittsford, the additional acreage was already contained in an agricultural conservation easement when they purchased the property. They now supplement their own 319 acres with an additional 300 acres of rented farmland thereby allowing the economies of scale to work to their advantage.

The Knickerbocker Farm is run with family only. Animals, orchards and vegetables require a lot of people to harvest such bounty. Accordingly, while mindful of the changing demands of the market place, the Knickerbockers continue to focus on growing corn, beans, wheat and oats that can be planted, nurtured and harvested with only family labor. Whether the farm will continue to be owned and run by Knickerbockers is not a certainty but it is reassuring that the Knickerbocker Farm will be forever a farm.

While the "Three Sisters" of the Seneca women were corn, beans and squash, the "Three Brothers" of the post-Seneca male[14] Pittsford farmer are corn, beans (kidney and soy) and wheat...pretty similar. In the main, corn and beans have been the staple of local agriculture for several hundred years. Local soils have also proven suitable for wheat and oats and these grain crops have made inroads as dictated by market demand.

In order to survive for centuries however, the heritage farms have had to be nimble; predicting market demand and altering their farm products accordingly.

---

[14] 140 of the 631 farms (22%) in Pleasant Valley are run by women

Dairy operations have been successful over many of the years the white man farmed the area surrounding Big Spring. Eventually these operations succumbed to the greater cost efficiencies of mega operations and the never ending challenges of "24/7- 365" animal care. Each of the area's

Century Farms were, at one time, deeply committed to dairy operations. The last iteration of the Lusk farm was mainly a dairy facility. In the 1920's, the Hopkins Farm milked sixty cows and the Knickerbockers had 30 head until the 1970's.

In the late nineteenth century, Rochester entrepreneurs used the same power from the Genesee that served to grind wheat into flour to run mills supporting a bourgeoning woolen industry. Raw material to supply these woolen mills was sheared from the one-half million sheep that grazed Pleasant Valley at the time. The agricultural lands that surround Pittsford are considered some of the country's most fertile and productive. Because this acreage was too valuable too squander on grazing land, these herds of sheep were relegated to less desirable properties closer to Lake Ontario.

The county was a major producer of potatoes for several decades in the twentieth century; at one time shipping more spuds than any county outside of Idaho. When L.C. Forman was breaking sales records with bottled pickles and piccalilli, local farmers reacted by planting and providing daily truckloads of freshly harvested cucumbers.

The twenty-first century proprietors of Pittsford's Century Farms were not without alternate career choices. While surely inculcated with the rich oral history of their respective farms by their fathers and grandfathers, the Lusks, Greenes and Knickerbockers were clearly not without non-farm employment options. Each has impressive educational credentials. Hal Lusk and Larry Knickerbocker are graduates of Cornell's prestigious College of Agriculture; David Knickerbocker completed the two year agriculture program there. Mark Greene earned his masters degree in Agronomy from the University of Wyoming.

Nor were they likely restricted from altering career paths. In order to survive in this competitive business, they have had to demonstrate the same drive, tenacity and business acumen necessary to compete successfully in the broader world of commerce.

They chose to farm. They "just knew". The call of the family farm was strong. They found great comfort in straddling the same well worn tractor seat as their fathers, grandfathers and great grandfathers.

37

Reflections on Big Spring

Does the Flap of a Butterfly's Wings in Brazil Set Off a Tornado in Texas? Edward Lornenz so postulated in his 1972 paper that introduced modern society to Chaos Theory. Likewise, does the marine crustacean gripping the hull of an Erie Canal barge in 1825 absorb limestone rich mineral nourishment from the molecules of water percolating from Big Spring as it passes through the village of Pittsford? Are the free-swimming larvae offspring of this crustacean swept into the Gulf Stream as the barge enters the Atlantic after a glacial crawl through Albany and down the Hudson River? And do they, in turn, find themselves in the bellies of the North Atlantic Haddock swept north and east to the coast of England? Are these Big Spring nourished haddock served fish and chips style at the pub in Pitsford, England? How do we measure the impact of that molecule of enriched sustenance from Big Spring on the diet of those in Pitsford, England?

Chaos Theorists reasonably contend that the so called "butterfly effect" of those who resided in Pleasant Valley and Big Spring over the centuries had substantial influence on the region and the world. How do we measure the full breadth of the impact of Cornplanter, Handsome Lake and Red Jacket? Is the world a better place because of Frederick Douglass and Ashley Sampson? Were our lives enriched by the contributions of George Eastman, Chester Carlson, Joseph Wilson and John Wegman? If so, how about Ike Hicks, Wilmer and the Dukes, Asa Dunbar and Bill Jarvis? Mel Morgan?

Yes Mel Morgan…part of contemplating the past is to consider what might have been if Mel had been allowed to live and contribute to the community for an additional sixty or seventy years rather than be a statistic of Vietnam. A world absent of war would have yielded a far different Pleasant Valley, Big Spring and Pittsford, New York.

The Seneca Tribe who roamed Pleasant Valley was the fighting crème de la crème of the Iroquois Confederacy. The New Englanders who immigrated to the great frontier of western New York State were of hearty stock and by nature, strong-willed risk-takers. From both of these sturdy gene pools, came generations of brave war heroes, inspirational politicians, compassionate humanitarians, civil rights leaders, creative inventors, and revolutionary entrepreneurs. Their influence has been substantial; both locally, within the state, throughout the country and the world. Many of them observed their own reflected image in the still waters of Big Spring.

Cornplanter's seminal decision to fight with the British had an indelible impact on the area and the Iroquois Confederacy. His devastating raids on Colonist's communities at Cherry and Wyoming Valleys prompted General Washington's retaliatory Sullivan Campaign. The latter placed the survival of the Iroquois Confederacy in jeopardy.

It is easy to second-guess the multitude of "what if" scenarios that surround the five hundred years that the Seneca Nation dominated the area. While initially advocating a neutral stance by the Iroquois Confederacy, Cornplanter's decision to allay with the British in the Revolutionary War was prompted by a combination of factors. Ever since the French, led by DeNonville, raided Seneca villages in Pleasant Valley and Big Spring in the seventeenth century, his people were strongly inclined to align with whoever opposed the French. The British were a natural benefactor of this contempt.

Secondly, he found Joseph Brant's arguments to the Confederacy so compelling that he decided to acquiesce. Brant, in turn, had been influenced by the fact that his sister had married the British officer William Johnson who became Brant's mentor and advocate. Johnson had been knighted by the King of England for his service to the Crown. Perhaps we can attribute the downfall of the Iroquois Confederacy to Brant's sister's choice of a mate.

If Cornplanter had decided that the Iroquois Confederacy would fight alongside the Colonists rather than the British, there would have been no need for the Sullivan Campaign, the Seneca would have hunkered down and survived just another brutal winter in Pleasant Valley and may not have been inclined to accommodate the white man's continued thirst to acquire Seneca lands.

Perhaps Cornplanter and Red Jacket's face-to-face discussions with Presidents Washington and Jefferson were the highest level of statesmanship ever conducted by local residents. Many contend that the United States Constitution was modeled after the Gayanashagowa; the constitution of the Iroquois Confederacy. Surely this qualifies as locally inspired political influence of substantial consequence.

The Big Three Iroquois Chiefs were the most admired and reviled of all politicians of Pleasant Valley. Red Jacket's cogent orations are classics but his propensity to overindulge in "firewater" constantly derailed his path to greatness. Imagine what a sober Red Jacket may have accomplished.

The paragon of Big Spring's statesmen was Handsome Lake. As the nineteenth century spiritual leader of the Iroquois Confederacy, he led a renaissance of his nation. "Handsome Lakers" still follow his teachings. Only if ....he had emerged sober twenty years earlier, his renaissance may have had far broader appeal and more lasting impact? Only if... he had retained the support of Cornplanter (and thereby the whole Iroquois Confederacy) by quickly distancing himself from the persecution of witches. Only if...he had been able to cease the continued sale of Iroquois land while there was enough remaining to allow his people to retain some semblance of their traditional way of life. Only if...

Perhaps it was simply a problem of "branding" and packaging? It took Handsome Lake or his disciples three hours per day for five days to fully explain his doctrine. A brief, pithy and memorable "elevator pitch" may have succeeded in sparking interest, building momentum and mass conversions?

While it is not certain that Red Jacket, Cornplanter or Handsome Lake resided long-term in Big Spring, it is reasonable to assume that each spent considerable time there. It is well-established that Big Spring was, at one or more times, a large Seneca village and was on a main path and trading route; connecting the Iroquois Trail to the Seneca capital of Ganonagan near Victor and to the sacred tribal birthplace at Clark's Gully on the southeast shore of Canandaigua Lake. Given the nomadic life of Seneca warriors and the extensive travels required of tribal leaders, it is a certainty that The Big Three of the Seneca Nation spent considerable time at Big Spring. Because there is a high probability that Big Spring was, in fact, the Capital of the Seneca Nation for a period of time, it is a equally likely that Red Jacket, Cornplanter and Handsome Lake resided in Big Spring for some portion of their lives.

John and Stephen Lusk, the first white settlers in Pleasant Valley, no doubt studied their likenesses in the still waters of Big Spring after moving from Indian Landing to Pittsford. Presumably they were joined by fellow Pittsford resident Asa Dunbar whose mixed-race family was the first non-native permanent residents of Pleasant Valley. Both families demonstrated the pioneer spirit and indomitable grit necessary to face the many uncertainties of the western frontier. The Dunbars had the additional burden of attempting to meld into a homogeneous white culture.

The "Hero of Charlotte" Capt Israel Stone, with his masterful charade to convince the British Fleet that his contingent of soldiers numbered in the hundreds rather than the dozens, is a among local legends. His timeless, quotable mandates ..."don't let them pollute our soil...if they come ashore, they will wade in blood knee deep" are examples of what makes the area's history compelling. Similarly, if Colonel Caleb Hopkins had not been able to quickly muster 600 reinforcements into his 52nd Infantry Regiment (of Pittsford), to come to the aid of Capt Stone, the British would have surely taken Rochester and the outcome of the War of 1812 perhaps significantly altered.

There were many inspired entrepreneurial leaders. Talented local business pioneers launched many successful business ventures. Tom Spiegel's Wagon Shop, Hicks and McCarthy's, L.C Foreman Pickles, the R.T. French Company and Burdett's Grocery are only a few enduring examples. Land speculators Israel and Simon Stone initially purchased the area that would become Pittsford for eighteen cents per acre. After creative refinancing of their debt, their ultimate cost per acre was just one penny!

While the essence of our capitalistic society is the "free" enterprise system, the most successful entrepreneurs have been those who have been able to limit others from mounting a serious competitive threat. Limiting competition equates to the ability to price your product at a level that the market "will bear" exclusive of such competition. This, in turn, usually equates to attractive profit margins. Hicks and McCarthy quickly gobbled up their sole competing ice cream shop within days of opening their store on South Main Street. They were smart enough not to price gouge the public but clever enough to make a handsome profit without the fear of price-cutting from local competitors.

Many local citizens (over age fifty) contend that Hicks and McCarthy's was "ruined" towards the end of the 20th century; ruined by the pervasive need to gentrify anything that harkened to an earlier time. Gone are the soda fountain, the penny candy display case and the back booths where one could nurse a cherry coke for the better part of the afternoon. Gone are the pleasures of a simple egg and olive or tuna salad sandwich.

Instead the "new and improved" Hicks' absorbed the adjoining space formerly occupied by Pierce Rylott's store. Yielding to purported contemporary tastes, the menu offers a wide array of organic, grass fed, totally sustainable free-range choices. All is not lost however... nostalgic citizenry can request a table precisely above the former location of Pierce's famous steps; former resting place to the keisters of multiple generations of citizens for whom "hanging around was an old custom".

Fred Dowling reportedly continues to be served "off-menu" creations that were former staples at the "old" Hicks'. He charms the waitstaff by reminding them of: his sixty years of loyal patronage, the fact that three of his sisters "worked the counter" many years ago and that the tuna on pesticide-free arugula (on the menu) can just as easily be served between slices of whole wheat toast as it was in the 1960's.

The Pittsford Inn held the preferred tavern franchise for decades. Lesser drinking establishments existed but offered only token competition. The PI had that special ambiance that you cannot quickly create; an atmosphere simmered to perfection over one hundred and fifty years. The aroma was subtle but distinct; coaxed into the cells of the wood floors and well-stained bar by thousands of spilled beers, millions of cigarettes, cigars and pipes and decades of assorted kitchen odors. Every once in a while, patrons would be treated to a superficial hint of Clorox that would awaken the olfactory like a dose of smelling salts and momentarily mask the comforting, familiar, ambient aroma.

Like the village itself, the Pittsford Inn's heritage consisted of multiple generations of pub patrons extending to the original Phoenix Hotel in 1807. Regular customers could take comfort in knowing that either their own great-great-great grandfather or his neighbor's, occupied the same bar stool a century earlier. The result was a classic hometown pub with broad appeal across socio-economic and generational lines. Factory workers arrived for "a quick one before dinner" in the late afternoon followed by the white collared contingent a couple of hours later. At all hours there was a smattering of 18 to 25 year-olds but they tended to dominate the evening hours. The core of older "regulars" who had frequented the PI for decades lived up to their moniker and were dispensed the opiate of the masses during all hours of business; the exception being when Wilmer and the Dukes were playing. On such occasions, they migrated to Tallo's or Hotel Stephany for "peace and quiet".

When the Pittsford Inn closed, there was panic among the Inn's regulars and not-so-regulars alike. The choices were not good. Much like a company reflects the principles and character of its chief executive, taverns mirror their proprietor. On that basis alone, the choice between the Hotel Stephany and Tallo's Town Tavern was bleak. Neither proprietor recognized the opportunity to solicit and welcome new customers and thereby become the preferred drinking establishment in the village. Both were mainly interested in milking the business for as much income as possible while enduring the least amount of stress.

Gerry Clifford changed all that. His timing was impeccable to capitalize on a perfect storm of serendipitous events. Hotel Stephany met the wrecking ball and Dom Tallo's liver gave out. Gerry swooped in, negotiated an agreement to buy Tallo's and the rest is history. Call it intuition, insight or blind luck, it makes no difference. The son of the longtime proprietor of the Maplewood Inn, saw an opportunity and seized it. He made modest improvements, enhanced capacity by adding an outdoor beer garden and, most importantly, hired bartenders who knew how to treat loyal customers with respect and dignity. Thirsty's is now the only game in town and they don't give patrons any reason to seek alternate venues. Call him a shameless monopolistic capitalist if you wish... or just say congratulations!

Some local "inventions" were not truly original while others failed to gain recognition beyond the local community. The Piccalilli that L. C. Foreman made domestically famous had been common in the pubs of Great Britain for centuries. On the culinary front, "white hots" have surely sustained loyalty among the locals but their traction in the greater world of food has been limited. But, "cream style" mustard as invented and popularized by Pittsford's R.T. French and Company remains a condiment staple in large parts of the globe and made a pungent, long-lasting impression in the world of food. What is a ballpark hotdog without an ample slathering of yellow "cream style" mustard?

Over the years, it was widely believed that Big Spring was home to both the first and the best of patents. Pittsford resident Samuel Hopkins was mistakenly identified and celebrated as the holder of the first U.S. patent for a unique method of processing potash. Much to the chagrin of the village elders of both Pittsford VT and Pittsford NY, the record was corrected to properly show that a different Samuel Hopkins (of Philadelphia) was the actual patent holder. Regardless, locals can take pride that Pittsford resident Chester Carlson's xerography patents are considered by many barristers as the best patents ever written; "best" from the standpoint of their breadth in providing overwhelming protection from those attempting infringement.

Likewise George Eastman's visionary insight to obtain tightly written patent protection on every new product or process development was integral to Kodak's long-term prosperity. Perhaps more so than ever, that strategy remains critical to the company's current and future financial success.

Pleasant Valley was home to some of the world's greatest "perfectors". Neither George Eastman nor Chester Carlson (Haloid/Xerox) meets the purest definition of "inventor". Both were brilliant, innovative and driven to succeed but neither originally conceived of the technologies that brought them fame and fortune. They vigorously studied, scrutinized, modified and perfected imaging processes that had been invented by others.

The roots of Pleasant Valley's rich traditions run deep. There is little doubt that George Eastman's father's admiration for Booker T. Washington and Frederick Douglass's efforts to bring equal rights to all people inspired him to become a conductor on the Underground Railroad. It is reasonable to assume that young George's ethos was molded in that image.

It is interesting to consider the degree to which Joe Wilson may have been influenced and inspired by George Eastman (and hence indirectly by Booker T. Washington and Frederick Douglass). Both led efforts to greatly improve existing imaging processes in order to make them commercially viable. Both protected the resultant proprietary technologies with inventive, tightly written patents. Both engineered innovative pricing strategies to allow their technologies to be affordable to the masses; Eastman's $1 Brownie and Wilson's five cent pay-by-the-copy system.

Mr. Eastman donated generously to African American colleges and built a school for black children near his summer home in South Carolina. Mr. Wilson fostered an environment that allowed Ursula Burns to excel in her career and ultimately become the first African American woman CEO of a Fortune 500 company. The neighbors of Eastman's South Carolina summer home were enraged that he appointed the son of former slaves as the manager of his property. The Klu Klux Clan boycotted Xerox products after Joe Wilson sponsored a documentary titled "Of Black America".

Both renamed their young companies by creating completely new words; each book-ended with hard consonants. Both became iconic brands[15].

Joe Wilson was one of the nation's greatest business leaders; visionary extraordinaire of Xerox and innovative Pleasant Valley humanitarian. He revolutionized office processes and, if he had lived longer, very well may have led the company to leadership in the age of personal computing and information technology. Through his incredible insight, Xerox Palo Alto Research Center (PARC) was commissioned to revolutionize office processes. Given an ample budget and infinite freedom to explore, Joe Wilson's scientists at PARC created Alto. Many feel that its unique combination of features represents the essence of the first personal computer (PC). The world has not been the same since. Many contend there has not been a more significant development since the Industrial Revolution.

Joe Wilson was decades ahead of his time in taking action to level the workplace playing field for minorities and women. Did the Great Spirit speak to Wilson on his brisk walks around Mendon Ponds? Was he reminded of the pre-white man centuries when proud Seneca women managed all of the core tribal resources, grew and harvested the

[15] The August, 2006 issue of <u>Business Week Magazine</u> rated the Xerox and Kodak brands as the 57th and 70th most valuable brand in the world respectively.

majority of food, organized and led community work groups, elected chiefs, unilaterally decided the fate of captured enemy warriors; all while raising the children? Indeed Pleasant Valley's native people had already proven that women could excel in management responsibilities. Joe Wilson was certain that women could make a far greater contribution to Xerox in leadership roles than could be accomplished from working exclusively on the factory floor or in the secretarial pool.

The ultimate impact of the gentle puff of air emanating from a single stroke of a butterfly's wing may not be realized for a longtime; perhaps months, years or even decades. Some of Joe Wilson's pioneering initiatives took time to yield significant results. Yet those results ultimately had long-term global impact.

He was far more than a gifted entrepreneur. His courage to create programs that brought dignity to the area's underserved, undereducated and underemployed Black community is a model in providing solutions to institutional racism. He established a new standard that ultimately made a difference far beyond Rochester's borders. From a stagnant number of six African American employees, he created the systems and the mandates to hire and train blocks of 20 – 25 at a time.

Wilson's Operation Step Up allowed job seekers to earn their high school diploma while working at Xerox. His pioneering public/private joint venture with the Department of Labor facilitated the creation of minority owned businesses as Xerox suppliers. This was a time well before "diversity" was a common sound bite used mainly by American industry to mollify stockholders and local constituents.

It was 1951 when Wilson first described Haloid's lack of female managers as a "disgrace". Exactly fifty years later, Anne Mulcahy was named President and CEO of Xerox. No doubt, this was not soon enough for Joe Wilson.

There are interesting parallels between Xerox's Chester Carlson/Joseph Wilson, Apple Computer's Steve Jobs/Steve Wozniak and Dell Computer's Michael Dell. Carlson was the introverted research nerd of xerography while Wilson was the visionary entrepreneur that made it commercially viable. Wilson was not at all certain what his Palo Alto Research Center (PARC) staff was likely to discover, if anything, but had the courage to set them free to create the first personal computer. It took the imagination of Jobs and Wozniak to recognize the true potential of the fledgling PC. They successfully refined the Xerox creation and introduced it to the world as the Apple Computer.

Much like George Eastman's obsession to make photography affordable to the masses by reducing the cost of cameras from $5 to $1, Michael Dell drove cost out of the PC industry to the point that there is now a PC on nearly every desk. Had Joe Wilson been ten years younger, perhaps the Genesee Valley would now be known as Silicon Valley and home to Sun, Cisco, Intel, Yahoo and Google.

If Pittsford had an official color, it would be yellow; yellow as in French's Mustard and those ubiquitous boxes of Kodak products. Perhaps Pittsford is Kodak Town? Pittsford residents Thomas Hargrove Jr., Albert Chapman, Kay Whitmore, Gerald Zornow and Louis Eilers all served as Chairman and CEO of Eastman Kodak during the most prosperous years of the company. Resident Antonio Perez has led the company since 2005. It is doubtful that any of their high school teachers labeled them as "not especially gifted" as George Eastman had been described. Fortunately, Eastman did not allow that early assessment to effect his self-confidence or deter his ambitious plans.

Perhaps Pittsford is Xerox Town? When Chester Carlson was busy revolutionizing the xerography process he sought solace at night and on weekends at his home in Pittsford. Perhaps Joe Wilson stopped for coffee en route from his Clover Street home to his brisk walk/planning sessions at Mendon Ponds Park?

The sure sign of an innovative leader is one who is not averse to taking prudent risk. Over the years, John Wegman had a couple of miscues in his attempt to diversify his business. His purchase of the Pittsford Inn in 1933 and the ill-fated venture to bring German food to the community via the Old Heidelberg restaurant was a mistake. Tom Spiegel and his German friends did not represent a sufficient business base to allow for continued profitable operations. It is understandable that Wegman felt confident that the company's knowledge of the food retailing business would be a transferable skill when attempting to vertically integrate into the prepared food sector. He, in fact, was proven correct in later years. He was just a classic case of being "ahead of his time"?

What motivates affluent white men and women to risk much by taking up a controversial cause? Who were these heroes who hid runaway slaves who were "following the drinking gourd" to freedom in Canada. Who could they trust with the knowledge that they were holding "freight" in their haylofts, basements and attics; that they were providing food, clothes and a day's rest before shepherding their charges to the next station under the cover of darkness? How did they explain the tunnels that crisscrossed the village with entrances hidden in their basements? Were their friends or neighbors members of the Ku Klux Klan?

The Rochester Race Riots of 1964 were fanned by the same prejudice that caused Presidents Washington and Jefferson to repeatedly break solemn promises that Seneca land would be forever Seneca land. The same prejudice led Red Jacket to accuse the white settlers of casting his red brethren into the same lowly class as the Black man. The same prejudice led Brigham Young to attach the death penalty to those who "mix their blood with the seed of Cain" and led to the indifference towards the death of the Black busboy in the Pittsford Inn fire of 1963.

Frederick Douglass was an inspiration to thousands of African Americans and abolitionists. He demonstrated incredible courage in risking his life and freedom by being among the first to speak out against slavery. Once legally free, how much easier the road would have been for him to relax and enjoy the fruits of his fame. While a lead conductor on the "last 100 miles" of the Underground Railroad that passed through Pittsford, it is safe to assume that he spent considerable time orchestrating the movement of "freight" through the multiple stations within the village. Perhaps he communicated regularly with Samuel Crump inquiring as to the availability of space in his barn adjoining the Four Corners? Maybe he checked on the welfare of freedom-seekers hidden in George Knickerbocker's mule shed by the Erie Canal or in the room-with-no-doors at the Lathrop House that was connected to the hidden stairs leading to the cavern below the village? Douglass must have been privy to or a co-conspirator in Ashley Sampson's ultimately clever charade to fool slave hunters.

Judge Ashley Sampson stands apart as one of Pittsford's premiere humanitarians. The early nineteenth century resident and owner of the Hargous-Briggs House (Saint Louis Church, 52 South Main Street) and station master on the Underground Railroad is credited with orchestrating the movement of hundreds of freedom-seeking slaves through Pittsford. His efforts to conceal his "station" were elaborate; the hidden stairs he had built extend from the basement (with its tunnel leading to the Phoenix Hotel and the Erie Canal) directly to the third floor attic with its cage and shackles. The latter were used to deceive fugitive slave hunters into believing that the "judge" had already captured the fugitives they sought. Perhaps his role as local judge, which theoretically obligated him to prosecute those in violation of the Fugitive Slave Act, was the ultimate guise that diverted suspicions.

Colleen Wegman, Anne Mulcahy and Ursula Burns are impressive business leaders that exert substantial influence on contemporary Pleasant Valley. But...being described as "the mother of us all" surely is indicative of the global impact Susan B. Anthony had in bringing equal rights to persons of all colors and genders. Thanks to these pioneers, women leaders will be even more dominant in the mid-century updating of this work.

Much has changed. Much has stayed the same. Spiegel's Wagon Shop succumbed to the ravages of fire. Sandy Allen and Mel Morgan were taken prematurely by the savagery of war. L.C. Forman Pickles and R.T French Mustard Companies were swallowed by companies higher on the food chain with a perceived need to broaden their product mix. The Phoenix Hotel pines for the days when it was the area's paragon of hotel/taverns. The proud Seneca Nation continues its struggle to survive.

The "faithful" still make the annual pilgrimage to Cumorah Hill near Palmyra each July to celebrate the Mormon Pageant. Locals make the daily pilgrimage to Kodak and Xerox toiling long hours in anticipation of "making it big". Aging Volunteer Fire Fighters respond with gusto to the wail of the village siren. The oppressive weather patterns remains static. "Hanging out" in the village remains a tradition and a cadre of "regulars" can be found at Hicks and McCarthy's during the day and at Thirsty's in the evening.

The Knickerbocker Farm is still on Pittsford's Knickerbocker Road and occupied by Knickerbockers. Caleb Hopkins' farm remains on Clover Street and his descendents still manage the operation. The woodlot that Caleb directed (in 1812) to be left untouched in perpetuity remains intact; its old growth timber succumbing only to Mother Nature. Harry (Hal) Lusk, descended seven generations from John Lusk, the areas first white settler, continues to till Pittsford's farmland. The fertile soil that drew settlers from New England 220 years ago continues to yield bountiful crops of corn, wheat and beans.

The cavern beneath the Four Corners remains unexplored by modern man or woman. Nobody knows when the five gallon can dropped by Bryce Chase into the cavern in 1964 stopped rolling. The tunnels that may, or may not, crisscross the village connecting basements in homes, churches, hotels and mule barns contain only the ghostly echoes of the footsteps of those who were "following the drinking gourd" to freedom.

Big Spring still silently feeds the village momentarily cooling the tepid Erie Canal. Its water is stirred occasionally by passing pleasure craft. Its reflections remain in the minds of the proud souls who passed this way before.

Epilogue

"The older you get, the more the relation of past and present grows on you, because you have more history to look at...No matter how old you get, you don't feel old. You're still the same guy inside, and so there is continuity there within yourself, you can't ignore it."

Wallace Stegner

When asked the pros and cons of living in Pittsford, a randomly selected patron of Thirsty's tavern responded...

Favorite aspects of living in Pittsford are: 1) fall colors and New England charm 2) the "old" Hicks and McCarthy's and 3) the wide variety of village characters

Least favored aspects of living in Pittsford are: 1) dreadful winter and summer weather 2) its known as Rochester's "wealthiest suburb" and 3) the wide variety of village characters

So what is it about the weather in Pittsford? Residents, who have lived most of their lives in the area, demonstrate an amazingly upbeat attitude regarding the oppressive climate. They stoically endure the long, dark, frigid winters, celebrate spring with gusto and are forgiving of the humid, mainly cloudy summers; no doubt preferring it to anything that must be shoveled.

Possible sources of their positive demeanor are twofold. First, perhaps some are not aware, or more likely prefer to ignore, that far more favorable climates do exist within the lower forty eight. "It's summer, doesn't everyone, everywhere stick to their car seats?" Secondly, this is not a highly mobile demographic group. Many residents are descended from original families that settled the area. The genes contained in the hearty stock that abandoned their New England roots and risked life and meager fortune for a new life on the western frontier, two hundred years ago are still evident in many of today's residents. They are quite accustomed to suffering a bit of pain in order to reap the delayed gratification of forthcoming milder seasons. Winters are something you endure so you can really appreciate spring...

Is the weather really that bad? It depends. For those who prefer sunny, dry climates, actually, it is. Readily available empirical climatic records of the area confirm that Pleasant Valley's weather is not for sissies!

Average relative humidity during the morning hours varies little between months. It averages 80% throughout the year. As one would expect, it is more humid in August and September when the averages in the morning hover between 85% and 90%. Afternoon average humidity is a little lower; averaging 60% to 70% in November through March and 55% to 60% the remaining months of the year.

Cloud cover is the very discouraging index. In the traditional "outdoor months" of June through October, the skies are cloudy or partly cloudy 75% to 80% of the time. In November through February, residents rarely see the sun as the skies are clear just 10% of the time. Only 14% of total days are characterized as "sunny"; just 51 days per year on average.

Annual rainfall in Pittsford is slightly less than the national average; 32 inches compared to 36 inches. Snowfall is heavy with average annual of 85.6 inches verses 25.2 average nationally. January's average low temperature is 17.6 bone-chilling degrees Fahrenheit.

Pittsford is no place for those who suffer from Seasonal Affective Disorder. According to a study conducted at Ohio State University and published in the Journal of Neuroscience, about six percent of the population suffers from the affliction during winter months when the days are shorter. This research indicates that mice brains shrink when they are deprived of sunlight. This may explain the source of winter blahs experienced by some people. When humans are deprived of sunlight, the hippocampus section of the brain produces increased levels of melatonin, a hormone associated with depression.

Residents of modern day Pittsford, have substantial pride in their village and town. Well informed villagers know that Pittsford was the first village founded in Monroe County (known as Northfield in 1796; Pittsford in 1814) and second in the area only to Canandaigua in age, population and commercial vitality for its first quarter century. Rochesterville did not incorporate until 1817 and did not surpass Pittsford in population until the mid 1820's.

While often eclipsed by Rochester, Pittsford's proud historians point to the fact that many of the county's "firsts" occurred in their fair village. These included the first: grist mill (1791), sawmill (1793), school (1794), library (1803), permanent church (1807), newspaper (1815) and post office (1811). The village also welcomed many of the first professionals in the county. These included the first: physician (1811), female physician born in the state (1860) and female licensed pharmacist in the state (1886).

What about the rich and famous? A contemporary inquiry for Pittsford's most "famous" residents yields superficial findings that focus on those living in the past few decades. There is mention of a token billionaire but mainly athletes and musicians of the late twentieth century dominate search results.

Musicians from the Jazz world include Steve Gadd and Chuck Mangione. Singer and songwriter Teddy Geiger resides in the village and pop singer-songwriter Wang Lee Hom was raised here.

Abby Wambach scored 27 goals in her first three games as a four year old in the Pittsford youth soccer league. In an attempt to level the playing field, she was transferred to a boy's team.

Her success trajectory has not slowed. She excelled through high school (Rochester's Sisters of Mercy) and college (University of Florida) before being selected to play on the US Women's National Team. In 2003, she was the leading scorer in the Women's World Cup and Female Player of the Year. In 2004, she scored the winning goal in overtime to defeat Brazil for the Olympic Gold Medal. She was the second player chosen in the WUSA soccer draft. She played for the US in the 2007 World Cup.

A broken leg incurred in an Olympic warm-up game against Brazil kept Wambach from the 2008 team. In 2009, she joined the Washington Freedom of the Women's Professional Soccer League. She is the paragon of the women's game and the most prolific female offensive player since (teammate) Mia Hamm. Despite her fame and busy schedule, she has continued hosting youth soccer clinics in Pittsford.

Surely Abby Wambach was the most gifted athlete spawned by the local community. But consider the "road traveled" by Neal Powless. Before attending Nazareth College, Neal grew up playing lacrosse on the Onondaga Nation reservation near Syracuse. One of three sons of Chief Irving Powless Jr., he earned college All-American honors three times, before playing four years for his Iroquois Nation team at the World Lacrosse Championships. He also played for the Six Nations Chiefs of the Ontario Lacrosse Association. His legacy to the area extends 500, 1000 or more years.

Billionaire, Tom Golisano, has a home bordering Oak Hill Country Club. He founded Paychex, the payroll processing company, headquartered in Rochester. He commutes to Buffalo to watch his hockey team, the Sabres compete in the NHL. Tom has spent an estimated $93 million of his fortune running for Governor of New York on the Independence Party ticket. On each of three occasions, he has lost to George Pataki. In 2002, he garnered 14% of the vote.

Modest residents of Pittsford prefer the village not be characterized as "Rochester's wealthiest suburb"; others move there for that very reputation. Many are attracted by the public school system. Both high schools appear annually on the U.S. News and World Report; list of the one hundred best public high schools in the United States. Class sizes are smaller than most schools and the expenditure per student is $9600 compared to the U.S. average of $6100. This results in correspondingly greater property taxes to fund these outstanding schools.

The population tends to be well educated with 95% of all residents holding at least a high school diploma. Thirty five percent have a four-year college degree and nearly 28% have graduate degrees. These percentages compare to just 15% and 7% respectively on a national basis.

If you like affluent neighbors, Pittsford is a good place for you. The median family income in 2007 was $67,359 with just 2.9% of the town's population falling below the poverty level. This is roughly 50% higher than the median family income for the U.S.

Management and professional careers dominate in the village with 62% describing their vocation accordingly. Another 32% of villagers spend their time in service and sales professions and only 6% describe their work as construction, production or transportation. Only one-quarter of one percent say that they work in agriculture but this number is higher when you consider the larger Town of Pittsford where the remaining farms are located.

Mr. or Ms. Average Pittsfordite commutes to their job via private car (84% do so) and their average commute time is about 22 minutes.

If someone is seeking ethnic diversity, there are better choices. While more diverse than forty years ago, the village is still nearly 98% white. The larger "town" is over 92% so. In 2000, there were 1400+ residents of the village and 27,000+ living in the town. By 2007, the village population had actually shrunk to 1331. The town is slightly more ethnically diverse than the village. In 2000, the ethnic make up of the area was:

Ethnicity	Village	Town
White	1389	25208
Black	8	435
Asian	8	1243
Native American	1	22
Hispanic/Latino	13	354
Pacific Islander	0	5
Mixed Race	0	209
Other	2	92

Residents "hanging around" the village talking politics have about an even chance of debating with a Democrat or Republican. Just 1.5% of the population identify themselves as Independents.

While Titus Lord was just thirteen when he integrated the Pittsford School in 1813, in the 1950's Pittsford Central School had only a single Black male student and he, for only a short period of time. During the first six decades of the twentieth century, the vast majority of students were of Anglo Saxon heritage; perhaps a few of Eastern European descent but very few if any Latino, Black, Asian or persons of mixed race. Given the above demographics, presumably there is greater diversity today in Pittsford's two high schools.

Fifty four percent of Pittsford residents describe themselves as "religious". Rochester is heavily Roman Catholic; Pittsford less so but still a robust 36% of villagers follow that faith. Just 11% of the village describe themselves as Protestants and 3% are "other Christian".

St Louis Church remains an important place of worship for local Catholics. The Hargous-Briggs House remains a center piece of the property. The church is the home of several art pieces of renowned local artist John C. Menihan[16].

With no synagogue, just 3% of the village's population is Jewish, although traditionally most members of Pittsford's Irondequoit Country Club are of that faith.

If you are committed to following or understanding Islam, local practitioners number only around six. This is about the same ratio of such followers in the U.S. Despite its proximity to Palmyra and Cumorah Hill, followers of the LDS Church represent less than one half of one percent of the population. This is two thirds less than the 1.57% of followers across the nation.

Present day Pittsford is no longer known as the "Condiment Capital of the World". Nor is it the home of French's Mustard, Foreman's Pickles, Pittsford Milling or Schoen Brothers Apple Drying. Rather it is known mainly as a suburban enclave for those who can afford the area's priciest residential property in exchange for an ample dose of New England charm, great schools, a strong sense of heritage, the feel of a college

---

[16] According to the church history,:" Saint Louis was most fortunate to be able to incorporate in the décor of the church the work of parishioner John C. Menihan, a prominent, eclectic artist and professor of art at the University of Rochester. The Shrine or St. Joseph mosaic, the large dossals and their companion banners, as well as the beautiful Nativity set are examples of his work that are enjoyed to this day. He was well known primarily as a portrait painter, and his touch is seen in the portrait of Father Reddington that hangs in the Manse. His landscape of the church and another of his works grace the rectory". His work also appears on the cover of "Reflections on Big Spring".

town, relatively safe neighborhoods and the assorted accoutrements of the affluent suburban lifestyle.

The aforementioned "charm" is partially attributed to a remarkable original collection of 131 nineteenth and early twentieth century homes located within the village. They represent a wide variety of styles ranging from Federal, Greek Revival, Gothic Revival, Italianate, Queen Anne, Eastlake and Colonial Revival. Many of these are listed and protected by the Register of Historic Places through the National Historic Preservation Act of 1966.

The architectural charm and excellent school system comes with a high price tag. The median price of a home in 2007 was $369,800; seventy percent above the median price of $217,200 for the country. Home values are clustered between the price range of $100,000 to $299,000 with 87% of all sales falling in that category. Just 9% of homes are sold for more than $300,000. Charm equates to "old charm" in some instances as 62% of the village's homes were built before 1939.

While villagers still lock their doors at night, they take comfort in statistics that reflect low rates of crime. On the well-recognized ten point safety scale (with 10 being the least safe), Pittsford consistently is rated a one. Rest easy residents of Big Spring!

The area's gentry come to Pittsford to mingle and play golf. The best known of the local country clubs is Oak Hill Country Club. They hosted the Ryder Cup once, the U. S. Open on three occasions and the PGA twice. Also within the town limits are Monroe Golf Club, Irondequoit Country Club and Locust Hill Country Club. The latter is home to the annual Wegman's LPGA tournament.

There are two colleges located within the Town of Pittsford; Saint John Fisher and Nazareth College. While this may qualify the village to be described as a "college town", the presence of students is something that may be noticed but is not a defining characteristic of the village.

Nazareth College was founded on Rochester's Lake Avenue in 1924 by the Sisters of Saint Joseph. It moved to its present day Pittsford campus in 1942. Until 1971, it was exclusively a women's college. Forty undergraduate and 20 graduate degree programs are offered to its 3000 students. While many of the Sisters of Saint Joseph continue to teach at the college, there is no longer an official affiliation.

Saint John Fisher began as a men's college in 1948. When Nazareth decided to accept men in 1971, St. John Fisher chose to accept women. "Teach me goodness, discipline, and knowledge" is the school's motto first uttered by its founders of Basilian Fathers.

The colleges 2700 students study business, education, nursing, pharmacy or arts and science. Summers are enlivened when the NFL's Buffalo Bills football team returns to its training facility on campus.

From Pleasant Valley to Flour City to Flower City, present day Rochester is known as the "World Capital of Imaging". The educational infrastructure to support that title is well in place with the University of Rochester's world class Institute of Optics and highly ranked Rochester Institute of Technology's Imaging Science Departments.

When including its Strong Memorial Hospital, the University of Rochester is the area's largest employer. Wegman's is the second largest source of jobs, followed by Kodak and Xerox.

The Erie Canal was the carotid artery of the village's vascular system. It expanded the market for the bounty of the area's farms by hundreds of miles. In return, dollars came back to the community; dollars that paid farm wages, allowed for the acquisition and cultivation of additional acres and for the purchase of modern, efficient farm equipment. These dollars were also re-circulated into local stores, blacksmith shops and taverns which contributed to the area's overall prosperity and continued population growth. Some portion of these dollars also ended up in the coffers of the tax collector who was obligated to "invest" in building a modern infrastructure for the community. This included water and sewer systems but, ironically, also a growing network of roads and eventually highways; highways that would ultimately make the Erie Canal functionally and economically obsolete.

The continued evolution of the nation's transportation infrastructure doomed the old Erie Canal's commercial viability. The Saint Lawrence Seaway absorbed a considerable portion of the Erie's barge freight when it opened in 1959. The remainder shifted to railroads and trucks as these modes became more efficient, versatile and cost effective. In the latter half of the twentieth century, the village saw the end of commercial barge traffic.

The old Erie Canal continues to provide a focal point to the village. Its main commercial value however is the "charm factor" afforded patrons of the retail and dining establishments that grace the former tow path on the north side of the waterway.

The Erie Canal is now a curiosity of the past; an ornamental bangle from an earlier generation. Functionally "Clinton's Ditch" still connects the adjoining "port" villages of Fairport and Lockport but it is mainly of interest to recreational boaters and the billions of mosquito larvae that find this opaque ribbon of tranquil water a perfect home.

While Big Spring/Pittsford is not an unpleasant place by most objective measures, it is not typically listed among the dream locations to live, work or play. The economy is far from robust, the topography is, at best, interesting and the weather is fit only for the most rugged. Home prices, taxes and the cost of living are well above the national norm. Nearby Rochester contains a days worth of arts and music scene but no big league sports franchises nor noteworthy entertainment or dining venues.

Who chooses to live here? Why?

Even in twenty-first century Pittsford, it is common for organized sports teams, congregations, school classes or a random row of bar stools to contain a good sampling of names whose ancestors arrived in the village in the nineteenth or early twentieth century. The Knickerbockers remain well represented in Pittsford with two families located on Knickerbocker Road. There are several Hopkins' including the descendents of Caleb Hopkins who still farm at the original site on Clover Street. The presumed heirs to the soda fountain dynasty Hicks and McCarthy's share dozens of Pittsford telephone listings.

Thomas Spiegel, 1860's blacksmith and wagon shop owner, has several descendents remaining in the village including Paul Spiegel, author of the Pittsford Scrapbook collection. Paul's nephew, Tom Spiegel, was commissioned to remodel Hicks and McCarthy's late in the last century.

Likewise, there are Hildreths who are presumably descended from the stage-line entrepreneur who operated from the stables at the Phoenix Hotel. A handful of Phelps' live in the village. They may be related to the original purchaser of the substantial acreage constituting the village; Oliver Phelps.

The first white settlers in the area, who arrived in 1789, still have progeny in the area. John Lusk's descendents have two listings; one of them, Hal Lusk, was the last to run the original family farm. The cousins Israel and Simon Stone, who built the first buildings near Big Spring, have descendents among the dozen or so listings in the local telephone directory.

The well-heeled residents surely travel to a wide array of memorable vacation destinations and sample a variety of cultures, climates, terrains, living environments and experiences. Yet many choose to live the majority of their lives in Big Spring. But...why?

What causes this stubborn grip on their souls? Are they not among the world's most upwardly mobile of societies? They are affluent, highly educated, well trained and surely employable in sunny, dry climes or cosmopolitan cities. Residents perpetually mutter about "gettin outta here for good" in the height of a long, cold, dark winter. Then they seem to so relish the first rays of spring sun that this threat is pushed to some deep recess of their mind; not to be resurrected until the following February.

Why stay? What causes the tenacious grip that the area seems to have on its residents? To a significant degree, it is because of the pervasive sense of heritage linking residents to their "home". While seldom verbalized, there is certain comfort in the familiarity of succeeding generations of village families continuing to reside, contribute to and thrive in the community. This contentment can be attributed to the knowledge that one continues in the footsteps of your parents, grandparents, great-grandparents and earlier generations. The comfort associated with this legacy, not only impacts those who share surnames with the early pioneers, but also those who arrived decades or a century later. There is peace-of-mind in knowing that succeeding generations have chosen to continue to live and work and raise families on the lands of their forefathers. Perhaps to "move away" from this homeland, in some way, would constitute a rejection of the revered judgment of family who preceded you. Such betrayal may dilute one's own sense of identity to their roots.

Exhibits

Exhibit #1

The seeds of racism were sown in Pleasant Valley a very long time ago. According to Mormon theology, the God of God's Elohim lived on a star named Kolob with his many wives. Their union begot millions of "spirit children". Prior to the creation of Planet Earth or the first mortal man or woman, two competing sons of Elohim proposed their respective plans of salvation; salvation of the spirit children upon their arrival on earth in the flesh. While both proposals called for the saving of the spirit children's eventual mortal souls, son Jehovah, who would later become Jesus Christ, did so in "the honor and glory of God" while brother Lucifer's proposal did so without such glorification.

Because Lucifer's plan lacked homage to the creator, his plan was summarily rejected and Jehovah (Jesus Christ) became God's favored son. This infuriated Lucifer. In retaliation, he convinced a third of the spirit children to join a heavenly revolt against God and his brother. This exacerbated God's fury with Lucifer. He changed Lucifer's name to Satan and expelled him, and his demon followers, from heaven. Lucifer and his followers were not the only group to be effected by this heavenly battle. Per Mormon doctrine, some of God's allies demonstrated greater valor in their support of the single righteous path than others. It was decided that while these less vigorous supporters of God and Jesus Christ, would be granted a mortal life on earth, they would not be permitted to become priests in the church. While most mortals may never have aspired to the priesthood and hence thought this restriction inconsequential, priesthood in the Mormon Church carries with it the promise of becoming a God in the afterlife and procreating for eternity. The latter had substantial appeal to many followers.

How would these less vigorous followers be identified in their mortal state? These "less valiant" souls were to be sent to earth through the ancestors of Cain. Cain, according to church doctrine, had killed Abel and, in response, God bestowed black skin upon him.

Mormons contend that they are not racists; rather they simply follow the will of God. It was God that placed the black skin upon Cain and it was God that mandated that the gospel not be taught to and the priesthood be denied the descendents of Cain. He declared these acts of segregation.

Church leader Joseph Smith added: "there is a reason why one man is born black and with disadvantages, while another is born white with great advantages. This reason is that we once had an estate before we came here, and were obedient; more or less, to the laws that were given us there. Those who were faithful in all things there received greater blessings here, and those who were not faithful received less" (Doctrines of Salvation 1:61). In 1863, Brigham Young stated further: "Shall I tell you the law of God in regard to the African Race? If the white man who belongs to the chosen seed mixes his blood with the seed of Cain, the penalty, under the law of God, is death on the spot. This will always be so" (Journal of Discourses, 10:110).

All was not without hope however. Parochial Mormon doctrine <u>did</u> allow for the salvation of the Black race and an everlasting life in heaven. The sole requirement was that they be "faithful all his days" on earth. The significant caveat was that they would reside forever in heaven... as the servant of the white man.

Exhibit #2

The Preamble of the Treaty of Buffalo Creek.

Articles of a treaty made and concluded at Buffalo Creek in the State of New York, the fifteenth day of January in the year of our Lord one thousand eight hundred and thirty-eight, by Ransom H. Gillet, a commissioner on the part of the United States, and the chiefs, head men and warriors of the several tribes of New York Indians assembled in council witnesseth:

WHEREAS, the six nations of New York Indians not long after the close of the war of the Revolution, became convinced from the rapid increase of the white settlements around, that the time was not far distant when their true interest must lead them to seek a new home among their red brethren in the West: And whereas this subject was agitated in a general council of the Six nations as early as 1810, and resulted in sending a memorial to the President of the United States, inquiring whether the Government would consent to their leaving their habitations and their removing into the neighborhood of their western brethren, and if they could procure a home there, by gift or purchase, whether the Government would acknowledge their title to the lands so obtained in the same manner it had acknowledged it in those from whom they might receive it; and further, whether the existing treaties would, in such a case remain in full force, and their annuities be paid as heretofore: And whereas, with the approbation of the President of the United States, purchases were made by the New York Indians from the Menomonee and Winnebago Indians of certain lands at Green Bay in the Territory of Wisconsin, which after much difficulty and contention with those Indians concerning the extent of that purchase, the whole subject was finally settled by a treaty between the United States and the Menomonee Indians, concluded in February, 1831, to which the New York Indians gave their assent on the seventeenth day of October 1832: And whereas, by the provisions of that treaty, five hundred thousand acres of land are secured to the New York Indians of the Six Nations and the St. Regis tribe, as a future home, on condition that they all remove to the same, within three years, or such reasonable time as the President should prescribe: And whereas, the President is satisfied that various considerations have prevented those still residing in New York from removing to Green Bay, and among other reasons, that many who were in favour of emigration, preferred to remove at once to the Indian territory, which they were fully persuaded was the only permanent and peaceful home for all the Indians. And they therefore applied to the President to take their Green Bay lands, and provide them a new home among their brethren in the Indian territory. And whereas, the President being anxious to promote the peace, prosperity and happiness of his red children, and being determined to carry out the humane policy of the Government in removing the Indians from the east to the west of the Mississippi, within the Indian territory, by bringing them to see and feel, by his justice and liberality, that it is their true policy and for their interest to do so without delay.

Therefore, taking into consideration the foregoing premises, the following articles of a treaty are entered into between the United States of America and the several tribes of the New York Indians, the names of whose chiefs, head men and warriors are hereto subscribed, and those who may hereafter give their assent to this treaty in writing, within such time as the President shall appoint.

R. H. Gillet, Commissioner.

Dao-nepho-gah, or Little Johnson, Da-ga-o-geas, or Daniel Twoguns, Gee-odow-neh, or Captain Pollard, Joh-nes-ha-dih, or James Stevenson, Hure-hau-stock, or Captain Strong, So-ne-a-ge, or Captain Snow, Hau-neh-hoy's-oh, or Blue Eyes, Haw-naw-wah-es, or Levi Halftown, Goat-hau-oh, or Billy Shanks, Hau-sa-nea-nes, or White Seneca, Howah-do-goh-deh, or George Bennet, Hays-tah-jih, or Job Pierce, Sho-nan-do-wah, or John Gordon, Noh-sok-dah, or Jim Jonas, Shaw-neh-dik, or William

Johnson, *Gaw-neh-do-au-ok*, or Reuben Pierce, *Shaw-go-nes-goh-sha-oh*, or Morris Halftown, *Shaw-go-za-sot-hoh*, or Jacob Jameson, *Gua-wa-no-oh*, or George Big Deer, *Joh-que-ya-suse*, or Samuel Gordon, *Gua-ne-oh-doh*, or Thompson S. Harris, *Gau-geh-queh-doh*, or George Jimeson, *Hon-non-de-uh*, or Nathaniel T. Strong, *Nuh-joh-gau-eh*, or Tall Peter, *Sho-nauk-ga-nes*, or Tommy Jimmy, *So-joh-gwa-us*, or John Tall Chief,*Shau-gau-nes-es-tip*, or George Fox, *Go-na-daw-goyh*, or Jabez Stevenson, *Tit-ho-yuh*, or William Jones, *Juneah-dah-glence*, or George White, by his agent White Seneca, *Gau-nu-su-goh*, or Walter Thompson, by his agent Daniel Twoguns, *Dau-ga-se*, or Long John, *Gua-sa-we-dah*, or John Bark, *Gau-ni-dough*, or George Lindsay, *Ho-ma-ga-was*, or Jacob Bennet, *On-di-heh-oh*, or John Bennet, *Nis-ha-nea-nent*, or Seneca White, *Ha-dya-no-doh*, or Maris Pierce, *Yoh-dih-doh*, or David White, James Shongo, *Ka-non-da-gyh*, or William Cass, *Ni-ge-jos-a*, or Samuel Wilson, *Jo-on-da-goh*, or John Seneca.

Tuscaroras:

Ka-nat-soyh, or Nicholas Cusick, *Sacharissa*, or William Chew, *Kaw-we-ah-ka*, or William Mt. Pleasant, *Kaw-re-a-rock-ka*, or John Fox,*Gee-me*, or James Cusick, *Ju-hu-ru-at-kak*, or John Patterson, *O-tah-guaw-naw-wa*, or Samuel Jacobs, *Ka-noh-sa-ta*, or James Anthony, *Gou-ro-quan*, or Peter Elm, *Tu-nak-she-a-han*, or Daniel Peter.

Oneidas residing in the State of New-York, for themselves and their parties:
Baptiste Powlis, Jonathan Jordan.

Oneidas at Green Bay:
John Anthony, Honjoit Smith, Henry Jordan, Thomas King.

St. Regis:
Eleazer Williams, *chief and agent.*

Oneidas residing on the Seneca Reservation:
Hon-no-ne-ga-doh, or Silversmith, (For himself and in behalf of his nation.) *Hoge-wayhtah*, or William Jacket, *Sah-hu-gae-ne*, or Button George.

Principal Onondaga Warriors, in behalf of themselves and the Onondaga Warriors:

Ka-noh-qua-sa, or William John, Dah-gu-o-a-dah, or Noah Silversmith.

Cayugas:

Skok-no-eh, or King William, Geh-da-or-loh, or James Young, Gay-on-wek, or Jack Wheelbarrow, D'yo-ya-tek, or Joseph Isaac, For themselves and in behalf of the nation.

Principal Cayuga Warriors, in behalf of themselves and the Cayuga Warriors:

Hah-oh-u, or John Crow, Ho-na-e-geh-dah, or Snow Darkness, Gone-ah-ga-u-do, or Jacob G. Seneca, Di-i-en-use, or Ghastly Darkness, Hon-ho-gah-dyok, or Thomas Crow, Wau-wah-wa-na-onk, or Peter Wilson, So-en-dagh, or Jonathan White, Sago-gan-e-on-gwus, or Harvey Rowe, To-ga-ne-ah-doh, or David Crow, Soh-win-dah-neh, or George Wheeler, Do-goh-no-do-nis, or Simon Isaac, He-dai-ses, or Joseph Peter, Sa-go-di-get-ka, or Jacob Jackson.

Witnesses:

James Stryker, Sub-agent, Six Nations, New York Indians. Nathaniel T. Strong, United States' Interpreter, New York agency.

H. B. Potter, Orlando Allen, H. P. Wilcox, Charles H. Allen, Horatio Jones, Spencer H. Cone, W. W. Jones, J. F. Schermerhorn, Josiah Trowbridge (To the Indian names are subjoined a mark and seal.)

SCHEDULE A.
CENSUS OF THE NEW YORK INDIANS AS
TAKEN IN 1837.
Number residing on the Seneca reservations.

Senecas	2,309
Onondagas	194
Cayugas	130
	2,633
Onondagas, at Onondaga	300
Tuscaroras	273
St. Regis, in New York	350
Oneidas, at Green Bay	600
Oneidas, in New York	620

Stockbridges	217
Munsees	132
Brothertowns	360

The Treaty of Buffalo Creek
(Selected portions thereof)

R. H. Gillet, Commissioner.
Jan. 15, 1838.

At a treaty held under the authority of the United States of America, at Buffalo Creek in the county of Erie, and State of New York, between the chiefs and head men of the Seneca nation of Indians, duly assembled in council, and representing and acting for the said nation, on the one part, and Thomas Ludlow Ogden of the city of New York and Joseph Fellows of Geneva, in the county of Ontario, on the other part, concerning the purchase of the right and claim of the said Indians in and to the lands within the State of New York remaining in their occupation: Ransom H. Gillet, Esquire, a commissioner appointed by the President of the United States to attend and hold the said treaty, and also Josiah Trowbridge, Esquire, the superintendent on behalf of the Commonwealth of Massachusetts, being severally present at the said treaty, the said chiefs and head men, on behalf of the Seneca nation did agree to sell and release to the said Thomas Ludlow Ogden and Joseph Fellows, and they the said Thomas Ludlow Ogden and Joseph Fellows did agree to purchase all the right, title and claim of the said Seneca nation of, in and to the several tracts, pieces, or parcels of land mentioned, and described in the instrument of writing next hereinafter set forth, and at the price or sum therein specified, as the consideration, or purchase money for such sale and release; which instrument being read and explained to the said parties and mutually agreed to, was signed and sealed by the said contracting parties, and is in the words following:

This indenture, made this fifteenth day of January in the year of our Lord one thousand eight hundred and thirty-eight, between the chiefs and head men of the Seneca nation of Indians, duly assembled in council, and acting for and on behalf of the said Seneca nation, of the first part, and Thomas Ludlow Ogden, of the city of New York, and Joseph Fellows of Geneva, in the county of Ontario, of the second part witnesseth: That the said chiefs and head men of the Seneca nation of Indians, in consideration of the sum of two hundred and two thousand dollars to them in hand paid by the said Thomas Ludlow

Ogden and Joseph Fellows, the receipt whereof is hereby acknowledged, have granted, bargained, sold, released and confirmed, and by these presents do grant, bargain, sell, release and confirm unto the said Thomas Ludlow Ogden and Joseph Fellows, and to their heirs and assigns, all that certain tract, or parcel of land situate, lying and being in the county of Erie and State of New York commonly called and known by the name of Buffalo Creek reservation, containing, by estimation forty-nine thousand nine hundred and twenty acres be the contents thereof more or less. Also, all that certain other tract, or parcel of land, situate, lying and being in the counties of Erie, Chatauque, and Cattaraugus in said State commonly called and known by the name of Cattaraugus reservation, containing by estimation twenty-one thousand six hundred and eighty acres, be the contents thereof more or less. Also, all that certain other tract, or parcel of land, situate, lying and being in the said county of Cattaraugus, in said State, commonly called and known by the name of the Allegany reservation, containing by estimation thirty thousand four hundred and sixty-nine acres, be the contents more or less. And also, all that certain other tract or parcel of land, situate, lying and being partly in said county of Erie and partly in the county of Genesee, in said State, commonly called and known by the name of the Tonawando reservation, and containing by estimation twelve thousand, eight hundred acres, be the same more or less; as the said several tracts of land have been heretofore reserved and are held and occupied by the said Seneca nation of Indians, or by individuals thereof, together with all and singular the rights, privileges, hereditaments and appurtenances to each and every of the said tracts or parcels of land belonging or appertaining; and all the estate, right, title, interest, claim, and demand of the said party of the first part, and of the said Seneca nation of Indians, of, in, and to the same, and to each and every part and parcel thereof: to have and to hold all and singular the above described and released premises unto the said Thomas Ludlow Ogden and Joseph Fellows, their heirs and assigns, to their proper use and behoof for ever, as joint tenants, and not as tenants in common.

In witness whereof, the parties to these presents have hereunto and to three other instruments of the same tenor and date one to remain with the United States, one to remain with the State of Massachusetts, one to remain with the Seneca nation of Indians, and one to remain with the said Thomas Ludlow Ogden and Joseph Fellows, interchangeably set their hands and seals the day and year first above written.

I have attended a treaty of the Seneca Nation of Indians, held at Buffalo Creek, in the county of Erie, in the State of New York, on the fifteenth day of January in the year of our Lord one thousand eight hundred and thirty-eight, when the within instrument was duly executed, in my presence, by the chiefs of the Seneca Nation, being fairly and properly understood by them. I do, therefore, certify and approve the same.

R. H. Gillet, Commissioner.

SPECIAL PROVISIONS FOR THE SENECAS.
ARTICLE 1.

The several tribes of New York Indians, the names of whose chiefs, head men, warriors and representatives are hereunto annexed, in consideration of the premises above recited, and the covenants hereinafter contained, to be performed on the part of the United States, hereby cede and relinquish to the United States all their right, title and interest to the lands secured to them at Green Bay by the Menomonie treaty of 1831, excepting the following tract, on which a part of the New York Indians now reside: beginning at the southwesterly corner of the French grants at Green Bay, and running thence southwardly to a point on a line to be run from the Little Cocaclin, parallel to a line of the French grants and six miles from Fox River; from thence on said parallel line, northwardly six miles; from thence eastwardly to a point on the northeast line of the Indian lands, and being at right angles to the same.

ARTICLE 2.

In consideration of the above cession and relinquishment, on the part of the tribes of the New York Indians, and in order to manifest the deep interest of the United States in the future peace and prosperity of the New York Indians, the United States agree to set apart the following tract of country, situated directly west of the State of Missouri, as a permanent home for all the New York Indians, now residing in the State of New York, or in Wisconsin, or elsewhere in the United States, who have no permanent homes, which said country is described as follows, to wit: Beginning on the west line of the State of Missouri, at the northeast corner of the Cherokee tract, and running thence north along the west line of the State of Missouri twenty-seven miles to the southerly line of the Miami lands; thence west so far as shall be necessary, by running a line at right angles, and parallel to the west line aforesaid, to the Osage lands, and thence easterly along the Osage and Cherokee lands to the place of beginning to include one million eight hundred and twenty-four thousand acres of land, being three hundred and twenty acres for each soul of said Indians as their numbers are at present computed. To have and to hold the same in fee simple to the said tribes or nations of Indians, by patent from the President of the United States, issued in conformity with the provisions of the third section of the act, entitled

"An act to provide for an exchange of lands, with the Indians residing in any of the States or Territories, and for their removal west of the Mississippi," approved on the 28th day of May, 1830, with full power and authority in the said Indians to divide said lands among the different tribes, nations, or bands, in severalty, with the right to sell and convey to and from each other, under such laws and regulations as may be adopted by the respective tribes, acting by themselves, or by a general council of the said New York Indians, acting for all the tribes collectively. It is understood and agreed that the above described country is intended as a future home for the following tribes, to wit: The Senecas, Onondagas, Cayugas, Tuscaroras, Oneidas, St. Regis, Stockbridges, Munsees, and Brothertowns residing in the State of New York, and the same is to be divided equally among them, according to their respective numbers, as mentioned in a schedule hereunto annexed.

ARTICLE 3.

It is further agreed that such of the tribes of the New York Indians as do not accept and agree to remove to the country set apart for their new homes within five years, or such other time as the President may, from time to time, appoint, shall forfeit all interest in the lands so set apart, to the United States.

ARTICLE 4.

Perpetual peace and friendship shall exist between the United States and the New York Indians; and the United States hereby guaranty to protect and defend them in the peaceable possession and enjoyment of their new homes, and hereby secure to them, in said country, the right to establish their own form of government, appoint their own officers, and administer their own laws; subject, however, to the legislation of the Congress of the United States, regulating trade and intercourse with the Indians. The lands secured to them by patent under this treaty shall never be included in any State or Territory of this Union. The said Indians shall also be entitled, in all respects, to the same political and civil rights and privileges, that are granted and secured by the United States to any of the several tribes of emigrant Indians settled in the Indian Territory.

ARTICLE 10.

It is agreed with the Senecas that they shall have for themselves and their friends, the Cayugas and Onondagas, residing among them, the easterly part of the tract set apart for the New York Indians, and to extend so far west, as to include one half-section (three hundred and twenty acres) of land for each soul of the Senecas, Cayugas and Onandagas, residing among them; and if, on removing west, they find there is not sufficient timber on this tract for their use, then the President shall add thereto timber land sufficient for their accommodation, and they agree to remove; to remove from the State of New York to their new homes within five years, and to continue to reside there. And whereas at the making of this treaty, Thomas L. Ogden and Joseph Fellows the assignees of the State of Massachusetts, have purchased of the Seneca nation of Indians, in the presence and with the approbation of the United States Commissioner, appointed by the United States to hold said treaty, or convention, all the right, title, interest, and claim of the said Seneca nation, to certain lands, by a deed of conveyance a duplicate of which is hereunto annexed; and whereas the consideration money mentioned in said deed, amounting to two hundred and two thousand dollars, belongs to the Seneca nation, and the said nation agrees that the said sum of money shall be paid to the United States, and the United States agree to receive the same, to be disposed of as follows: the sum of one hundred thousand dollars is to be invested by the President of the United States in safe stocks, for their use, the income of which is to be paid to them at their new homes, annually, and the balance, being the sum of one hundred and two thousand dollars, is to be paid to the owners of the improvements on the lands so deeded, according to an appraisement of said improvements and a distribution and award of said sum of money among the owners of said improvements, to be made by appraisers, hereafter to be appointed by the Seneca nation, in the presence of a United States Commissioner, hereafter to be appointed, to be paid by the United States to the individuals who are entitled to the same, according to said appraisal and award, on their severally relinquishing their respective possessions to the said Ogden and Fellows.

Acknowledgements

Much of this historical account of the Genesee Valley and Pittsford, New York was drawn from the fine research of others. Material in this book not listed below came from readily accessible public documents, data bases, news reports and reference works. These resources included the websites of public companies and institutions discussed in the text. These included Kodak, Xerox, Wegman's, Hickey Freeman, The University of Rochester, Saint John Fisher College and Nazareth College. While popular sites that allow unstructured editing without qualifying contributors were occasionally consulted, information accessed from such sources was vetted elsewhere to confirm accuracy.

Paul M. Spiegel was particularly helpful. He is the author of the five volume set titled "Pittsford Scrapbook" which contains a treasure of photos that capture many of the seminal moments in the history of the village. Mr. Spiegel was most generous in allowing the reprinting of selected photographs contained in his outstanding series of books. Without his creativity and commitment, much of the area's history would have been lost. Mr. Spiegel also offered cogent suggestions on an early draft of my manuscript.

The proud and dedicated archivists at Bausch and Lomb Incorporated, Eastman Kodak Company, The George Eastman House and Xerox Historical Archives were generous with their time in providing images for this project. New York taxpayers are well-served by the gracious public servants at the New York State Museum in Albany, New York. I appreciate their alacrity in providing unique images of Seneca Longhouses contained in this book.

Charles D. Ellis' book "Joe Wilson and the Creation of Xerox" is strongly recommended. It contains many insightful anecdotes useful in understanding the incredible gifts and interesting peccadilloes of a remarkable business pioneer. His work was useful in my attempt to capture the essence of the person behind the amazing success story of Xerox.

While seeking information on the tunnels that reportedly run throughout the village of Pittsford, I consulted with the, most capable, Pittsford Town Historian, Ms. Audrey M. Johnson. She was very helpful in directing me to several references and provided much-needed encouragement on an early manuscript draft. I appreciated the guidance and encouragement of Mr. Joe Maxey, President of Historic Pittsford.

I am further indebted to: Paul Knickerbocker, Larry Knickerbocker, Harry Lusk, Mark Greene, Lynn Sanger, Douglass Drake and Sally Schrecker.

Sarah Bradbury created the chart titled "The Seven Villages Descended from Northfield" which provides great clarity to what was heretofore a complicated puzzle of names and dates. The talented artist Alicia Ivelich, labored long in creating her unique depiction of "Underground Railroad Routes of the Genesee Valley". I believe her rendition of Capt. M. Pouchot's 1754 map of the Seneca Villages of the Genesee Valley is a significant enhancement of the original.

Invaluable candid feedback and editing assistance was provided by Trudy Richter, Kristin Gasteazoro, Susan Mathews, Paul Spiegel, Audrey Johnson, Joe Maxey, Hal Lusk, Susan Scott and Peter Menihan.

My daughters, Kelsey McNellis and Kerry McNellis, demonstrated incredible patience, fortitude and listening skills while seeming to appreciate my enthusiasm for people and places contained only in their imagination. I could not be more proud of them.

Most significantly, I am immensely grateful for the support and encouragement of my wife, Erica Richter. She offered sage advice regarding the broad scope of this endeavor. She listened and laughed at my dinner table descriptions of the day's discoveries and provided unending encouragement, inspiration and wise guidance. In the final stages of this project, her deft editing skills contributed greatly to the clarity of the text.

Front & back cover art by:

JOHN C. MENIHAN, AWS, ANA, 1908-1992

John C. Menihan was born in 1908 in Rochester, NY. During his six-decade career, Menihan was one of the most prominent and beloved artists in western New York. A well-known regionalist painter/ printmaker, he documented the local scene with his landscapes and portraits in a wide variety of media throughout his life. In 1947, he won an unprecedented four First Prizes – in oil painting, watercolor, printmaking, and drawing – in the Finger Lakes Exhibition at Rochester's Memorial Art Gallery. Mr. Menihan was Associate Professor of Fine Arts at the University of Rochester. He also taught at the Memorial Art Gallery. His many commissions can be seen in regional institutions, businesses and homes. John C. Menihan's papers are held by The Smithsonian Institute's Archives of American Art. For further information see www.johncmenihan.com.

Cover design by:

Tom Menihan, the son of cover artist John C. Menihan, grew up in Pittsford, New York. Tom is a watercolor artist and graphic designer living in Boston, MA. He and his wife, artist Ginny ONeil, work at their studio/galleries in Jamaica Plain and Oak Bluffs, Martha's Vineyard. During the winter months, they are the artists-in-residence at Jake's Resort Hotel in Treasure Beach, Jamaica. For further information see www.twoboatsgallery.com.

References

Hart, Isabella. *History of Pittsford.* Pittsford, New York: Historic Town of Pittsford, 1 August 1970.

Spiegel, Paul M. *Pittsford Scrapbook, Volume 1, Bicentennial Celebration.* Pittsford, New York: Published by the Town of Pittsford, 1976.

Spiegel, Paul M. *Pittsford Scrapbook, Volume 2, 1900 – 1920.* Pittsford, New York: Published by the Town of Pittsford, 1977.

Spiegel, Paul M. *Pittsford Scrapbook, Volume 3, The 1920's and 1930's.* Pittsford, New York: Published by the Town of Pittsford, 1980.

Spiegel, Paul M. *Pittsford Scrapbook, Volume 4, The 1940's Thru 1960.* Pittsford, New York: Published by the Town of Pittsford, 1982.

Spiegel, Paul M. *Pittsford Scrapbook, Volume 5, A Kaleidoscope.* Pittsford, New York: Published by the Town of Pittsford, 1985.

Wolfe, Andrew D. *Pittsford at 200, Portrait of a Community, 1789 – 1989.* Pittsford, New York: Wolfe Publications, Inc., 1989.

Spiegel, Paul M. *Echoes of Old Pittsford, 1879-1880, "A few social notes and exciting events in Pittsford in 1879".* Collected at random by Paul Spiegel largely from the *Rochester Democrat and Chronicle.*

MacNab, Thompson and Shirley Cox Husted. *Northfield...on the Genesee. The Story of a Frontier Town of Monroe County, N.Y.* Rochester, New York: The Monroe County Historian's Office, 1981.

Archer, Michael. *A Patch of Ground, Khe Sanh Remembered.* Hellgate Press, 2005.

Waldman, Carl. *Atlas of the North American Indian.* New York: Facts on File Publications, 1984.

Wallace, Anthony F.C. *The Death and Rebirth of the Seneca.* New York: Vintage Books, 1969.

Carl Waldman, *Encyclopedia of Native American Tribes.* New York: Facts on File Publications, 1987.

Parker, Arthur Caswell. *The Code of Handsome Lake, The Seneca Prophet.* Forgotten Books, 2008. First published in 1913.

Levitt, T. "Marketing Myopia", _Harvard Business Review_ July- August, 1960.

Walton, Cindy Lou. "_The Hamlet of Pittsford 1800-2002_". Pittsford, Michigan, Pittsford Area School.

Ellis, Charles D., _Joe Wilson and the Creation of Xerox._ Hoboken, New Jersey: John Wiley and Sons, Inc., 2006.

Brayer, Elizabeth, _George Eastman: A Biography._ Rochester, New York: Reprint edition by the University of Rochester Press, 2006.

U.S. Department of Agriculture, New York Agricultural Statistics Service, "_2002 Census of Agriculture, County Profile_", Monroe County, New York.

Klees, Emerson. _Underground Railroad Tales With Routes Through the Finger Lakes Region._ Rochester, New York: Friends of the Finger Lakes Publishing, 1997.

Klees, Emerson. _The Iroquois Confederacy, History and Legends._ Rochester, New York: Friends of the Finger Lakes Publishing, 2003.

Maxey, David W. "Inventing History: The Holder of the First U.S. Patent." _Journal of the Patent and Trademark Office Society,_ Volume 80, 1998, Pages 155-170.

Devoy, John. _Rochester and Post Express: a history of the city of Rochester from the earliest times,_ Rochester, N.Y.: Post Express Print. Co., 1895.

Peck, William F. _Semi-centennial history of the city of Rochester._ Syracuse, N.Y. : D. Mason & Co., 1884.

Parker, Jenny Marsh. _Rochester: a story historical._ Rochester, N.Y.: Scrantom, Wetmore & Co., 1884

Index

303

About the Author

David McNellis was born in Detroit, Michigan to Canadian parents. He graduated from Pittsford Central School in 1962. His interest in the area's past began when he was a resident in the 1960's. Intriguing historical anecdotes told by local teachers, merchants, farmers, barbers and bartenders prompted him to study the area's fascinating history and ultimately share his discoveries in this book.

Since earning a B. S. degree from Michigan State University and an MBA from the University of Oregon, he has lived and worked mainly on the west coast. He is the proud father of two remarkable young women and lives in San Carlos, California with his wife Erica. Reflections on Big Spring is his first book.

CPSIA information can be obtained at www.ICGtesting.com
Printed in the USA
BVOW02*2228171213

339409BV00005B/115/P